CYTHEREA'S BREATH

CYTHEREA'S BREATH

BY

SARAH ALDRIDGE

the
Naiad
Press
inc.
1982

SARAH ALDRIDGE   Photo by Donna J. McBride

Novels By Sarah Aldridge

THE LATECOMER
TOTTIE
CYTHEREA'S BREATH
ALL TRUE LOVERS
THE NESTING PLACE
MADAME AURORA (1983)

*Aphrodite — golden, irresistible
goddess — violet-crown'd Cytherea*

*To
MH
and
TW*

CYTHEREA'S BREATH

PART I

Emma stood on the sidewalk at the foot of the stone steps, staring up at the tall, arched door of the big red brick house. She looked down again at the card in her hand. This was it, No. 9 Cushman Terrace, and the date was right, Wednesday, April 25, 1906. With a nervous gesture she turned the card in her fingers to read again the name engraved on the other side—Miss Margaret Bell. With one more glance upward, she walked quickly up the steps. Having come this far there was no point to hanging back now. The cloud of eager confidence that had borne her along so far suddenly threatened to dissolve but she would not give it time to vanish altogether. She had only to be clear and positive in explaining what she wanted to do, the goal she wished to attain. She had not had a moment of doubt during the long train ride from the north, nor in the brief walk from the railway station. She had been busy marshalling her facts, ordering her thoughts for the presentation of her project. People listened if you had something definite to say and could say it simply and directly.

Besides, there was no reason why she should be ill-at-ease. Mrs. McHugh had assured her that the women she was about to meet already knew her history, the record she had made in college. Several of them had contributed to the fund that had paid her way through medical school. She had only to explain why she felt so overwhelming a need for some further financial assistance.

She stood before the tall door and willed it to open quickly before her eagerness ebbed. To distract herself she looked around at the empty, silent Baltimore street, lined with other square, massive houses whose large windows were heavily draped with dark velvet and white lace curtains, each with a long white tassel hanging motionless in the center of the pane of glass. There was the impress of wealth here in the lack of movement and the absence of people. Even the noise of St. Paul's street, a block away, did not break the opulent calm. How unlike the teeming, dirty, raucous slum streets that clustered around the big, overburdened city hospital where she had spent her year's internship.

The big door opened silently. A spare, middle-aged black woman in white apron and cap stood motionless, just inside, waiting for her to speak.

"Miss Bell is expecting me. I am Emma Wycliffe."

The maid stepped back for her to enter and then walked silently away on the deep carpet of the vestibule, leaving Emma to stand alone, listening to the intense stillness of the house. But a door opening somewhere let escape the sound of women's voices. It formed a background to the maid's return. She followed the woman across to the drawing room.

As Emma entered the room there was a brief, sudden silence and then she heard Mrs. McHugh say, "Dr. Wycliffe, I am so glad to see you."

Emma stepped toward the short, round, greyhaired woman who had risen to greet her. Mrs. McHugh's soft blue eyes and rosy face, smiling up at her, reassured her and she was ready to be introduced to the others.

Mrs. McHugh said to the slight, plain woman in the dark brown, high-necked dress, who sat in the tall-backed chair, "Margaret, this is Emma Wycliffe. Emma, this is Miss Bell."

Emma glanced briefly at Miss Bell, seated so erectly, her narrow white hands motionless in her lap. As she responded, Mrs. McHugh said, "My dear Emma, as soon as you have had a cup of tea, we are all eager to hear what you have to say. Come, do sit down."

Emma sat down and the maid handed her a cup of tea that Miss Bell had poured. She drank it thirstily, thankful that Mrs. McHugh went on talking, while the others eyed her curiously, still speaking to each other.

Presently Mrs. McHugh said, "We all here feel that we know you well, Dr. Wycliffe. We know the fine record you made in medical school."

"Yes," said Emma, "and I am so grateful for all the help you have given me. I'm determined to show you how much I appreciate it. That is why I have come here now to ask you to support me for one more year. I want to go abroad to study. If medical women are to show what they can do, that they can really be equal to medical men, they must not be cloistered and unaware of the great advances that are being made in the medical centers of the rest of the world. If I could spend just one year in London, in one of their great hospitals —"

Mrs. Vickers, a large, placid woman who sat on the other side of the teatable, looked curiously at the tall, golden-haired girl whose blue eyes were so bright with enthusiasm. Why, she wondered, listening as Emma went on speaking, did so beautiful a girl wish to take up a life that would bring her in contact with the more sordid aspects of life. Such a girl could easily find a suitable husband, a man of substance —

Mrs. Vickers' musing was interrupted by Emma's voice, answering Mrs. McHugh's adroit questions, asked for the purpose of drawing out the details of her aspirations. Yes, said Emma, she was her parents' eldest child. Her father was a professor at one of the eastern colleges. His reputation as the mentor of brilliant young men was well established. No, she had no sisters, only brothers, five of them.

Mrs. Vickers, her interest caught, asked, What of them, what of her brothers? Were they clever young men? Oh, yes, said Emma. They were the reason why she had sought outside her family for financial aid. Her father's income could not possibly provide the boys with the sort of education they should have and at the same time pay for her professional advancement. Her nearest brother was already a lawyer, married, with a growing practice and a young family to provide for. The next had just graduated from Cornell University and was even now on his way across the Pacific as a budding naturalist with a scientific expedition. Her father's income was needed for the younger boys, eager, precocious. She could not jeopardize their future by demands for herself.

Glancing quickly at Miss Bell, Emma saw that she had made a breach in that wall of reserve. Miss Bell's eyes, green with flecks of warm brown, were fixed on her face, but they shifted away at once.

Mrs. Vickers' slow, calm voice was saying, "It must be very satisfying to have such a decided call to guide one through life. But I cannot help but think that a medical career is a rather dreadful choice for a lovely young girl like yourself. You must be called upon to face many distressing things."

Emma's laugh was lighthearted, indulgent. How often she had

met with this protective, kindly, uncomprehending solicitude. She had learned to parry it without hurting the feelings of the women who voiced it.

"But, Mrs. Vickers, I am not a child! I am twenty-seven years old and I've had quite a lot of experience!"

Miss Bell's soft voice interrupted. "Twenty-seven! I should never have thought it. But of course it takes time to earn a medical education."

Emma, alert to respond to her, said, "And I was late starting. It took me a year out of college to find support for medical school—your support, Miss Bell, and that of some of these other ladies." Her glance round showed her that she was breaking through the reservations, the latent disapproval in some of the women who listened to her. "I have had," she went on gently, "moments of uncertainty, of self-questioning. But I have never seriously doubted that I was meant to be a doctor."

She went on speaking, in a serious voice, of her year's internship—of the ambulance calls in the night to dismal, fetid slum dwellings where there was no privacy even for a woman moaning in difficult childbirth, of the miserable, wretched children brought to the hospital too malnourished to survive the diseases and accidents that filled their hopeless environment. Caught up in her own zeal, she found herself launched into an account of a struggle to save a woman from dying of blood poisoning, the result of a desperate attempt to avoid the birth of another unwanted child through the use of buttonhooks and knitting needles.

But she stopped abruptly, aware in a warning flash that these women, though they might know that such things happened, would be indignant at having these horrors thrust upon them in the muted elegance of Miss Bell's drawing room.

Mrs. Vickers said, her voice full of distaste, "It is very terrible that such things should exist."

Emma was surprised by Miss Bell's voice, suddenly decisive. "They will not cease to exist until there are more young women with Dr. Wycliffe's determination to confront and banish them."

Mrs. Vickers brushed cake crumbs from the lace front of her dress. "Yes, I daresay." Her eyes lingered with obvious pleasure on Emma's golden hair, straight features and sparkling blue eyes. "But it is hard to imagine you in a sickroom."

Mrs. McHugh laughed. "But wouldn't she brighten any sickroom, Adelia?"

Miss Bell asked, "Does your mother approve of what you have decided to do?"

"She has never disapproved," Emma answered. "Though sometimes she has misgivings about the obstacles I shall find besetting my way. But I point out to her that obstacles are only there to be overcome—as she herself has taught me to believe."

Miss Bell's brown-flecked eyes lingered on her for a moment. "She must be very proud of you—she must be very proud to have such a daughter." She paused for a moment and then added, "We must see that at least lack of money is not one of those obstacles."

Emma's heart bounded but again some impulse prompted her to hold back from effusive thanks. Instead she said gravely, "I shall always be grateful to you, Miss Bell."

There was more general conversation then as the group of women talked among themselves. In the hubbub of voices that came with the break-up of the gathering, Emma heard Miss Bell's voice say in her ear, "I am treasurer of our group and doubtless my own convictions will have weight with my friends."

Various of the women bowed to Emma as they said goodbye to Miss Bell and then passed out through the massive front door held open by the maid. Mrs. McHugh asked if she was staying in Baltimore. Emma said no, she must return at once to New York. Mrs. McHugh said that in that case she must come with herself and Mrs. Vickers, that they would take her to the railway station. Miss Bell, standing silent, bowed as they said goodbye.

Seated in the velvet-lined glass box that was Mrs. Vickers' electric brougham, Emma was quiet, conscious of fatigue and of the letdown after the prolonged strain of getting ready for this confrontation. But as Mrs. Vickers moved the horizontal driving-stick to guide the brougham into the station yard, Mrs. McHugh said, "I think your visit has been quite successful. You can be confident about your plans to go abroad. Miss Bell has made up her mind to back you and where she leads the rest of us will follow."

Emma, seated in the train, listening to the clack of the wheels carrying her back north, felt a great happiness engulf her. She would go to London. She would spend her year in a great hospital there. Then when she had got beyond this long period of preparation she would be able to justify herself, prove that her dream could be satisfying reality.

*   *   *

Emma stood at the window, leaning her head against her arm.
Her bedsittingroom, at the top of a tall house, overlooked
London's river. The long summer evening was still light and she
could watch the tugs and barges moving up and downstream. Of
course she was tired. Ever since she had reached England two
months ago she had been on the stretch, trying to absorb the sights
and sounds and habits of the great city, in the midst of the
relentless program of attending lectures, walking the wards of the
hospital to observe doctors in charge of difficult cases, being on
call for maternity and street accident cases, sitting in on demon-
strations and consultations.

"Don't worry, Mother," she had reassured her mother in her
letters. "You know I thrive on work, on activity. It is idleness
that kills, that destroys the value of life for me. You would be
surprised at the number of people I have got to know here already.
Everyone warned me when I first came here that by getting myself
a lodging like this, by myself, I would be isolating myself. It
hasn't been like that at all. Of course I had Father's introductions
to the people who knew him so well when he was my age. There
are a number of scientific and scholarly families I visit now. I
have told you about them in my other letters. And they have all
introduced me to *their* friends, so that sometimes I am harassed
by having to choose among several invitations for one evening.
That sounds very vain, doesn't it? But I did not come to London
to enjoy a social season and I do sometimes need to study."

Nevertheless she had found that she could get through an
enormous amount of work in a day and be ready in the evening to
go to the theater, the music halls, to a dance at the house of a
family with sons and daughters her age or younger. At such times
as these she had learned to gloss over her professional activities.
She was amused by the slight stiffness, the nervous hesitation
shown by her hostesses or the young men to whom she was
introduced, faced with a clever young medical woman from
America. Then she was glad that her physical beauty, her natural
manner when she was wearing a silk and lace gown, almost
instantly disarmed them.

She did not mention in her letters to her mother that she had
met socially Sir Maurice Colburn. A few weeks after she arrived
she had encountered him at the hospital. Her name had been
mentioned to him among those of a few picked graduate students

assigned to observe his operation on a woman with a prolapsed uterus with complications. She had not expected him to notice her. She supposed that to a man of his standing in the medical profession the students who clustered around him were just so many faces, so many nonentities. Perhaps because she was a woman he had glanced at her quickly and then a second time, his eyes brightening. She was used to these sudden glances of surprise and admiration and gave it no further thought.

But a day or so later, when she was hurrying along the hospital corridor, she had met him face to face and he had broken off his conversation with another doctor to stop her and chat.

"Dr. Emma Wycliffe?" He smiled down at her. She was a tall woman but he topped her by half a dozen inches. His long, narrow, handsome face was tanned. She had been told that in his holidays he was a mountain climber, that he had recently taken part in the ascent of a hitherto unconquered peak in the Austrian Alps. "You are from the States? Your father is Edward Wycliffe. My father was one of your grandfather's disciples. The scientific tradition runs through all your family, doesn't it?"

She had nodded, too nonplussed to speak.

Colburn went on again. "I understand you are here for a year's graduate study. What are you specializing in?"

This at last gave her an opening and she found herself explaining in detail what her purpose was in coming to London. He seemed to listen attentively and then said abruptly, with a sudden pat on her arm, "Good for you! I hope to see more of you." He had then turned away and walked on down the corridor with his companion.

Emma was aware, when she resumed her walk in the opposite direction, that several nurses and students had noticed the encounter. She saw various expressions on their faces, of surprise, envy, mockery, and wondered why the brief interchange should arouse such interest. But in the pressure of her work she forgot the incident.

She was astonished later in the day, when she sat in the small room used by the women on the staff as a place for a few moments' rest, by the sudden remark made by the big girl from Australia who was training as a midwife. "You've caught Lord Byron's eye, haven't you?"

Emma looked at her blankly. "Lord Byron?"

The girl, good natured, laughed at her bewilderment. "Sir

Maurice Colburn, of course. Don't you know that is what they call him? He never fails to notice a goodlooking woman."

Emma put down her cup of tea. "He knows my father's family. That is why he stopped to speak to me."

The girl, pouring hot water from the urn into the teapot, said over her shoulder, "Oh, yes, I dare say. Has to have an excuse, doesn't he? Well, you must be used to that sort of thing. The men don't pass you by, do they?"

Emma, her vexation growing, retorted, "I don't like this sort of talk. *I* do pass *them* by, you know, unless there is good reason not to."

"Oh, all right! Don't lose your temper. You know he's married, of course?"

"Of what consequence is that to me?" Emma's vexation broke out in anger.

"Just thought you might not know. He doesn't let it stand in his way where women are concerned."

Emma said hotly, "I've no interest in his personal life."

She tried to forget this conversation when she encountered Colburn thereafter, but she was aware that it had aroused a certain wariness. It was a handicap, she thought, for a woman who had the professional interests that she had, to have also the sort of physical beauty that inevitably attracted men. In idle moments she often considered her reflection in the looking glass. To her mother her loveliness had always been a special gift, an extra boon in having an only daughter in a family of sons. To herself it had often been a nuisance, a distraction from more important things. She had been a tomboy when she was growing up and her brothers had given her no special attention because she was a girl. Her mother had never made a requirement of lady-like behavior. She had quickly learned, when she had first met boys outside her family, that her natural friendliness had to be checked, for it was misinterpreted. During her medical training, men, if they were not benevolent autocrats, became chiefly obstacles to be circumvented.

So with Colburn she became restrained, only sometimes, in the eagerness generated by a medical problem, responding quickly to his singling her out from among the other students. As a clever, resourceful surgeon her admiration for him grew. A good many of his patients were women. He was in constant demand, called in by the fashionable medical men who specialized in the diseases of women. Emma overheard many conversations in which his surgical skill, his knack for dealing with wealthy and pampered women, the size of the fees he charged, were discussed at length. He was frankly spoken of as a womanizer. It seemed he did not mind the reputation he had in this line. His wife, Emma was told, had long ceased to concern herself with him. She was a wealthy woman and lived most of the year abroad.

But Emma noticed that he did give generously of his time to the poorest women. He made no distinction professionally between the women who enjoyed the comforts of private rooms and those who lay in beds in the crowded wards. Even the streetwalkers received the same care, overlaid with an exchange of bawdy humor, as if on the basis of equality.

When they met in the hospital he was impersonal, exacting, professional. But when she found herself of an evening in the same drawing room or with the same theater party he was Lord Byron indeed. She laughed a little to herself at the frankness of his pursuit of her.

A week ago he had invited her to come with him to the theater, to see a revival of Shakespeare's *The Winter's Tale*, with dinner afterwards at a fashionable restaurant. Emma, feeling the challenge of his approach, had said yes easily. Now this was the evening and, watching the quiet water traffic glide by on the river in the still, clear light of the London June evening, she found she was uneasy about the hours ahead. It would be the first time she had gone to the theater and dined alone with a man who was a comparative stranger. She doubted that Colburn would realize that this was the case. She half wished that she had declined his invitation. A discreet reserve was always safer for a woman. But a sudden surge of recklessness swept through her. She had not come to London to be safe, to be a dedicated hermit, to live the life of a sheltered spinster. Her scope was to be wider and she might as well begin to act on her own at once.

The small traveling clock on the table chimed and she saw that it would soon be time to go downstairs to meet him. She put on the one gown she had that would be suitable for the occasion and re-did her hair, piling the golden coils up onto the top of her head. Then she took the hatbox down from the shelf of the wardrobe and placed it on the table. This was the climax of her arraying herself. It had dwelt in the back of her mind all the while she was dressing.

It was an extravagance, this wide-brimmed, befeathered creation, its elegance emerging from the tissue paper. A theater-hat, it was called. She had worn it on a few occasions and had been both pleased and amused to notice the glances of other women who instantly recognized it as both fashionable and expensive. She could read in their faces the question, How could she afford such a luxury?

The answer was that she could not. Or could not have, if it had not been for Miss Bell's generosity. For the first few weeks in London she had really not noticed the limitations of her budget. The grant of money made to her by the women in Baltimore was just enough to feed and house her. But by midsummer she had begun to chafe at her poverty. Therefore she was delighted as well as amazed when she received a letter from Miss Bell enclosing a draft for the equivalent of fifty dollars. It was, said Miss Bell, to provide her with the means of enjoying a few amenities beyond the day-to-day necessities.

A thrill of pleasure went through Emma when she held the draft in her hand. That amount of money gave her a sense of independence. The feeling of being penniless vanished. She reproached herself that, when she tried to remember Miss Bell more clearly, all she could call up was the sober elegance of the Baltimore house and the figure of a slight, middle-aged woman in a dark, unfashionable dress. She was ashamed that she had given no special thought to the woman who, if Mrs. McHugh was right, had made the decision that had sent her to London. Fingering the draft absently she wondered if Miss Bell had had an inkling of what this extra money would mean to her.

Emma put the big hat on her head and fastened it securely to her luxurious pile of hair. She smiled at her own reflection. She wondered what Miss Bell would think of the use to which some of her money had been put. When she had written to thank her, she had said nothing of how she would spend it. Miss Bell had written again, this time a friendly little note that spoke casually of events in Baltimore that she thought might interest a fellow country-woman abroad. Emma felt a twinge of chagrin at the recollection that this second letter lay unanswered in her writing case. She hoped Miss Bell would excuse her dilatoriness on the ground of pressure of work.

The clock in the nearby parish church striking the quarter after the hour reminded Emma that she was already probably awaited downstairs. She dismissed Miss Bell from her mind and hurried to pick up her gloves and evening purse. As she came down the last flight of steps she saw a man's head illuminated by the hall lamp.

*   *   *

Colburn looked up to greet her. She saw his eyes widen in admiration as he took in her whole appearance, ending with the big hat. It was obvious that he had not expected such splendor. As they left the house and he hailed a hansom cab, he kept glancing at her, as if fascinated by a revelation that had taken him unawares.

He took her to the Old Vic and she was entranced by the play. Afterwards at dinner she did her best to maintain an air of sophistication. She was careful not to drink too much wine. Some inner caution held her back when she realized that Colburn pressed sherry and claret and champagne on her as the meal progressed and at the end suggested a liqueur. So sparing was she that finally he asked her if she was a temperance advocate.

Lifting her glass slightly so that the light caught the color of the drink, she said, "I can scarcely be that, surely?"

His touch of seriousness vanished at the lightness of her tone, but she was aware of the persistence of his efforts to keep her glass filled. She became more and more uneasy at the way he hovered over her, at his catching her hand whenever he could and fondling it. At last she suggested that it was time that she returned to her lodging. The night was pretty well gone. He agreed readily, but she noticed that he hesitated for a moment, as if about to say something that he finally did not voice. When they reached the house where she lodged and she had unlocked the door, he followed her into the vestibule and stood for a while looking up the dimlit stairway.

Suddenly understanding his meaning, she said quickly, "It is quite safe! I shan't need an escort to my own door!"

He did not reply but stood between her and the stairs, smiling faintly in the overhead light that cast shadows over his face. Before she was fully aware of what he was doing, he caught her around the waist and tilted her head back so as to avoid the wide brim of her hat. He was speaking to her as he did so and she realized that he was quoting from the play they had seen — "sweeter than the lids of Juno's eyes Or Cytherea's breath —." As he brought his lips close to her she was suddenly swept by a feeling that she could not control. She thrust at his chest with all her strength. The suddenness and the violence of her action threw him off balance and he was obliged to let go of her and catch the newelpost to prevent himself from falling backwards. When he had regained his balance he stood staring at her for a long moment. She stared back, glad to be released from his grip and at the same time chagrined at the vehemence with which she had pushed him away. At first she saw only anger in his eyes but then a more thoughtful look appeared, as if there was something in her own expression that disconcerted and puzzled him.

"I beg your pardon," he said finally, straightening his collar. "I had better say goodnight."

Emma stammered, "I'm sorry I —"

But he cut her short. "Please accept my apologies. I misjudged the situation."

He stepped past her as he spoke and opening the door walked out, closing it firmly behind him.

Emma stood for a moment collecting herself. All through the evening she had had a sense of some such attempt on his part. She had been prepared, in a way. And yet she had flung him off with a violence that surprised herself. She should have acted with more suavity. But her impulse had been instant, ungovernable. And it was not simply Colburn. She realized that it might have been any man. When she finally gathered herself together and climbed the stairs to her room, she still wondered at herself. She had never before shrunk from kisses and hugs. This was something different, a man's embrace. And she did not want it, would never want it. She felt a wholeness in herself. She would allow no man ever to invade her, ever to breach that wholeness.

She spent a wakeful night, sleeping fitfully. Anxiety fastened itself on her, as it seldom did. She wondered what Colburn might do, whether he would seek some sort of petty revenge. She was certain he was a man who would not overlook a rebuff. He would be able, she knew, to make her remaining stay in London miserable. Worst of all he could hinder her professional life. Instead of justifying to the ladies in Baltimore their support of her, she would fail to obtain the honors she sought.

The next morning, as she finished dressing and left the house to go to the hospital she continued to dwell on the problem. Colburn had an operation scheduled for that afternoon at which she was to be present. Her thoughts kept straying to the question of how he would act towards her. When the time came to go to the operating theater, it seemed at first that Colburn would not take notice of her presence among the others. But afterwards, when he lingered, as he often did, to talk in a relaxed and indulgent fashion to the students who gathered around him, he came face to face with her. His easy smile vanished for a moment and he gave her a somber glance. Then his expression became impersonal and he said, "Ah, Dr. Wycliffe, I have here a note from Mr. Simpson reminding me that I promised to arrange for you to make rounds at St. Bartholomew's as an observer. I'm sorry I've forgotten to do so till now."

He drew a visiting card from his wallet and wrote something hastily on the back. Holding it out to her he said, "That should do it."

With a flood of relief and gratitude she smiled at him. He looked at her now for a long moment, as if considering something. But in the end he said nothing more before turning away. After that, whenever she met him in hospital hours he was casual, more brusque than he had been, passing by her with the same lordly cordiality he used with all his students. Occasionally she met him at the houses of other friends. Then he was more gallant, singling her out, sitting by her for an hour or more, sometimes even offering to take her home. She never accepted. She noticed that on each such refusal his expression changed for a moment, to a half-angry frown. But it was a mere glimpse of his inner feeling. He did not again invite her to go out with him.

*   *   *

"Mother dearest," wrote Emma, "I spent yesterday evening with a group of English suffragettes—members of Sylvia Pankhurst's National Women's Social and Political Union. Now don't worry. I'm not going to get myself arrested and clapped into prison, though my sympathies are very much with them. I must remember my ladies in Baltimore. They would be upset if they heard that I had involved myself in political protests, especially since this would interfere with the purpose for which they sent me here to London. But it is thrilling to talk to some of these women, who are ready and willing to make any sacrifice to achieve a wider sphere for all of us. You know how it was, five years ago, when I first went to medical school in Philadelphia and the girls in my class were jeered at by some of the men and upbraided in the newspaper for being unwomanly. How silly, to think that being a doctor is unwomanly! How threatening the men seem to find us if we make the slightest show of independence!''

Emma laid down her pen thoughtfully. Her mother's letter had contained several phrases that betrayed the uneasiness she felt over her only daughter's choice of career. Her mother had said, ''Yes, my darling. I know you will succeed in what you so earnestly seek to do. You have never really been defeated or checked in your life. May you never know what true disillusionment is. May that brightness of yours never be dimmed. It is too precious to me and will ever to be anyone who is discouraged or hopeless or frozen within themselves.''

Emma went on with her letter. ''This evening I am going to a gathering at Angela Bigwood's flat. Usually Angela has no time for frivolity. She is secretary of a society that teaches illiterate servant girls to read and write and the rest of her time is absorbed in working for the National Women's Social and Political Union. She daily expects to find herself in prison with Mrs. Pankhurst. She often tells me that Englishwomen will obtain the right to vote before us Americans. But tonight we are celebrating a minor success—I haven't time to explain to you what it is—and Angela says there will be a little sherry wine and some cakes and we can dance to her gramophone. I'll give you an account when I write again.''

When Emma reached Angela's flat the long summer evening was still light. The sound of many voices all talking at once greeted her as she climbed the last flight of steps. Angela's big room was crowded and it was some time before she had met and chatted with all the people she knew.

At last she found herself sharing a window seat with a slender young girl whose hair shone red-gold in the rays of the setting sun shining in at the window. The girl, laughing at Emma's efforts to get out of the worst of the crush, shrank back into her corner to make way for Emma's more ample skirts. She said, ''You'll be quite squashed, if you don't sit down here.''

''Thank you. Everyone seems very animated.''

''Oh, yes!'' The girl gave her a closer look. ''You must be Angela's American friend.''

''Has she only one?''

The girl laughed again. ''Oh, dear, no! I mean, you must be the doctor who has come here to study. Angela has spoken of you

often. She is so impressed by all you've done. She says you make
the men sit up and take notice.''

"I'm Emma Wycliffe. Yes, I'm here for graduate study in
medicine.''

"I'm Alison St. Claire. I really have very much wanted to meet
you. It is wonderful for a woman to be doing all the things you
are doing. My own efforts seem so puny in comparison.''

"And what are they?''

"I am a slum visitor for the London Women's Rescue
Mission.''

Emma said, surprised, "You look very young!''

Alison laughed. "So everyone says. It comes of being so fair.
I'm your age, I'm sure, or nearly. In any case, I'm tired of the
idea that women must always be sheltered. We're not, you know,
unless we have dependable fathers and husbands. But of course!
You must know all that better than I. You're a physician. You
must be fully aware of what happens to women in those dreadful
tenements —''

"Too many children and not enough money to feed and clothe
them, so that some of them take to the streets out of despair —''

"Or sell their little girls into sexual slavery.''

"I did my internship in a large public hospital in New York
City.''

"Ah, then, of course you know. Why can't we do something
effective to change these things? Angela and her friends say we
can do everything when we have the vote. But that seems so far
away.''

"I know very little about political affairs. But it seems to me
that all I can do as a doctor is try to cure the disease rather than
prevent it.''

They went on talking for a while until suddenly Alison put her
hand on Emma's arm. "Will you come with me some day when I
make visits? I wish you could see what it is like here.''

"I should like to—when I can find a free moment.''

In the weeks that followed Emma found an occasional morning
or afternoon when she could join Alison. She became aware,
observing the wretched, crowded rooms, dirty, fireless in cold
weather, inhabited by the broken, hopeless women whom Alison
came to succor, that she was coming to grips with reality as she
had not done before. She had seen squalor as extreme, women as
abject, when she had served her internship. But then she had been

protected from too intimate a sense of this underside of life by the lingering effects of the sort of upbringing she had had. Absorbed in her professional problems, urged on by the need to gain medical experience, she had walked through those dreadful streets, done her work in those dreadful tenements, untouched by doubts about the unchangeability of such human misery. Looking back, she saw that she had preserved a sort of invincible innocence, invincible until now. Now, with the growth of her professional vision, she began to see clearly that there were things that could be done, reforms that could be made. A fire began to burn in her that gradually consumed the childish awe with which she had started out on her medical career, that wiped out the docility with which she had once accepted the authority of her elders and the views they laid down as laws.

*   *   *

Her new friendship with Alison made the biggest difference in her life. They formed the habit of spending their leisure time together. She taught Alison to play tennis, which she had played in her college days, and sometimes on weekends they went bicycling, or punting on the upper reaches of the Thames with young men whom Alison knew. Invariably they wound up these lighthearted sessions at Alison's flat, alone, cheerful and relaxed from the vigorous exercise and fresh air.

"Oh, Emma, it's such fun to be with you! I've never enjoyed anything so much."

"We do get along very well together, Alison. We seem to think alike."

They stood close together beside the table on which were spread the remains of a late tea. Alison picked up the remains of a crumpet and held it close to Emma's mouth. "You're still hungry. I can tell."

Emma opened her mouth and bit into the crumpet, at the same time without conscious thought taking Alison around the waist.

Alison laughed and leaned against her. "Dear Emma! I used to be lonely sometimes, when I hadn't enough to do. Oh, I know, there's Charlie Armstrong and David, but I can't have them here at all hours. And they do get a bit tiresome."

Emma swallowed the bite of crumpet. "You're not serious, then, with either one?"

"No. I know that my mother and dad are waiting for me to say

I'm engaged, to one of them or some other suitable young man. I am certain that is the only reason they agreed to my coming to London to be an independent woman. She can have her fling, they think, and then she will be ready to settle down to a normal life.''

"Perhaps they are right. What is a normal life, to them?''

"Oh, that I should marry someone with an established future—a solicitor or a bank clerk or someone like that and then live in a suburban house and have several children.''

Emma laughed. "Is that a picture of your parents' life?''

"Almost exactly—except that I am an only child and a girl—that, I am sure, was unforeseen. My father is a doctor in a country town in Hampshire. He and my mother distrust London. There are too many strange creatures like you about.''

"Like me!''

Alison grinned up at her. "Only they are thinking of the male sex.''

"I am safe, then?''

Alison hesitated. "To tell the truth, I haven't mentioned you at home. I'm quite sure that they would think a female American doctor would be a dangerous influence.''

Emma, still holding her around the waist, looked down into her face. "Why would that be? You have quite a few medical women here in England. You're ahead of us, really. Is it because your father does not want women in the medical profession?''

"Oh, he is very conservative, of course. But I don't think his objection would be really that. It is simply that they think of Americans as—unpredictable, rather temperamental.''

Emma laughed again. "I'm very predictable, Alison. At least, you seem to know when I'm hungry—and when I'm discouraged and need cheering up, or when I'm vexed and need an outlet for my annoyance —''

Alison interrupted her by putting her fingers on Emma's lips. "Emma, you're such a joy! Of course I can tell your feelings! You never try to hide them. And it pleases me so to be able to comfort you when that is what you want or to be merry with you when you are happy.''

"You're a darling, Alison—my darling," said Emma, gathering her up in her arms and kissing her.

No one found it strange that soon Emma and Alison chose to share lodgings. There was the obvious saving in money for rent and food. And they already shared professional interests and friends. Between themselves the decision and the acting upon it seemed something that happened spontaneously, not the initiative of one rather than the other. They fit into one another's life easily, comfortably. Alison, naturally talkative and cheerful, could be quiet and unobtrusive when Emma needed to study. When Emma put aside her books she was ready to talk, laugh, argue. Emma, watching her at times when she sat absorbed in writing the reports she prepared for the Mission, thought, What a wonderful companion she is.

The first night they spent in the new lodging their tacit understanding rose to the surface. The moving of their belongings had been done hurriedly, separately, in a few moments snatched from a busy day. Emma, bringing her trunk and her books in a cab and directing the cabman to carry them up the steep, dark stairs to the top flat, had found Alison's things already there, hastily disposed in a sort of order. In the evening, when she returned from the hospital, she was greeted by Alison. Alison, recognizing her step on the stairs, opened the door and ran out on the landing, crying, "Oh, Emma, how lovely! You're early!"

"I came as soon as I could."

Alison pulled her into the room and hugged her. "We're going to celebrate, Emma, all by ourselves. I haven't told a soul that we moved in today. See, I've brought some wine to have with our dinner."

It was a happy meal. Alison, with her mixture of merriment and sudden little sharpnesses of manner and words, dispelled any remnant of dejection and irritation that Emma might have brought with her from the hospital. After they had eaten and had cleared away the table, Alison all at once stopped talking.

Emma, surprised at her abrupt silence, looked over her shoulder from across the room, where she had been placing the cups and saucers in the cupboard. Alison stood still in the middle of the room, the dishtowel hanging from her hand.

Emma asked, "Why, what is the matter?"

Alison's little laugh was unsteady. "It all seems so — so lovely — and so improbable."

"What does?" Emma came over and stood looking down at her.

"That we're here together like this. It has all been so easy, as if it was meant to be —"

Puzzled, Emma said, "Of course it has been easy. Why

shouldn't it be? We both wanted to make the move. It is not such a strange thing for two women like us to share lodgings.''

"Oh, no. But you and I, Emma —''

Emma put her arms around her. "Well, what about you and me?''

Alison dropped the dishtowel and put her arms around Emma's neck. "Oh, Emma, Emma, I do love you so!'' She buried her face in Emma's shoulder.

Emma said nothing but held her closer, kissing her gently on the ear closest to her. Alison shivered and made a half-hearted effort to push her away. "Oh, Emma, don't! I can't stand it!''

Emma held her away to look at her. "Why, what is the matter? Don't you like that?''

Alison clung closer. "Oh, no, that's not it! It's just too much! I feel you right down to the marrow of my bones!''

Emma laughed as she pulled her close again and began to kiss her all over her face. When she reached her lips she touched her tongue to them and found them slightly parted in readiness. For a moment they stopped and gazed at each other, as if measuring the distance they had come. Then they drew close once more, feeling the beat of the blood in their bodies.

In bed that night, the light out and only the moonlight in the room to show them each other's eyes, Alison lay curled in Emma's arms. Their naked bodies clung together, their skins moist from the close contact, their hands eager to find the sensitive spots in each other. Where one led the other followed, turn about, each discovering a new delight, each teaching and being taught, till the leap in the joined bodies brought a breathless pause. Only when the moon had vanished and the room was dark did sleep overcome them, still wrapped in each other's arms.

*   *   *

The coming of Alison into her life gave a magic quality to all sorts of ordinary things. Emma found now that her feet had wings when she went about the thousand pressing details that filled her day. She never seemed to tire, as if the thought of being with Alison in the evening banished any sense of effort. She found herself responding to people, to the patients she was called upon to treat, the nurses who helped her, the doctors who supervised her, with a new sensitivity, a more open sympathy. The spring of happiness that flowed so freely within her gave a glow to the

world. She was keenly aware of the pleasure of walking through
the streets of London in the moist, fresh May mornings, of the
beauty of the May trees in full bloom. Even the sights and smells
of the hospital lost some of the depressing effect they often had on
her. She noticed that many of those she dealt with were affected
by her own enthusiasm, that a nurse would suddenly look up at
her from the task of feeding a patient, that someone's head would
turn in the corridor as she passed by, as if her joyous passage was
a magnet.

She had not known that there was this immense new dimension
in the range of her feeling. There seemed now an inexhaustible
scope for her spirit within the physical movements of her daily
life. The weeks and months passed by in a tremendous surge of
energy and achievement. The days were crowded with the
demands of her professional life. In the pressure of each moment
she exulted in the sense that she was learning, developing,
reaching out as she had never done before. And at the end of the
day there was Alison and their private life together, the sharing of
experience, the joy of easy, comfortable companionship, and at
last, in the still peace of the night, Alison in bed with her, seeking
the bliss of her love as she sought Alison's.

The tempo of her medical work increased. In the New Year
came greater duties and opportunities, more exacting require-
ments. One opportunity she especially prized was that Colburn
chose her as one of the select group of students who accompanied
him on his own cases. She was surprised and grateful to him. He
never paid special attention to her. Surrounded by the whole
group of students, he kept up his usual manner, casual,
impersonal, sometimes satirical. But more than once she had
looked up to find his eyes on her, speculative, thoughtful. He
must still wonder about her, probably still resented the recollec-
tion of her rebuff. But these were only brief glimpses of his
personal feelings. Quite often, in rotation with the other students,
he chose her to follow a particular case through to its conclusion.

One of the most serious of these was that of a woman with a
massive infection of the uterus and hemorrhages resulting from a
bungled abortion. Medical care had come too late and Colburn
himself obviously thought the woman doomed. Emma could not
get the memory of the woman's hopeless face and ravaged body
out of her mind. Numbers of times during her internship she had
had to repair the damage caused by a woman's furtive attempt to

rid herself of an unwanted conception. Then she had still accepted without question the attitude of her teachers, that no reputable doctor would perform an abortion except in the most extreme emergency. But now, with her growing experience, she began to be troubled by a sense of cowardice when a wretched slum dweller begged her for help. Colburn's patient was a woman in her thirties, a governess with no friends or relatives who would brave the disgrace in coming to her aid. Emma thought, What could have induced such a woman to seek help from an unqualified abortionist, except desperation in the face of the refusal of help by a reputable doctor? She would certainly die. The disgrace she had sought to hide would outlive her.

Emma was with her when she died. Meeting Colburn as he came in response to a summons, too late, Emma merely looked at him silently. Colburn, at the sight of her face, said, "She is dead?"

Emma nodded, still silent. Colburn, upset, said harshly, "Well, it was inevitable. Why do these women do these things?" When Emma did not answer, he said in a gentler tone, "Well, buck up. You must learn to face this sort of thing."

Emma said, "It is so unnecessary."

"To every physician the loss of a patient in death seems unnecessary somehow."

"I don't mean that. I mean, it seems so unnecessary that a woman in her situation should need to risk her life so."

He looked at her closely. "She evidently thought it very necessary, in order to protect her reputation."

"But why should she have had to?" Emma demanded, her sense of outrage overflowing at last in speech. "Why should it not have been possible for her to have professional attention at the beginning?"

Colburn's expression changed to impatient indulgence, "Because, my dear Dr. Wycliffe, the law does not permit a physician to perform an abortion at will, to cover up indiscretion. It is the penalty a woman must pay in sinning against society, if not against God."

"In that case, how about the man? A woman does not conceive by herself."

Colburn, as if irritated by her statement, turned away. "It is assumed that a woman, being of the purer sex, should have a stronger sense of virtue, which she neglects at her peril."

"That is nonsense and you know it is!"

He spun around to glare at her angrily. "Don't be a fool! What I say is what our society accepts. If you question such things, keep your questioning to yourself. It will do you no good, in your professional life, to break the rules. I will give you that advice once. I'll not tolerate any further such remarks."

She stared back at him, at first indignant at his tone of voice and ready to retort. But her indignation was checked. She said, "I'm sorry. I spoke so simply because I feel strongly the injustice of the situation."

He shrugged. "That is beside the point. I advise you to think first of your professional responsibilities. A physician must not lend himself as an accomplice to illegal acts."

"Unless the persons involved are wealthy enough to escape the consequences."

His anger shone forth again in his face but he suppressed it. "It is one of the privileges of the wealthy to afford what others cannot."

Emma, repelled by his statement but unable to answer it, sat down on the edge of a hard chair and gazed at the floor.

Colburn's voice cut into her thoughts. "Cheer up. Confronting misery is one of the hazards of a medical career. You will get used to it."

"I don't think so — not when that misery can so evidently be avoided."

Colburn burst out impatiently. "Oh, you women! You're always bringing your personal sensibilities into every situation! That's one good reason for keeping you out of the medical profession!" For a few moments he fumed silently and then said in a quieter tone, "Don't let your feelings run away with you. If you want to make reforms, remember that they will take a long time—especially when it comes to changing the nature of man and woman."

*   *   *

That evening Emma, as she made her way home from the hospital, longed for the solace of Alison's quick sympathy. In the brief period of their coming together the flat had become thoroughly home, Alison the anchor of her life. Alison was always instantly aware of her state of mind, always ready to soothe and cheer.

Alison's quick, light step sounded in the room before she had reached the top of the stairs. The door was open when she got to it.

"Emma, darling!" Alison pulled her into the room. "I'm so glad you've come! I am tired of writing this report."

"I'm glad to be home."

Alison gave her a second look. "There is something wrong."

"Wrong? Not more wrong than usual."

"Oh, yes, there is! You're a goose, Emma, if you think I can't see it. Something is worse than usual."

Emma did not answer as she took off her hat. Alison, casting covert glances at her, gathered up the papers strewn on the table.

Emma said, "I ought not to bring my problems home to you, Alison, but I cannot help it. I must unburden myself somehow."

Alison answered quickly, "Of course. What is it now, Emma?"

"We've had a particularly bad case—one of Colburn's—of a woman who has died of a bungled abortion. He will not admit that something might have been done to prevent it — Oh, he is a dedicated man, a first-rate surgeon. But he refuses to believe that a reputable doctor may give women advice that would avoid the need for an abortion or aid them when they feel they must have one. That is the attitude that drives women into the hands of unscrupulous practitioners."

Alison's glance was shrewd. "So you have had another argument with him."

Emma sighed. "Yes. Oh, Alison, all this turning away, this denial that something might be done! We're not living in the Middle Ages, to say that it is simply God's will that someone must die in agony. It is merely washing one's hands of someone else's misery —"

Alison put her hand through Emma's arm. "Now, do quiet down, Emma. After all, it is against the law for a doctor to do anything for a woman unless her life is in danger. At least, that is what you have told me. I've always heard that a doctor can lose his right to practice if he does."

"Yes. We are all such cowards. But, Alison, wealthy people can always get relief, competent help. Wealthy women don't die of bungled abortions. It is only the poor devils whose lives are so miserable anyway —"

"Emma, do be careful. I know that you are indignant about

such injustices. So am I. But Colburn is right. You must not
jeopardize your reputation. A woman is twice as vulnerable as a
man in such circumstances. There are only too many people eager
to find ways of discrediting a woman doctor.''

''I know that very well. But, Alison, it is not everywhere in the
world that people are so benighted. I have heard of clinics in
Holland where women can go and get advice about preventing
conception and devices for that purpose. I wish I could visit there
and see for myself before I go back to the States.''

''You cannot?''

''I haven't the money. By the time I finish my course here I
shan't have a penny more than my fare home. Unless —''

''Unless?''

''Well, you know, I've just thought of it. I wonder if Miss Bell
would lend me the money to visit Holland before I go back.''

''Oh, Miss Bell!'' There was a little laugh in Alison's voice.
''Emma, she certainly is very generous. Didn't she send you
money at Easter?''

''Yes. You remember, we had a glorious week in the Lake
District on it. I should never have got there otherwise. However,
if I ask her for money to go to Holland, I certainly cannot tell her
why I want it. I shall have to say I want to go to Paris for a quick
visit to the hospitals there. I wonder if she would respond.''

''Well, you can only write and ask.''

For a while Emma mulled over the thought of asking Miss Bell
for the money but she did nothing. At first she told herself that
she was too busy even to snatch a few moments to compose a
letter. As it was, she received more letters from Miss Bell than
she wrote. Her replies were always delayed and only prompted by
the arrival of a second letter before she had answered the first. Yet
she had come to look for the envelopes with the Baltimore
postmark with as much eagerness as she did those from her
mother. Miss Bell was well acquainted with London—in fact,
with France and Italy as well. She was, Miss Bell had said in one
of her letters, in the habit of spending a couple of months abroad
each year. She spoke about the things in London she looked
forward to, Covent Garden and the Opera, the Royal Academy
show, the Shakespeare revivals. Gradually Emma had been
forming a picture of Miss Bell in her mind's eye that was
somehow separate from her recollection of the rather prim woman
in the staid Baltimore house.

When she thought about it, she was worried by the fact that she could not distinctly remember how Miss Bell looked. In the excitement and emotional stress of her visit to Miss Bell's house, she had failed to see her clearly. Mrs. McHugh she recalled easily—the fair, faded hair, the sympathetic blue eyes, the rosy complexion of a cheerful, plump woman of fifty. But Miss Bell's face eluded her.

Miss Bell's letters were surprising. They were not such as she would have expected an elderly spinster to write. Sometimes they made her laugh, with their turns of phrase and sharp comments. Miss Bell often quoted the Greek and Latin classics and sometimes the bawdier passages. There was something Elizabethan about Miss Bell's style of writing, thought Emma, thinking of the passages in Shakespeare that, as an adult she had found were expurgated from the plays as she had been taught them in school.

Once she had commented on this and Miss Bell had replied, "Fortunately, I had a classical education—the sort that is usually reserved for boys. I have never been able to understand why girls should not learn the classics. It was Juvenal who said that it was folly to lock up a woman. She is quite clever enough to make use of her guards to free herself."

But presently Emma had to admit to herself that there was really another, underlying reason why she shrank from writing to Miss Bell now. That reason was simply that by doing so she had to acknowledge that the end of her stay in London was fast approaching. In a few short weeks she must part from Alison and yet even the idea of this seemed like death. She could not imagine being without Alison. When she faced the coming of June and her own departure she found herself inventing all sorts of fanciful possibilities. Alison would persuade her parents to let her visit the States and Emma's family. Alison would seek some sort of employment that would provide her with passage across the Atlantic and a means of livelihood when she arrived—as a companion, perhaps, to a wealthy woman or as a governess. Emma was shy of mentioning these thoughts, not knowing how Alison might see such suggestions.

And Alison herself worried her. As summer approached Alison sometimes made an allusion to their impending separation. Occasionally she burst out with a cry of, "Oh, Emma, what am I going to do when you're not here!" But as the days went by

Emma was aware of a subtle change in their dealings with one another.

It was chiefly a difference in the way Alison responded to her caresses. Sometimes when they went to bed Alison would melt lovingly in her arms. But often now she would protest for a while, lying on the side of the bed, gently pushing Emma's hands away. There seemed to be an ambivalence in her attitude, as if her body sought Emma's coaxing and fondling, while her mind held her back, instructed her to defeat Emma's wooing. Aware of this Emma tried harder to cajole her and in the end Alison, with a sudden laugh, would give in.

But Emma was left wondering. More and more the spontaneity of their feeling for each other seemed to be ebbing. In the mornings, when they first got out of bed, Alison was gay and happy, ready to play as they bathed and dressed. She was unwilling to say goodbye when they parted for the day and always looked forward to the evening when they would be together again. But when evening came she seemed reluctant to come out from behind the facade of the brisk, capable Miss St. Claire, who had little time for frivolity.

Little by little Emma had learned about Alison's people. Almost every weekend Alison was away from London, visiting her parents in the Hampshire town. When she came back from these visits she was even more talkative than usual, full of sometimes critical remarks about her parents. Emma saw that, under this bright, cheerful disdain, Alison had withdrawn from their life in common, as if being back as a child with her parents had aroused in her self-doubts and feelings of guilt that centered on Emma. She tried to evade intimacy in both bodily contact and in conversation. When they went to bed on the evenings when Alison returned from these visits, she was especially unwilling to surrender to Emma, especially unyielding in accepting Emma's loving caresses. Emma, dismayed, began to protest against these weekend visits.

"But, Emma, I must go and see them, as often as possible. I promised that when they finally agreed to letting me come to London. Oh, I know, you think that is childish. I'm twenty-four years old and ought to be able to do what I think I should. But you don't know my parents. They are very staid. They will never believe that I should do as I like until I'm married and then it must be what my husband wants. One is an eternal child with them.

They feel, I'm sure, that they must require me to visit them as often as possible, so that they can keep tabs on me."

"Then you must come to the States with me—assert your independence!"

"To the States! Why, Emma, that would be impossible!"

"Is it? How could your parents object to your coming with me to visit my parents?"

Alison was silent and looked down at the floor. Emma, excited at having finally voiced what was in her mind, pressed on. "Alison, there is no reason why you cannot come with me—or at least follow after me soon. I cannot bear the idea of leaving you here!"

But still Alison hesitated, embarrassment preventing her from replying.

Emma pleaded. "Alison, my darling, I've spent hours trying to think of some way that we should not be separated. Surely you are as unhappy as I am about my going back. Don't you realize that it is only a few weeks now and we shan't be together?"

Alison suddenly burst out, "Oh, Emma, of course! I dread it as much as you do. But there is something I haven't told you." She stopped abruptly.

"What? What is it?"

Alison, hearing the alarm in her voice, said soothingly, "My parents are making a question about my staying on in London any longer. They have never liked the idea that I should be here alone and mingling with people they know nothing about."

"But you're not living alone."

Alison did not look at her. "I haven't told them that I am living with you, with another girl."

"Why?"

"Because they would not like it. I would have had to tell them who you are and they don't like Americans. At least, they are uneasy about Americans. My mother thinks all American girls are fast. I have told you this before."

Emma burst into a laugh. "You would not like to disillusion her by taking me with you to visit them?"

Alison did not join in her laugh. "No, Emma. I don't think it would be a good idea. You'd look like—such a rare, splendid, exotic, creature—they'd take fright right away."

Emma eyed her seriously. This was not the carefree, joyful, uncalculating Alison she had first known. A dreadful feeling of impending disaster suddenly stirred at the bottom of her heart. Something was happening to her Alison and she could not tell what it was.

Alison, relieved by her less tense tone, went on. "I couldn't possibly mention the idea of going across the Atlantic with you. You see that, don't you? They are anxious, you see, that I should meet a suitable young man and marry. After all, I shall soon be getting to be an elderly spinster!"

Emma said in an artificially calm voice, "And that is what you look forward to?"

Alison turned away from her and looked out at the window for a few minutes. Turning back she said, "Emma, I shall never be as happy as I've been here with you. I know that. I cannot ever expect to find someone else like you, someone who loves me the way you do, who has so many surprising things to say, who is always just a little ahead of me—oh, someone who is not you! But, Emma, this cannot last. It could not even if you weren't going away. We cannot, my darling, do such a wild thing as to stay together this way. If you weren't such a romantic old thing, you'd have seen that before now."

Emma sat perfectly still, stunned into complete silence. She heard Alison speaking, repeating what she had just said in other words, talking faster and faster to try to break down her shock. But it was as if she heard someone else's voice, talking to someone other than herself. This was not possible. This was not Alison saying these things to her, Emma.

At last Alison stopped. Emma said in a voice that sounded strange even in her own ears, "Alison, are you seriously thinking of marrying?"

Alison answered in a rush, "If you mean, right now, right away, why, no. But, Emma, I don't really have a lifework, like you. Of course, I have been doing something I think is useful and important. But I can't say I won't lay it down at once if the right man presents himself. If he doesn't—well, I won't be worse off than most women. With most women, you know, anything they do before marriage is just a makeshift. My parents feel that way and they would think it tragic if my makeshift turned into a lifework."

"That is not the way I see my life."

"Oh, for you, Emma, it is very different. But even you might think otherwise if circumstances change."

"Circumstances will not change with me."

Alison heard the bitterness in Emma's voice and it touched her heart. This after all was Emma, her Emma. She went over quickly and put her arms around Emma, pulling her head against her breast. "Oh, my darling! Let us forget all about your going to the States. It won't be for a while yet."

And Emma, too wounded to want to probe the pain, gave in and pulled Alison down on her lap.

But the realization of what lay beneath the surface with Alison stood in the way, for Emma, whenever they made love. She had known before that Alison, after the first few unfettered days of their being together, needed a few moments at the start of their love-making in which to exorcise the strict restraints of her up-bringing. Under Emma's gentle coaxing the initial shrinking generally wore off. With a man, thought Emma, the sort of man her parents would want her to marry, Alison would be passive and reluctant. She had confessed to Emma that she feared penetration by a man. When she was with Emma, attraction and rejection warred within her until the touch of Emma's hands drove away her fears. Then in the momentary release of desire she clung as closely to Emma's body as she could. Very often she would weep softly for a few minutes before settling to sleep in Emma's arms, her tears tickling Emma's neck as they ran down into the pillow.

One Friday evening Emma was surprised on arriving at the flat to find that Alison was preparing a meal. She had expected her to be packing a few belongings, ready to depart for the train that would take her to her parents' home.

Alison gave her a vigorous kiss but did not linger before going back to the stove, saying over her shoulder, "I thought you'd like a real meal for a change, Emma. I was properly taught the house-wifely arts, though you may not think so."

Emma asked sharply, "Is there something the matter?"

Alison paused before replying, in a careful voice, "Why, no! Why should you think so?"

"Because by this time of a Friday evening you are always on your way to Paddington station. Are you staying in London this weekend?"

Alison busied herself with the food. "Yes. That is, something has come up. I've had to make an engagement for tomorrow that can only be made on the weekend. I sent my mother a telegram to explain."

"But you didn't bother to tell me."

Alison was forced to turn around. She dropped her eyes at the sight of Emma's angry face.

"I didn't think it would matter. You're always busy at the hospital on Saturday and Sunday."

Emma's voice was charged with anger. "Of course I am. My time in London is limited. I cannot afford to waste any of it. But if I had known that, for once, you were staying in town, I should certainly have arranged some free hours. It is too late now."

Alison's voice faltered. "I'm sorry, Emma. I didn't think —" She left the sentence unfinished and turned back to her task.

Emma took off her hat. The May evening, fine and calm, came in at the open windows. She suddenly felt aggrieved, with a longing for carefree, idle hours in the open air, away from the sights and sounds and tensions of the hospital. Since Alison was silent, she finally asked, "What is your engagement? Is it something to do with Angela and her suffragettes? Are they planning a demonstration in Hyde Park?" She tried to make her tone jocular.

Alison answered hurriedly, "Oh, no! At least, yes, it has something to do with the Freedom League. They don't like the way Mrs. Pankhurst runs things. They've been receiving some legal advice from—from someone—he is a sympathizer. He thinks women in England have received very shoddy treatment under the law. He says it is a disgrace to a civilized country. He has been donating his services —"

Emma walked across the room and putting her hands on Alison's shoulders turned her around. "Alison, what are you talking about? What has this got to do with your staying in town?"

Alison shrank away from her. "Oh, Emma, I promised Arthur that I would stay in town and spend some of Saturday and Sunday with him. He has been so kind, all this past month, whenever we've needed help of any sort. I can call on him at any time and he will come as soon as he can. I've told you about these worrisome cases we've had with landlords who won't provide the most necessary repairs to those awful tenements —"

Emma, taking her hands away, said nothing as Alison's hasty, half-incoherent explanations flowed on. At last Alison stopped in mid-sentence. For a while there was silence in the room as she made the last preparations for their meal. Then she said placatingly,

"There, that's safe. It can wait till we are ready. I bought a bottle of wine, Emma. The beaujolais you like. Shall we have some?"

Emma looked at her for a long moment. Resentment mingled with a more thoughtful impulse in her. Obviously Alison had shirked telling her of this engagement, had thought to soften the effect of its announcement by going to great effort in preparing a careful meal. The bottle of wine climaxed it.

Emma demanded, "Who is Arthur?"

Alison put the bottle of wine into her hands. "Arthur Clifton. Open the wine, Emma."

Automatically Emma took the corkscrew from her and began to unstopper the bottle. "And why are you staying in town to spend the weekend with him?"

Alison said testily, "I'm not spending the weekend with him. He asked me to stop in town so that we might have dinner together and go the Philharmonic concert. He has asked me so often and I have always said No, that I had to go to my people. Finally I gave in. My parents know him. They think — they think —"

"They think he is a suitable husband for you."

"Yes. They would like me to marry him."

After a pause Emma said, "This does not sound like something that has happened suddenly, Alison. Yet you've never told me anything about it."

Alison turned her head away. "I couldn't bring myself to speak of it. I haven't really encouraged him, Emma. I thought that he would get tired of hanging about me —"

"But he hasn't."

"No, he hasn't." Alison paused and then burst out as if she could restrain herself no longer. "He has asked me to marry him, I have put him off again and again. He expects a definite answer tomorrow."

"Are you going to marry him?" Emma's voice was like a lash.

Alison stood silent with downcast eyes.

"Well?"

"I don't know. I scarcely know whether I want to marry at all."

Emma, stung by this admission, could not respond to the troubled sadness in the other girl's eyes. She raged, "So you have had no real thought of me then when we've been alone! Or when I believed we were alone, just the two of us, with no one else present in body or spirit. Arthur has been with us. You've been thinking of him, whether you should marry him or not. You have deceived me, Alison."

Alison flushed hotly and angrily. "No, no, I have not, Emma. But surely you must see that this is wrong—that what we are doing cannot continue."

"What is wrong? What are you talking about? There is nothing wrong with what lies between us. Only if we deceive each other, only if we allow others to determine how we feel towards each other. Alison, I love you. I thought you loved me."

Alison's brief anger fled. "Oh, Emma, of course I love you. I'll never love anyone else as I love you. But there are things — I can't marry you. We can't have a household and a family. We must conform to what the world demands—what our consciences demand."

"Our consciences! Don't speak for mine!"

They quarreled, bitterly, striving to wound each other as deeply as possible. At the climax of their quarrel Emma left the flat and walked doggedly for an hour or more, unheeding the crowds in the street who jostled her in her distrait mood. Her anger and her anguish rose as nausea in her throat as she thought of going back, and yet the next moment some recollection of Alison made her long to return and unsay the words she had spoken. At last she did return and as she opened the door Alison flew into her arms with a cry of relief and joy.

But their conflict was unresolved. On Saturday when Emma came home from the hospital Alison was not there. She had left a note on the table reminding Emma that she was to spend the afternoon with Arthur and had no idea when she would be back. She did not return in fact till late in the evening, coming in alone to find Emma still sitting at her work table with books and notes scattered before her.

She had purposely taken leave of him downstairs, thought Emma, while Alison chattered on, too lightly, about her afternoon out. On Sunday morning, as she left for the hospital, Emma remarked as casually as she could, "You might as well bring him upstairs when you get back from the concert." and Alison did so.

The young man who came in with her was tall and lean-faced. His clear brown eyes gazed at Emma in open admiration. He had heard a great deal about her, he said, from Alison. He said frankly that he was impressed by Emma's record as a pioneer woman in the medical profession. He was articulate and shrewd and well-informed. He kept glancing at Alison as if sharing with her much of his thoughts.

When he left, Emma was in a bad humor and Alison suffered the reaction of the nervous strain under which she had been dwelling. Again they quarreled, as violently as before. She would leave the flat, Emma declared. She could not stand this anomalous situation, this loss of Alison as wholly hers. She would not share her with anyone, in any way. Alison retorted that after all Emma was leaving London, perhaps forever, in only a few weeks. What would then become of their meaning to each other? Emma, reminded that she had given no real heed to this inevitable parting, said resentfully that a permanent separation was not necessary, could not be, that somehow they would have found a way to be reunited.

"But how, Emma?" Alison demanded, anguished. "How? Oh, Emma, we can't go on like this forever! We must part. I must settle my life properly. I cannot hurt my parents. It is best that we make a clean break now, before we get too committed."

"Too committed! Alison, I cannot be more committed!"

In the end, after a series of such quarrels, exhausted, emptied of resentment, of the anger they felt towards each other, they reached a calmer shore, salvaging some of the fondness, the pleasure in each other's company. But to Emma it was obvious that something had been lost—the delight, the exhileration, the special luxury of their first weeks together. They were too careful of each other's feelings, too sore from their combat to invite each other into the inner recesses of their separate daily lives.

Besides, thought Emma, if what she says is true, Arthur must have first place with her. A special resentment dwelt in her heart which she could not eradicate. Alison had never really accepted her as her lover. For moments—precious moments—Alison had given in to the seduction of love in her arms. For moments Alison had forgotten the pattern of life to which she had been bred. But never for more than fleeting moments. She had, in fact, lived with a sense of horror at what they were to each other. Thinking this, Emma finally resigned herself to the loss of Alison. I never really

had her, she thought in this low spot of sadness. I deceived
myself. And poor Alison. If she has always felt this way, she
must sometimes have been very unhappy.

Their new, calmer friendship fed chiefly on their common
interests. Alison's attention was taken up more and more with the
demands of her work. Attempts were being made in Parliament to
change laws that might improve the lot of slum dwellers and
elderly paupers, and Arthur came more and more often into these
affairs. Emma, in an effort to forget her own heart sickness,
welcomed the heavier schedule of work and study that her
approaching departure from London entailed. She found herself
beginning to long for the end of her stay. She wanted to be away
from Alison, away from London, away from the constant
reminders of that short-lived bliss, that brief, golden time of her
first days with Alison.

                    *   *   *

She sat down and wrote to Miss Bell and asked her for the
money to go to France. And then she immersed herself in her
work. She was restless and half-angry in spite of this. Alison,
noticing that she was short-tempered and moody, made a special
effort to comfort her. Grudgingly she tried to respond. But living
with Alison now was something quite different from what it had
been. They stood on another footing with one another. Emma felt
that the ground they stood on was made of glass, that it would
crash to a thousand fragments at too heavy a step. She saw that
Alison had the same feeling. They treated one another with a
careful consideration that precluded real intimacy. They kissed,
they tentatively caressed one another, but both of them were
aware that something alive and precious had gone out of their
lives.

Then all at once Emma awakened in the middle of the night and
thought of Miss Bell. She realized that enough time had gone by
now for her to have received a reply. She thought of Miss Bell's
gifts, of the big hat—a momentary gleam of cheerfulness came to
her thinking of it lying in its wrappings on the cupboard shelf. She
had really very little use for it but it seemed a symbol of gaiety
and the lighter pleasures of life. Miss Bell would probably be very
surprised at the use some of her money had been put to. She
thought of the letter she had written, trying to recall its phrases

and wondering if there had been something she had said that had checked Miss Bell's impulse of generosity. Perhaps it was simply that Miss Bell, like many people with an abundance of means, was ready to give freely at her own whim but drew back at a forthright request. Lying in the dark awake beside the quietly sleeping Alison, she tried to imagine what Miss Bell's reaction might have been. Perhaps she thought the request for money to visit Paris was frivolous, that Emma had used the excuse of visiting medical Paris as a means of covering up a less serious objective. But I could not, Emma reminded herself, tell her that I really wanted to visit The Hague and Dr. Rutgers' clinics. That she could scarcely approve.

During the day Emma had little time to think about her personal affairs and the time slipped by ever more quickly. Her mother's letters came with their usual frequency, the note of anxiety about her clearly underlying the family news she related. Her mother obviously worried about her life of dedicated work and study, with no hint of pleasures and cheerful companionship. Her mother, of course, knew nothing of Alison—at least, knew nothing of what Alison meant to her. With a pang, Emma's mind ran off at once to Alison. Would she ever learn, she wondered, to avoid that first moment of yearning when a brief respite from other preoccupations left her free to think of Alison. That first moment was so quickly followed by the inevitable, painful recollection that Alison was no longer her refuge, her reassurance. She pushed away the images of Alison that came crowding on her— Alison beside her in bed at night, Alison singing happily as she brewed the tea and toasted the muffins for their breakfast, Alison waiting to throw her arms around Emma when she arrived in the evening after the day's separation.

The days went by and the final moments of her London stay drew closer. She prolonged her evenings at the hospital, filled every waking moment with study. If only she could hear from Miss Bell. But no letter came. Then she grew discouraged and decided that even Miss Bell had deserted her, that Miss Bell had taken offense at her request, that she would not hear from her.

Her last day at the hospital arrived and she spent a part of it taking leave of those among her colleagues who had become friends. She gave no thought to Colburn. She doubted that he would remember that this was the day of her departure. So she was astonished when late in the afternoon, while she was alone for a few minutes in the women staff members' duty room, he appeared in the doorway.

"Ah, so you leave us to go back to the States," he said. "Well, I want to tell you that I shall miss you and that I am certainly not alone in that feeling."

Emma, trying to regain composure, said hastily, "I am tremendously grateful to you, Sir Maurice. There is a great deal that I shall always owe to you in my professional life."

"Yes, yes." He walked about the room restlessly, one hand in his pocket. "We've not always agreed but I do hope you will succeed in what you want to do. But let me warn you. You are an impulsive young woman and sometimes with the best of intentions you may put yourself in awkward and dangerous situations."

He is thinking of that argument over the woman who died of an abortion, thought Emma. "Thank you. I shall try to consider important problems carefully."

He circled around the room again and came back to her. "You are going straight back to the States?"

Emma, thinking guiltily of Holland and Dr. Rutgers' clinics, said hesitantly, "Well, there may be a chance that I shall be able to visit the Continent before I go home."

"That would be a very good thing. In fact, it would be an excellent thing if you could visit not only Paris but Berlin and Vienna. There are many things being done in medicine abroad that a young physician would profit from observing. You have exceptional gifts, Dr. Wycliffe. I admit the fact, though you know that I do not welcome women into the profession."

"It is very kind of you —"

He cut her short. "In case you do have the opportunity of going to the Continent, I shall give you some letters of introduction to medical colleagues there and I shall suggest that some of your other instructors do likewise."

"Oh, thank you! I am leaving London tomorrow."

"Then come and pick them up at my consulting rooms before you leave. They will be ready for you."

She was almost speechless. He lingered for several moments longer, staring at her with a strange, brooding look, as if he could not take his eyes off her. At last he turned on his heel and went out of the room.

*　　　*　　　*

Emma finished the afternoon in half a daze. When she got to the flat there was no sign of Alison. But on the stand in the hall where the mail was usually deposited, she saw at once the letter from Miss Bell. It was, in fact, a small packet. She tore it open impatiently, reckless of what it might contain, and the bank draft fell at her feet. For a moment she stared at the white paper, unnerved. Miss Bell had sent her money after all.

She picked up the draft and held it folded while she looked more carefully into the packet. There were several small white envelopes, their flaps turned in. She drew out the letter itself and read.

"My dear Dr. Wycliffe. I am most gratified that you should think of me as a friend to whom you can appeal in such a moment of your professional life. I am — we are all, here in our Baltimore group — so proud of you, of what you have achieved during your stay in London. I think your plan to visit Paris very sensible. After all, a means of comparison of methods must be of great value to a doctor. But I do not think you should limit yourself to France. I believe that Berlin is at present the mecca of medical people. And then there is Vienna and Geneva. It would be a great shame for you to return without at least a glimpse of the Continent, when you have such access to it from London. I hope you will allow me to provide not only the means for you to visit France and Germany, but also Italy. You deserve, I am sure, a holiday to recruit your strength, for I know how dedicated you are to your studies. Italy is a special joy to me. I have spent a number of winters there, in Rome and Florence and Venice. Even such a brief visit as yours must be to these cities of ancient civilization will be a refreshment to you. We need not think of this as a loan, as you suggested. It is my extreme pleasure to provide the means for such a worthy purpose."

For a long moment Emma stood with the letter in her hands, folding and refolding it, confronting her own feelings. The letter was longer than the brief messages that had accompanied Miss Bell's other gifts and there was a warmth in its tone that surprised her. Evidently she had touched a chord in Miss Bell's heart in speaking of a desire to travel on the Continent. Of course she could not accept Miss Bell's generous offer as a gift but there was no need at the moment to raise an argument. In answering she would simply demur, speaking of future repayment in general terms.

Then she remembered the bank draft still in her hand. She unfolded it and read the sum, stunned. Two hundred dollars. It was almost half of the amount of the grant of money she had been given for her year's stay in London. For another moment she simply stared at it, bewildered. Then she looked at the small envelopes, caught together with a ribbon. Miss Bell had placed a note with them.

"These are letters of introduction which I hope you will find useful. Since I shall not be going abroad this summer I believe those to whom they are addressed will be glad to receive you in my place. Mr. and Mrs. Knight in Paris are old friends, with a wide circle of acquaintances. Dr. Prinz in Berlin is an eminent specialist in women's diseases. Frau Kunz in Vienna once taught music here in Baltimore. Dr. Lenoir in Geneva is a professor in the University of Geneva and a specialist in nervous disorders. In Florence I should like you to meet the Wakemans. They are English people who can remember Robert Browning."

Emma read the note through twice, thoughtful. So Miss Bell intended that she should not only travel but that she should have enough money to mingle with people of cultivation and means. The sum of money was not that intended for the pilgrimage of a poor student. "I shall buy some new clothes," thought Emma, "in Paris."

Her reverie was interrupted by the sound of Alison's latchkey. Alison came in, saying in the carefully brisk, determinedly cheerful voice she used each evening when they met,

"Emma, you're early! I thought I should be here ahead of you tonight." She had parcels in her hands and Emma took some of them from her and they went up the stairs to their flat, Alison saying over her shoulder, "I am so glad that we shall be alone together for the evening. It is your last and tomorrow you will be gone."

And then, thought Emma, you will be alone with Arthur. As her mind wandered through a maze of unhappiness, her sense of irreparable loss warring with the surge of self-confidence that Miss Bell's letter had given her, she watched Alison moving purposefully about preparing the special meal she had planned. At last, rousing herself, Emma responded to her cheerful talk and they ate in friendly good humor, both of them anxious to ignore the uneasiness that lay beneath the surface. But as they finished the meal and began together to clear up the kitchen, the pauses in their talk grew longer and more frequent. It was in the midst of a long silence that Alison suddenly asked,

"Are you all packed, Emma?"

"Carter Patterson have already picked up my trunk. I have two bags besides. You know, Alison, if women did not wear such ridiculous clothes, traveling would be much simpler."

Alison laughed. "Yes, but at least we don't have crinolines and bustles. There has been some improvement, Emma, in women's lot."

After another pause Emma said, "I'm not sailing directly to the States. I'm going to the Continent first."

Alison cried in astonishment, "Why, Emma, how have you managed it?"

Emma picked up the packet from Miss Bell. "Miss Bell has sent me a draft for two hundred dollars and half-a-dozen letters of introduction."

Alison gasped. "Two hundred dollars! Forty pounds! Emma, why didn't you tell me at once!" Impulsively she threw her arms around Emma's neck and kissed her. "Why, darling, you will be able to do everything you wanted to. How wonderful! What an extraordinary person your Miss Bell must be!"

In the outburst of her enthusiasm she hugged Emma with the old spontaneity, the old wholeheartedness. Emma, in spite of herself, caught her fast in her arms and for a while they clung together. Alison murmured into her ear, "Emma, Emma."

But presently they broke apart and Alison, to cover the awkwardness of the moment, said, "How long will it be before you go home?"

"Perhaps six weeks or two months."

"But you will not be in Holland all that time?"

"Oh, no. In fact, Miss Bell does not know that I am going to The Hague nor my purpose in going there. She has sent me the money to visit France, Germany, Austria, Switzerland and Italy."

"My, what a wonderful sound that has! Oh, Emma, darling, do enjoy it! Do forget your unhappiness. Then you will be sailing at the end of August."

"About then."

After a silence Alison said, in a quiet voice, "Arthur and I shall be married by then. My mother is anxious to have the wedding soon." Alison suddenly laughed. "Perhaps she thinks I shall change my mind—or Arthur may get cold feet. I have told Mrs.

Grey that I cannot keep the flat when you leave. And I've given the Mission people notice. If I'm in London after that, I can always stay with Angela for a day or so. My mother wants me to come home and get ready for the wedding there.''

"Yes.''

"There is always such a lot to do for a wedding and my mother is counting so on it.'' Alison's voice faltered and she burst out, "Oh, Emma, I can't pretend any more! I do not know what you must think of me, but I cannot help it. It's like death to think of losing you.''

Emma, lost in a cloud of remoteness, tried to rouse herself to be comforting. "It can't be helped, Alison. You've told me over and over that you could never reconcile yourself to life with me, with a woman. It would mean giving up too much that is important to you. Since that is the case, you have made the right choice. Come, don't cry. We've thrashed this all out before. Don't let us make ourselves miserable all over again.''

Alison saw that she was very pale. "It would be easier, Emma, if you felt as I do—that our love is something forbidden, no matter how sweet it is. It is wrong, Emma, wrong!''

"Wrong for me to love you as I do? No, it is not. I shall never believe it to be wrong.''

"Then we shall never agree. I am fortunate in finding Arthur. He is kind and generous. You yourself have seen, Emma, that he sincerely believes that women should have the same freedom, the same opportunities as men. You know he agrees that a wife should be her husband's equal in every way, that a husband should not have any kind of property rights in his wife.''

"Any marriage is mere slavery otherwise.''

"Yes, yes. Arthur and I are of one mind there.''

"Then, as you say, you are very fortunate.''

Their conversation stopped there and for a long while they sat in silence, while the last light of the long evening faded out of the sky. It must be nearly ten o'clock, thought Emma. Their flat, in a side street off Chiswick Road, was close enough to Kensington Gardens for the sound of the keeper's voice, calling "All out'' before the gates were closed, to be heard. It would be one of her memories of London, thought Emma.

Alison spoke suddenly, close to her, and she realized that she had come to kneel by her chair. "Oh, Emma, if it could only be you!''

"Me? What do you mean?"

"Oh, Emma, I can scarcely bring myself to say it! But when I am in bed with you it is so rapturous—so overwhelming. I want you then. Any price is as nothing to pay for that. I cannot imagine allowing anyone else—any man—even Arthur —" Alison faltered to a stop.

"Don't worry about it, Alison. Many women feel that way, brought up as you and I have been. But if you love him, you'll get over that with Arthur. And familiarity takes away fear."

"Oh, Emma, Emma," was Alison's only reply, as she clung to her more closely.

*   *   *

The demands of travel were a welcome shield for Emma against her own misery. She had arranged to go first across the North Sea to the Hook of Holland. The stay at The Hague, crowded with the professional observation of the clinics she had come to study, absorbed her waking hours. But in every leisure moment, in the long reaches of the night, she could not escape the desolation wrought by the loss of Alison. At first she felt she would never again enjoy quietness of soul, that forever afterwards she would have this battle to fight with herself to subdue the bitter rebellion that was always waiting to possess her.

She had thought that being separated from Alison, being free of her daily presence, would be a relief to her feelings, would make forgetfulness easier. But the opposite seemed to be true. She could not banish the longing for Alison, the remembrance of Alison's soft yielding body in her arms, the fragrance of Alison's apple-blossom skin. A growing bitterness invaded her. Perhaps Alison had never really been sincere in her loving attentions. Perhaps the little mocking phrases that Alison had used, which at the time she had taken for endearments, had really been mockery. Emma told herself that this could not be true. But the sense of having been deceived, having been made use of, warred with her loyalty to the Alison who had first come to her arms. Never, never, never again would she be so vulnerable, so easy to manipulate. Never again would she show anyone the core of her heart.

By the time she was ready to leave Holland and go on to Paris she had reached a certain calm, an embittered calm easily overset, but at least it was a step towards self-control. In Holland she worked with a frenzied sort of energy, allowing herself as little time for rest as possible, so that sleep might overcome her as soon as she got into bed.

There were two letters from Miss Bell awaiting her in Paris. Of course she had said nothing, in her letter of thanks, about the fact that she would be in Holland for two weeks or more. No doubt Miss Bell was wondering at her failure to respond. But then she had been a poor correspondent all during her stay in London. Miss Bell would probably excuse her as being too busy with professional activities.

Reading Miss Bell's letters, Emma was conscious of a sort of peaceful pause in her inner harassment. Miss Bell recommended certain places to shop, certain places to visit, reminded her of the friends to whom she had letters of introduction, who would be delighted to take her to the Opera, to the more famous restaurants.

Thereafter, throughout the rest of her trip, she came to depend on the quiet, even friendliness of Miss Bell's letters. She found herself looking first among the envelopes she picked up at each new stopping place, for Miss Bell's characteristic, erratic handwriting. She has become a friend, thought Emma, sitting reading the most recent of the letters in a public garden in Vienna. I would never have expected to become as well-acquainted with anyone by letters as I have with her. Without Miss Bell's introductions she would have had few opportunities to enjoy the more leisurely moments of her travels. She would be eternally grateful to Miss Bell.

On board ship, crossing the Atlantic, Emma sat in a sheltered corner of the promenade deck and read through once more the last letter she had received, picked up in Liverpool before embarking.

"My dear Dr. Wycliffe. At last you are homeward bound. I am sure your parents are anxious to have you with them once more. And of course you will have many professional demands on your time. However, I hope I can persuade you to consider a proposal I have to make. The suggestion has been made that you should come to Baltimore for several months, to give a few lectures about your experiences abroad and the professional observations you have made of new methods in the medical centers you have visited. I have no idea what your plans may be for the coming year, but I put forward this suggestion for your consideration. Should you find it acceptable, it would delight me if you would come and stay with me during your visit to Baltimore. I realize that your time abroad has been taxing and you must need rest. But at least here with me you will be saved many inconveniences.''

How like her! thought Emma, putting the letter down. Of course it was Miss Bell herself who had arranged the course of lectures. How like her to present the matter impersonally, as if she was only the mouthpiece for others. Emma knew at once that she would accept. After all, it behooved her to please Miss Bell, in some repayment for all her help. And besides—yes, self-interest told her that in Miss Bell she had a willing backer. A young woman setting out in the medical profession would find a backer very useful. In Miss Bell she had a person rather than an institution to back her.

And in the next second Emma felt a sense of shame. Before meeting with Alison she would never have dreamed of calculating like this. But now she no longer had Alison and her memories of Alison were somehow tarnished. There could never be anyone to stand in relation to herself as Alison had stood. So, she thought, I shall shut it all out. I'll go and see Mother and then I'll go to Baltimore.

And she began to feel as if in Miss Bell she had a refuge, a shelter from the danger of emotional disaster.

*   *   *

PART II

The late September afternoon was warm, hazy, dusty as the train carried Emma south. It had been a long trip, from New England to New York, across the Hudson River on the ferry to Jersey City and the train for Baltimore. It would be over soon. Emma thought of her mother. Her visit at home had not been long and a good deal of it had been taken up with satisfying the curiosity of her brothers, her friends. Her mother had been chiefly an absorbed listener, her attention closely fixed on Emma's appearance, Emma's manner, the answers Emma made to her father's questions about London, his friends and old associates there.

Her mother had protested at the presents she had brought.

"Of course I love them, my dearest. But you've been very extravagant. I don't *need* French gloves. Nor all those fine cambric chemises and the lace-trimmed peignoir."

Emma laughed gaily. "Of course you don't *need* them, Mother. That was not the reason I brought them."

"Then your own wardrobe—Emma, you have four or five gowns and frocks that must have cost a fortune."

"And where did I get the money? Why, from Miss Bell, of course. They are not the wages of sin, Mother dear."

Her loving mockery vexed her mother. "I would not suppose they were. Nevertheless, I can't imagine that Miss Bell expected you to spend her money on frivolities. Don't you have to account for it?"

"To her? Oh, no. She has never asked me any questions about how I spend her money. She simply sent me a draft from time to time—in amounts she must have judged I would need. She has, I must say, large ideas about the scale on which one should live and travel."

"But, Emma, surely you should not have spent all of the money simply because she sent it to you! You should have used as little as possible and returned the rest."

Emma was silent for a few minutes. How to make her mother understand? She finally said, "I'm quite sure that is not what

Miss Bell intended. In any case, if I am mistaken, I shall soon
know. She has invited me to come and stay with her for a while.
She has used her influence to obtain for me an instructorship in
the Medical School in Baltimore. It is just for this semester and
I'll chiefly be reporting on the new methods I observed in
hospitals abroad. But it is certainly a great help to me in orienting
myself. Miss Bell must know that I am out of funds.''

"Oh, dear, Emma! You will be more and more in her debt.''

"Mother, don't worry so! I think I understand Miss Bell's
motives in helping me. She wishes to forward the establishment of
women in the medical profession and I afford her an opportunity
to give practical assistance in that line. She is a wealthy woman.
If I have miscalculated the extent of her generosity, she will soon
let me know, I'm sure.''

Her mother had been checked by her peremptory tone and had
looked at her keenly, as if noticing a new hardness in her manner.
When Emma had left on her journey south, her mother was still
uneasy, still troubled by unspoken questions about what had
happened to her while she was in London.

*   *   *

Miss Bell's carriage was at the railway station in Baltimore
waiting for her when Emma arrived. As it took her to Cushman
Terrace, she thought ahead, trying to focus on what she knew of
Miss Bell outside her letters. Mrs. McHugh had told her—long
ago, it seemed—that Miss Bell was the youngest of three
daughters of a wealthy Baltimore merchant. Her American friends
in Paris had said casually that her oldest sister was the wife of a
man powerful in Baltimore politics and that the other sister had
married young and moved to California, where she now lived
surrounded by several children and grandchildren. The Paris
friends had also made veiled allusions to the fact that Miss Bell
had never married because she feared fortune-hunters.

The pianist in Vienna had talked about Miss Bell chiefly as a
music-lover, a dependable patron of musicians. The Swiss doctor
had said a few circumspect things about the emotional problems
of women of means who had no husbands or children on which to
expend their energies. The elderly English couple in Florence had
surprised Emma when they spoke of Miss Bell as their "young
friend," "a charming girl, so much more modest and cultivated
than one expected of an American young woman." The cousin in

the Embassy at Rome had spoken breezily of "Oh, yes, Cousin Margaret. She always has some bee in her bonnet about women's rights." Emma had had the impression that he was about to add, "Are you her latest cause?" but good manners had stopped him.

Miss Bell awaited her in the big, shadowy drawing room. Emma saw before her the same slight, straight-backed, soberly dressed woman she remembered, rising from her chair with punctilious politeness to greet her.

Miss Bell began bravely enough, walking determinedly toward her across the deep-piled carpet. Her soft voice said, "Dr. Wycliffe —," as if she intended to say something further, but stopped in midair, as if diffidence had defeated her. For a moment she stood tongue-tied, as abashed as a schoolgirl. Emma examined her face frankly, anxious to fill in the blank that she had been aware of all during her absence. The clearcut, bony eye-sockets, the thin, slightly aquiline nose, the narrow chin—this was not the nondescript face of a middle-aged woman, the face she had assumed.

Emma reached out and grasped both of the delicate, fine-boned hands. "Miss Bell! How I have looked forward to seeing you again! I have so much to tell you! So much to thank you for!"

Color came up into Miss Bell's face and she moved her lips as if she wanted to speak. Not succeeding, she drew her hands out of Emma's grasp and made a slight motion towards the two massive, carved mahogany chairs placed near each other. As Emma moved to sit down she suddenly regained composure enough to say, "Or perhaps you are tired from your journey and would rather go at once to your room?"

"Oh, no," said Emma, sitting down and throwing back her light wrap. The late September weather in New England had been considerably brisker than the languid warmth of Baltimore. Her bright blue eyes were fixed on Miss Bell's face with candid interest. "Traveling in such luxury does not tire me."

Miss Bell avoided answering her gaze. "I have always enjoyed travel, even sometimes when it involved hardship. It depends upon the interest either of one's destination or the events along the way."

"You usually go abroad each year, don't you? But not this year. Your friends all spoke of how disappointed they were not to have a visit from you."

Miss Bell was vague. "No. I did not feel it right to go abroad this summer. We have had, you know, a serious bank panic. As I am treasurer for several charities, I felt I should stay home and do what I could to safeguard their investments.''

Emma remembered that Miss Bell's friends in Paris had spoken of her as having a man's grasp of finance. It was a pity, they said, that she had not been born a man, for she would undoubtedly have been a worthy son to succeed her father in the business world.

"Perhaps, then," said Emma, remembering the long gap in Miss Bell's letters, "it was not too convenient for you to have provided me with such a large gift."

"Oh, no! That gave me no concern at all. Ah, I am sure I must have caused you some anxiety by not answering your request more promptly. But you see, it was because of Flora's accident. My cook." She gave the barest glimpse down at her hands, folded in her lap.

Emma reached over and took one of them in her own, gently turning it about to examine it. There were faint white lines on the back, reaching up over the wrist. "You have been burned."

"Yes. Flora's apron caught fire from the stove. We had to act quickly to save her. Dr. Richards says the scars will fade with time.''

"I hope so." The light, thin hand lay passive in Emma's. The fine symmetry of the bones, the clear silkiness of the skin, impressed her. It would be a great pity to spoil that delicate beauty. Emma raised her eyes to look up into Miss Bell's brown-flecked green ones gazing down at her. Miss Bell looked away and drew back her hand.

"Do they pain you now?"

"Oh, no. They're quite healed."

"Are they stiff?"

"Only a little—in the morning, before I have used them."

Emma took hold of both her hands and manipulated them gently. "You should exercise them regularly. Do you play the piano?''

Miss Bell gave a deprecating little laugh. "No. I do not play well enough to bear my own playing."

Emma sat back and released her hands. "There must be something else. I shall massage them for you each day. Was Flora badly injured?''

"No. She had only superficial burns. She healed quickly. But you see, that was the reason I was so long in responding to you. I

thought of asking Mrs. McHugh to write in my place but then it
occurred to me that you might prefer that I did not, that you
would like it to be a matter between the two of us."

"That was kind of you, Miss Bell."

They went on to talk about Emma's travels. Miss Bell seemed
to lose her nervousness. She laughed at Emma's account of a
concert she had attended in Paris, where the playing of some of
Debussy's latest music had caused a fracas among the critics.
Miss Bell, it turned out, was a devotee of Debussy's music. It was
a new departure, she explained, that had not yet received unquali-
fied acceptance in Baltimore's musical circles. Emma listened,
entertained by the same witty quickness of mind that she had
come to enjoy in Miss Bell's letters. Miss Bell, animated now,
talked easily, like a much younger woman. "Our young American
friend," Emma remembered the English couple in Florence had
said.

Perhaps because she noticed how quiet Emma had become,
Miss Bell suddenly broke off and said, this time in a positive
voice, that Emma would undoubtedly like to retire to her own
room.

*   *   *

Within a week of Emma's arrival, Miss Bell gave a dinner party
to introduce her to some of her closest friends. Mrs. McHugh and
Mrs. Vickers noticed at once Emma's Paris gown and the new air
of sophistication with which she wore it.

"Mrs. McHugh murmured, "She is perfectly splendid—really,
like a goddess. I've never seen such a dazzlingly beautiful
woman. No wonder we've heard tales of her conquests in
London."

"It has made a difference in her. I don't know just what it is.
She was a beautiful young woman before she went. But there is a
change."

"More assurance, perhaps? Certainly she does not seem aware
that the decolletage of that gown is a little extreme."

"By Baltimore standards. Not by French." Mrs. Vickers' tone
was authoritative.

"Of course. But she seems oblivious to the fact that it may
make a decided impression here."

"I should have thought that perhaps Margaret might have said
something about it. Though there is nothing vulgar about her."

"If it were anyone else—but she disarms one. That blue satin sets off her bosom and shoulders very well—and such glorious golden hair."

Both women watched Emma as some of the men came into the drawing room, leaving the cigar smokers in the dining room. She had sat down at the piano and, playing softly, was demonstrating to Miss Bell the way in which she had heard the latest of Debussy's *Images* played in Paris.

"She is remarkably versatile," said Mrs. Vickers. "She does not play like a professional, but she is able to project the effect she wishes."

Mrs. McHugh sighed. "It is marvelous that so many extraordinary gifts should be given to one woman—beauty, brains, a musical talent, the power to charm —"

"That certainly she has. Look at the men."

Several had gathered around Emma, so that Miss Bell, in a dark brown velvet gown with long sleeves and a high neck, was lost to view.

"Do you notice how she treats them? She is not in the least affected by their manner, even when they try to provoke her with remarks about women's suffrage or women doctors."

"They never go very far."

"They are afraid of her, I believe. See how closely they watch her, as if ready to back away at the least sign of danger."

"They know she knows too much about men's lower natures—as a physician, I mean. It is strange to think of a young, unmarried, well-bred young woman like her being in contact with so much that is gross and sordid—as she must have been in her hospital training."

"She certainly cannot be treated as an untried girl."

"She has more the air of a gifted, ambitious young man."

"That, I think, is what these emancipated women approve."

"But the men won't like it. It will be difficult for her to find a husband."

"I wonder if she wants one," murmured Mrs. McHugh just before Miss Bell, having escaped from the crowd around Emma, joined them.

*   *   *

The spare, grizzled black woman laid the dish of bacon and eggs down in front of Emma. Two places had been set at the table, with squares of linen on the highly polished dark wood and large, solid silver knives and forks.

"Miss Bell is not up yet, Dorcas?" asked Emma.

"Oh, yes, ma'am, but she ain't back yet." At Emma's raised eyebrows, she explained, "Miss Margaret always goes to seven o'clock church. She told me to have your breakfast ready when you came downstairs. You weren't to wait."

"Then I shall not see her this morning. I shall be gone by the time she gets back."

Dorcas bowed her head in agreement and held out a basket of hot biscuits. "Miss Margaret said Thomas was to have the carriage ready for you when you want it."

"But how did she get to church?"

"She walked. She goes to St. Michael and All Angels and that's just a step away."

Emma was silent, coping with the idea of Miss Bell's carriage awaiting her command. She looked up to see the maid's intelligent eyes fixed on her.

"I don't need Thomas and the carriage, Dorcas. I have my bicycle. I put it under the steps at the back door."

Dorcas nodded to show that she knew this. "But Miss Margaret didn't think you were going to use it to go to work, miss."

"Well, I shall. I learned to use a bicycle in England. I can go anywhere on it."

Dorcas raised her eyebrows slightly, as if doubtful how Miss Bell would view this. But she left the room without saying more about it.

Emma broke a biscuit open and put butter on it. She was due at the Medical School at eight. She thought back on the last few days. She arrived in Boston with only a few coins left in her purse. She had borrowed the train fare to Baltimore from her father. She wondered how Miss Bell had guessed at this state of things. For the day after she had reached Cushman Terrace, Miss Bell had suggested delicately that no doubt she would like the convenience of a bank checking account and opened one for her with a large deposit. Mother would be even more upset about that, thought Emma. And if it wasn't Miss Bell, I would not accept it. But with her—and I do need pocket money till I get my first honorarium, whenever that will be.

Very quickly Emma's life in Miss Bell's house fell into a pattern. Every morning except Sunday she ate breakfast hastily,

served by Dorcas, and left for the Medical School before Miss
Bell came back from communion. On Sundays she accompanied
her. Her weekday mornings were spent at the Medical School, but
she shortly found herself a member of the staff of the city
women's hospital. After that she had no more leisure, only a brief
hour or two snatched for exercise and recreation. She undertook to
answer calls to deliver babies in the dirty, crowded tenements
filled with the new immigrants from Russia and eastern Europe,
flooding into Baltimore to provide labor for the food canning
factories and the new steel mill at Sparrows Point. Sometimes she
was called late at night and came in yawning after Miss Bell was
already seated at the breakfast table.

Whenever she could she came home early, eager for a game of
tennis. Miss Bell, discovering that she enjoyed the game, had
arranged a membership for her in a local club with courts nearby.
Arriving home she wheeled her bicycle up the narrow walk that
ran between the high brick walk of the carriage house and that of
the main part of the house, passing under the windows of the
room Miss Bell used as an office and sitting room. The walk led
to the back door and under the steps there was a sheltered space
where she could leave her bicycle before going in through the
kitchen.

At first her entering the house by this way shocked Flora the
cook. But soon—had Dorcas said something? Emma wondered—
Flora accepted it as one more eccentricity in an already unaccount-
able person. Flora was an ample, talkative, light-colored woman
whose lively eyes examined with interest Emma's face and
clothes. Sometimes Emma, tired and thirsty, dropped into a chair
beside the kitchen table to drink a glass of the cold cider Flora
offered her. In the beginning Flora hinted broadly that she could
not understand why such a beautiful young lady, used to living in
luxury, should want to go doctoring people, but since Emma gave
her only humorous answers, she gave up this line of inquiry.
Instead, she regaled Emma with detailed pictures of Miss Bell's
Baltimore world as seen from her kitchen.

Flora, Emma discovered, was Thomas the coachman's wife and
the couple lived in the upstairs rooms of the carriage house. There
were no other servants except a woman who came to clean several
times a week. When Miss Bell gave a dinner party—something
she did quite often, since Flora's reputation as a cook was
considerable—she hired waiters and a kitchen maid—all relatives

of Flora and Thomas. Emma noticed that Dorcas was treated with a careful respect. Dorcas had been longest in the employ of the Bells. She had been a servant in the house when Mr. Bell had been alive.

Before dinner Emma joined Miss Bell in the drawing room, where Dorcas brought them two glasses of sherry on a small round solid silver tray. Miss Bell was always there ahead of her, seated in one of the mahogany chairs, the tinted light from the heavy frosted glass lampshade falling on her white hands folded in her lap. She almost always wore brown silk or velvet. The dark heavy material seemed to diminish even more her slight body.

On these occasions Miss Bell liked to talk about her visits to Europe. Last summer, she told Emma one evening, she had been taken on a tour of southern France—out-of-the-way places difficult to reach—in one of the new motorcars, owned by friends of hers.

"A most interesting experience. I should never have seen these things otherwise. Have you ever ridden in one of these motors? I do not mean an electric brougham, such as Mrs. Vickers has. They are driven by combustion of a gasoline fuel."

"Yes," said Emma, "once or twice while I was in England. Some people have them there."

"Several families of my acquaintance have acquired motor cars. In fact, my older sister and her husband have a large touring car which they use chiefly on Sunday afternoons for a drive through Druid Hill Park. I went with them the weekend before you arrived for a drive out towards Ellicott City, to see the beginning of the autumn coloring along the banks of the Patapsco."

"Have you thought of having a car of your own?"

Miss Bell was thoughtful. "I have. But there are certain difficulties. Thomas is no mechanic and he is too old to learn and yet not old enough to pension. Besides, I do not have much use for such a vehicle here in Baltimore. If the carriage is inconvenient, I walk."

"Perhaps you should learn to ride a bicycle. A bicycle gives one a remarkable freedom in moving about."

Miss Bell's face lit up with a delighted smile. "A bicycle? Why, I never thought of that possibility!"

How much younger you look all at once, thought Emma. She said, "I don't see why you shouldn't. It would give you a wonderful sense of freedom."

"I'm afraid I'm too old for anything like that."

"Too old? Of course not. I'm sure age would not prevent you. But perhaps you have the habit of thinking such things beyond you."

Miss Bell considered her words. "Those of my generation grew old faster than girls of yours. You have been given the opportunity for far more active lives. You do not think of age in the same way."

"I do not think of it in connection with you, Miss Bell. I feel you are much closer to being my contemporary."

Miss Bell burst into a startled laugh. "My dear girl!"

Emma smiled. "I like to hear you laugh. It makes you much younger."

Miss Bell was serious at once. "I'm afraid you find me rather formal. I believe it is because I've always lived with those older than myself. Both of my sisters are much older than I."

"And I have only younger brothers."

"It must have been a different experience altogether. I've never been used to young people. Although, a few years ago I took my nieces—the children of my second sister who lives in California—abroad with me."

"Did you enjoy that?"

"Yes. But I'm afraid that my elderly ways may have dampened some of their high spirits."

"I really don't believe that. I don't believe you would spoil anyone's fun—not even for silly young girls. And you would not have let them know if they spoiled yours."

She saw the deep blush rise in Miss Bell's pale face. "I do not believe in deceiving myself. I find it ridiculous for elderly people to pretend they are ready companions for the young."

"But you may go to the opposite extreme. I think, with you, it is nothing but the habit of a lifetime. Come. Let me teach you to ride a bicycle and play tennis."

Emma thought for a moment that she had gone too far. Miss Bell did not look at her and for a while they were both silent. Then presently Miss Bell said, "You are a very kind young woman."

*   *   *

As winter came and the evenings drew in early, Emma with regret gave up tennis. Besides, she was getting busier as she became better known both in the hospital's charity wards and to other patients. If a woman whom she had treated once asked for her on a second visit, she always responded, sensing behind the request a longing for the sort of sympathetic attention only another woman could give. She refrained from talking about her daily work in the slums, where she frequently treated women too exhausted and apathetic to take the most necessary precautions to prevent disease in themselves and their children. She came home to the luxury of Miss Bell's house often burdened by the despair and anguish she had been surrounded by in the dark, noisome dwellings of ignorant and wretched people. Especially was she saddened by the women who came to stand in the doorways and hallways to watch her come and go. Sometimes they stopped her with clumsy and halting attempts at conversation. She soon learned that their intent was to question her about ways to avoid further pregnancies, burdened as they were already with more children than they could care for. The bolder and more embittered ones did not plead but demanded information from her. Rich women, they said, avoided having too many children. Everybody could see that. How was it done? Couldn't she tell them how it was done? Or was she too rich and comfortable herself to care? And at this point they looked her up and down, eyeing the quality and elegance of the clothes she wore.

Emma answered them with as much sympathy as she dared display, phrasing her reply with as broad a hint as she could that they should have the cooperation of their men. With the more aggressive women this brought only derisive retorts and with the meeker a hopeless turning away.

Sometimes, after an especially harrowing case, she returned in the evening too cast down to achieve a normally cheerful air by the time she joined Miss Bell in the drawing room. She did not realize at first that Miss Bell was always aware of her mood and would keep silent until she was ready to talk. But one evening, when she was especially distraught, Miss Bell said,

"Dr. Wycliffe, forgive me, but is there something that is giving you anxiety?"

Emma, roused from a brown study, said with surprise, "Why, no, there is nothing wrong."

"I thought perhaps your mother was not well."

"Oh, no. My mother is quite well. Why did you think that?"

"Because you seem anxious."

Emma said nothing for a while. Miss Bell was also silent. Presently Emma said, "I am sorry I am not better company. I find it hard sometimes to forget the problems I face during the day. I know I should banish them from my mind when I get home."

"Perhaps if you spoke of them to me —?"

By no means, Emma thought vehemently. If it is hard for me to face the misery I see every day, used as I am to its existence, however would you manage, who have only an abstract knowledge of it?

Aloud she said, "I cannot bring such things into your pleasant house."

"I am not a hothouse plant! I know there are many here in this city who live in tragic circumstances!"

Emma gazed with interest at the sudden color in Miss Bell's cheeks, the flash in her eyes. "Of course. You must, since you help to manage so many charitable funds. But though one may know that want and dirt and vileness exist, it is something else to spend hours with those who suffer them."

Miss Bell's indignation died away as suddenly as it had flared up. "Yes, I understand. It is presumptuous of me to compare my efforts with your experience."

"It is not presumptuous at all. I merely mean that there is no point in my harrowing your feelings simply to assuage my own."

"Perhaps you do really need a rest."

Emma shook her head. "It is not a rest I need. It is the opportunity to do something really effective towards ending the sort of misery I see women afflicted with." She stopped herself abruptly and after a pause, aware that Miss Bell was looking at her expectantly, said, "When I was doing my internship in the slums of New York—it was my introduction to a personal experience of human degradation—I told myself that there was no point to my bewailing the conditions I had to work in. If I could not control my own dismay at what I saw, I could be of very little use to those I was learning to treat. I remind myself daily of this now. It does seem sometimes, however, that it is like trying to stem the tides of the sea."

Miss Bell said, "It is often discouraging to deal with people in the mass. But I fear that you are more affected by what you see than you will admit. I think you should have a respite from your work."

"Perhaps in a while," Emma temporized.

*   *   *

Dorcas put the basket of hot biscuits down on the table near Emma's hand, as she did each morning. But this time she remained standing silently instead of going out of the room.

Emma looked up at her, surprised. "Do you want to speak to me about something, Dorcas?"

"Yes, ma'am. Miss Emma, you're a regular doctor, ain't you?"

Emma laughed. "Yes, of course."

"Miss Margaret said so."

"So that means I must be," said Emma, smiling. She waited for Dorcas to go on. Watching the black woman's face she saw a hint of inner distress in the usually impassive features.

Dorcas leaned closer to her. "Ma'am, could you do something about my sister's child?"

"What is the matter with her?"

Dorcas was slow to answer. "She lost her baby and she ain't been right since."

"How old is she?"

"Fourteen."

"Your sister's child, Dorcas?"

"Well, her grandchild. But my sister has raised her. Her mother's dead."

"You say she lost her baby. Do you mean she had a miscarriage? She is pretty young. That happens to young mothers often enough and there may be complications."

Dorcas did not answer and Emma, sensing some further problem, looked at her keenly. "What is the story, Dorcas? I cannot help unless I know the circumstances."

Reluctantly Dorcas said, "Ma'am, I'm ashamed to say it, but the girl got fooling with a man —"

Obviously, Emma thought, waiting patiently while Dorcas hesitated.

"A no good, trifling nigger," Dorcas said bitterly. "She wasn't raised that way, Miss Emma. I swear to God, she hadn't no call to behave that way."

Emma, seeing the distress in the black woman's face and hearing it in the deterioration of her way of speaking, said sympathetically, "Dorcas, young girls often act thoughtlessly, especially if they live in an environment where temptation is easy.'' Especially black girls, she thought, growing up in a community that half-expected them to be promiscuous and early the mothers of illegitimate children.

Dorcas, as if reading the meaning behind her words, said hotly, ''Miss Emma, I tell you she was looked after. She knew better. She knew what my sister expected of her. She's a disgrace to us.''

''Yes, but now you say she needs medical attention,'' said Emma, striving to bring Dorcas back to the main point. ''She hasn't recovered from the miscarriage?''

Again Dorcas was reluctant to speak and Emma waited, buttering her biscuit. There *is* something more to this, she thought.

Finally Dorcas said, ''She hurt herself.''

Emma's voice was sharp, ''Hurt herself?''

''She didn't want the child. She didn't want us to know what she'd done.''

''You mean she aborted herself?''

Dorcas, a little doubtful of her meaning, said hesitantly, ''She got rid of it. But she hurt herself.''

''I see,'' said Emma, and thoughtfully ate her biscuit. ''Probably she has not healed and has an infection. She could have killed herself. Dorcas, does Miss Bell know about this?'' She must, thought Emma. She seems to know everything about her servants and especially about Dorcas.

But Dorcas shook her head. ''No, ma'am. I haven't told Miss Margaret nothing. My sister is too ashamed. She won't let me tell her. She don't want Miss Margaret to know that Demetria hadn't any more pride than any other silly girl—when Miss Margaret thought she had a real good mind and was paying for her schooling.''

''Oh, that's it! Well, you can't be too hard on her, Dorcas. I'm sure she has had plenty of temptation and bad examples.''

Again Dorcas was quick to pick up her meaning. She said angrily, ''No, ma'am. My sister don't bring up her children like trash! Demetria should have known better. And my sister trusted her.''

''Well, don't be harsh with her, Dorcas. Yes, I'll examine her. Probably she'll have to come to the hospital. And, Dorcas, I shall have to tell Miss Bell about this.''

Slowly Dorcas nodded, as if accepting the inevitable.

*   *   *

"Yes, it is discouraging, but, as you say, one cannot expect too much of a girl in her circumstances. However, her grandmother has been strict with her." Miss Bell spoke in a resigned tone of voice.

It was Sunday morning and they sat together, having been to communion and breakfasted.

"From the degree of Dorcas' disappointment, I gather that quite a lot was expected of her."

"She is an intelligent girl—what Dorcas must have been at her age. It is a waste of human material not to give such a child an education, so that she can improve on her background. Will she recover fully?"

"Oh, yes. I operated on her at the hospital yesterday. It was a simple matter. I don't know what sort of instrument she used to induce the miscarriage. She will not tell me all the details. Fortunately she did not perforate the wall of her uterus or she would be dead now. It was chiefly curretting she needed, to clear away the infection."

"Perhaps she will have learned something from this. I have always thought she was a strong-willed girl, genuinely eager to advance herself. She may yet, if she realizes the folly of saddling herself with illegitimate children. I am encouraged by the fact that she has done this desperate thing rather than spoil her life—now that she is safe."

"Dorcas thinks she was ashamed to admit to her grandmother—and to you—how irresponsible she had been—that she was afraid that you would lose all interest in her."

"Well, perhaps that may have swayed her to an extent. But I believe, really—from what I know of her—that she was chagrined at the idea of losing out on the chance to better herself. She is a determined girl and one who is inclined to be reckless in seeking what she wants. She is clever enough to be bitter at the lack of opportunity for such as she is. She does not have the docility that would make her life easier. Dorcas forgets that she herself had to learn resignation to her lot—as most of us do."

"You are going to continue to help her?"

"Yes. I'll provide for her a little longer, till I see how things go. I hope her grandmother and Dorcas don't chide her too much and make her defiant. Then she will be lost sure enough. She would become rebellious. And that would be a pity."

After a moment's silence Emma said, "Mrs. McHugh saw me with her in the ward yesterday. Mrs. McHugh is a regular visitor in the wards where the black women are. She brings them little luxuries. She is a kind woman."

Miss Bell gave her a quick glance. "Yes, Martha thinks it is important for us to keep a sharp eye on how these people are looked after—which means in many cases our own servants and their relatives. So by now Martha knows all the details. Demetria's aunt is Martha's cook."

Emma laughed. "You're all interrelated, above and below stairs, aren't you?"

Miss Bell smiled in answer and then said seriously, "Martha, of course, warned me that my efforts with Demetria would be fruitless—that there is no use trying to change the nature of negro servants—that they don't have either the wish or the capacity to adopt our outlook on life."

"Dorcas was angry when I hinted that she shouldn't be too hard on the girl since both her natural impulses and her environment were bound to defeat her. Dorcas was angry—as if what the girl has done was a personal affront to herself."

Miss Bell's smile was thin. "Dorcas is an unusual woman. I don't agree with Martha and other well-meaning people who see no advantage to be gained by educating negroes—that is, beyond their usefulness as servants. I am convinced that as individuals they should have an opportunity to prove themselves."

Emma looked at her with interest. "These are revolutionary ideas here, aren't they?"

Miss Bell said drily, "This is not a part of the world where they would be well-received."

*   *   *

It was Miss Bell who suggested that perhaps Emma should go to see her parents on Thanksgiving. "It is an especially important family occasion in your part of the world, I know."

But Emma shook her head. "My parents do not make much of it. They are English-born, you know, and my mother thinks of it really as a sort of Harvest Festival. In any case, they will be with my brother and his family. They do not expect me home."

So instead she was invited with Miss Bell to Thanksgiving dinner at the Harms'.

Dorcas, who always helped Emma dress when it was for an

occasion that required the wearing of a corset and the fastening of an evening dress, came to her room as soon as she had finished dressing Miss Bell. Since the episode of Demetria, the black woman was more talkative with Emma.

She said now, as her thin, bony black fingers neatly passed the laces through the corset eyelets, "Miss Margaret is right glad to have you here, Miss Emma. You make her a lot more cheerful."

Emma glanced back at her curiously. "Has she said this to you?"

"No, ma'am. She don't need to. I can see."

"You have known Miss Bell all her life, haven't you, Dorcas?"

"Since she was a little thing. She had no mother and her mammy was my mother's youngest sister. I came to work in the kitchen here when I was a young woman. Miss Susanna ran the house then. The first thing that happened after I came here was Miss Hester got married. There was a big wedding. Miss Hester was twenty years old and very pretty. She married and went to California. It was lucky for her that there was Miss Susanna to look after Mr. Bell and Miss Margaret. I don't think she could have stood waiting the way her sister did."

"Waiting?"

"Miss Susanna waited to get married till Miss Margaret was ten years old and could go to boarding school." Noticing the surprise on Emma's face, Dorcas went on. "Mr. Bell didn't show any signs of marrying again and somebody had to stay and look after him and Miss Margaret."

Dorcas paused while she picked up Emma's gown and dropped it over her head and began fastening it at the back. Emma said nothing, aware that part of the black woman's mind was still dwelling on the past. As she expertly gave the finishing touches to Emma's hair, Dorcas said, "Miss Margaret is too solitary. She always has been too quiet. That is why it's a good thing you've come here, Miss Emma."

"Why, Dorcas, Miss Bell sees her sister every few days and she has many friends. She entertains often. I don't think you can really call her solitary."

"That's not just the same thing. She speaks her mind to you, Miss Emma. I've noticed that. She never did to anybody else— except Miss Cordelia and she's in Europe."

"Miss Cordelia?"

"She and Miss Margaret were girls together. Her husband, Mr. Drummond, is an important man in the government now. She's been away for a long time. So she hasn't been here to talk to Miss Margaret. Miss Margaret, she always tries to carry her own burdens without telling anybody."

"Well, I expect that is because she grew up alone, with no brothers or sisters her own age."

Dorcas nodded and held the elbow-length glove for Emma to put her hand into. "Everybody used to wonder why Mr. Bell didn't marry again. Even Miss Susanna didn't know why until he died, but Miss Margaret found out when she came home from school. She never told Miss Susanna nor Miss Hester but kept it to herself."

Emma paused in buttoning her glove. Obviously Dorcas wants me to realize something here, she thought. "What was the reason?"

"He had a woman he liked but couldn't marry. She was a right smart woman, goodlooking, high-colored. Some folks couldn't tell she had black blood. She knew just how to manage him and when he died she came and showed the lawyers deeds of gift he had given her for several pieces of land right here in the middle of Baltimore. That's how Miss Susanna found out. But Miss Margaret knew all along. That woman is a rich woman now."

"The family did not question her claims?"

Dorcas shook her head. "Miss Susanna didn't want a scandal and Miss Margaret said it was what her father wanted and she didn't think they should interfere. Mr. Harms was pretty mad about it."

After a thoughtful pause Emma said, "What is it you want me to understand about this, Dorcas? Did Miss Bell and Mrs. Harms quarrel? Is there still some resentment between them?"

"No, ma'am, they didn't exactly quarrel. Miss Susanna was terribly upset because Miss Margaret knew about something like that when she was just a young girl. She thought Mr. Bell should have been a lot more careful about not letting her know. I think she blamed herself for going off and leaving Miss Margaret, so that Miss Margaret found out for herself. But I don't think Mr. Bell realized that Miss Margaret had found out. She never said anything to him."

Well, thought Emma, as Dorcas put the fur-trimmed wrap around her shoulders, now I have an interesting background for this evening's gathering. I wonder if Dorcas intended that.

*   *   *

On the few occasions when she had met Miss Bell's sister, Emma had felt herself firmly rebuffed. It was Mrs. McHugh who explained part of the reason. It was, Mrs. McHugh said, because she was a physician. Emma had heard of Dr. Osler of Hopkins' famous remark, that human kind might be divided into three groups—men, women and women physicians. From the other medical women with whom she worked she knew that acceptance in Baltimore society was not something to be taken for granted. Mrs. Harms, it seemed, was one of those most rigid in this prejudice.

Mrs. McHugh had said, with an apologetic laugh, "She does not want to accept you as a physician—to admit that you are one—because she knows she must accept you as Margaret's friend."

"You mean, it would be impossible for her to accept me both socially and professionally?"

Mrs. McHugh's laugh was replaced by a look of vexation. "It is an old-fashioned attitude, Dr. Emma. Most of us have overcome the idea that women physicians have forfeited the right to be thought ladies. But Susanna does not change her views easily."

In the carriage, as Thomas drove them to the Harms' house, Miss Bell said, "As I have remarked to you, there will be only kinfolk and a few intimate friends at Susanna's tonight. You have met most of them. I think only James West will be new to you. He is related to my brother-in-law, from a branch of Preston's family that has been impoverished ever since the Civil War. He was a promising boy and Preston undertook to educate him. He is a lawyer now and he has served in the State Attorney General's office. Preston considers that he has a brilliant political future. And so he does, with Preston's backing."

"He seems a fortunate young man."

"Yes. Beyond that, my sister is very fond of him. He is like a son to her."

"She is childless."

"Yes. Susanna has never wanted children—to bear and raise, that is. But she likes having a grown son and James fills that role with her. He is, I think, a few years older than you and unmarried.''

"Is that a hint or a warning?"

Miss Bell, startled, said, "Why, neither!" and then, seeing Emma smile, laughed. "He is considered a very good catch but so far he has shown no inclination to marry."

The Harms had a large new house, surrounded by an ample garden, in a newer, fashionable part of the city. Miss Bell had said that her brother-in-law was one of Baltimore's older political chieftains, still someone to be reckoned with in city affairs. Though he himself had never held public office he was the power behind other men who did. He had inherited an old Maryland fortune, Miss Bell said, one that had survived the Civil War and which he had built up by skilful manipulations. Emma, aware of ramifications in the subject beyond her grasp, did not ask for details.

Susanna, greeting them in the drawing room, wore a gown of deep purple velvet, high-necked, lace-trimmed. Her husband, a somber man with watchful eyes hooded by a drooping fold of skin, stood behind her. Susanna had her sister's own spare uprightness but she was a taller woman, unbending even as she went punctiliously through the forms of greeting. My sister, she seemed to say, has her own endeavors, her own associates, but they are not mine. Please keep a certain distance from me, at least until I have reached an estimate of your character, your acceptability.

I shall never, thought Emma, half-amused, arrive in Susanna's good graces.

"Good evening, Miss Wycliffe." Susanna as usual did not acknowledge Emma's professional title. I am only, thought Emma, somebody her sister has befriended in connection with some charitable scheme.

Emma was introduced to James West. He was a ruggedly built man, brown-haired and clean-shaven, whose alert grey eyes quickly took in her face, her bare shoulders, the swell of her bosom, her lowcut gown. She was aware that he watched her closely from across the room until they went in to dinner.

At the dinner table she was placed between two elderly men, one of whom wanted to tell her everything about the great fire that had wiped out the business center of Baltimore.

"Just three years ago this Christmas, Miss Wycliffe. It has made many changes. Baltimore is not the same. Ah, so much was swept away—so much of the charm of the city. It had, you know, a real Colonial aspect. I miss that—many of us do."

"Yes, I can see that it would be distressing. But some benefit has come from it, hasn't it? You have many new buildings and a modern water supply now, I am told."

The old man looked at her in surprise. "Why, yes, that's so." He paused for a moment. "You have scientific interests, I believe. Someone has told me that. That's very unusual for a young woman—and such a beautiful one!"

Emma laughed.

After dinner after everyone was back in the drawing room James West was at her elbow. He hadn't had a chance to meet her before, he said, because he had been down at Annapolis looking after the horses. His uncle—he explained he meant Preston Harms—had a farm on the Severn River where he bred racehorses.

"There is good hunting and fishing and boating in that part of the world," he said. "Perhaps you can talk Cousin Margaret into bringing you down there."

"That is nice of you. But it depends on whether I should find the time."

He paused to look at her closely. "That's right. You're a doctor, aren't you?" As he asked the question his quick eyes once more took in her face, her hair, her bare shoulders. "Well, maybe you could manage it anyway. Or if Cousin Margaret doesn't want to come, Aunt Susanna can bring you."

Emma, aware that Susanna was watching them from across the room, thought, That is highly unlikely. But aloud she said, "Does Miss Bell like hunting and fishing and boating?"

James, catching the tone in her voice, laughed loudly. "Cousin Margaret has never been on a horse or held a firearm or a fishing rod in her life, so far as I know. Sometimes she has been on my uncle's yacht for a few hours."

"That is what I supposed was the case." Emma was smiling but she felt a growing irritation at James' persistence in eyeing her.

He seemed to realize her annoyance but also seemed to enjoy the idea that she was conscious of his scrutiny. He was a man, she thought, who liked to impose himself on women and who furthermore was used to women allowing him to do so.

"I've heard about you. You've stirred up a lot of my friends and kin."

"Stirred them up?"

"Why, you know—a lady doctor. They're not used to the idea. They think it is another of Cousin Margaret's fancies."

"She doesn't strike me as being a fanciful person."

James smiled. "That's because you hold the same opinions as she does—about women's rights."

"It seems to me that a good many women here in Baltimore have done as she has in the last ten years. She is not alone."

"You're thinking of the Johns Hopkins Medical School and how the women refused to put up the money to bail it out unless women were allowed in. Oh, yes. Cousin Margaret was one of those. But a good many of our kin didn't like the idea and still don't. They think it is all part of the lunatic fringe that is taking over the country with TR's help."

"Do you really think Mr. Roosevelt is so radical?"

"I don't. And I'm not going to stand in any woman's way."

As long as she does not cross you, thought Emma. "That's kind of you!" she said.

He laughed again, appreciating the implication of her remark. "There are no flies on you, are there?"

Emma said sharply, "I shouldn't have expected you to find any."

The covert anger in her voice made him suddenly serious. He was still eyeing her closely. "Well, I expect you like horses. We are grooming a young filly for the Preakness next spring. I hope you'll still be here to see the race."

"Perhaps," said Emma. She looked up to notice that now Preston Harms' attention was focused on them. He sat a little way from them, silent as usual, giving the impression that he was listening to a male friend who sat next to him. Or perhaps was preoccupied by a train of thought that had nothing to do with the scene at hand. But now his brooding, watching eyes were fixed on Emma attentively. Unable to bear the scrutiny she got up and walked to another part of the room, trailing James behind her.

On the way home Miss Bell was largely silent and Emma, subdued by her withdrawn manner, said very little. When they arrived home they both went at once up the stairs. On the landing, outside Emma's bedroom door, Miss Bell lingered. Emma waited for what she wanted to say, watching the silent conflict reflected on her face.

"I hope the evening was not trying for you, Dr. Wycliffe."

She saw and understood everything that happened, thought Emma. "Oh, no. I hope I said nothing that would offend your sister."

"I am sure you did not. Susanna is a difficult woman. She does not mean to appear inhospitable."

"She did not. It is simply that I know so little of your customs and interrelationships here."

"We are indeed a rather insular society." Miss Bell paused for a moment. "Susanna was very conscious of the attention James West paid you. She would not altogether like it."

"I would as soon he had not paid me quite so much attention."

Miss Bell said in a gentle voice, "You must be very attractive to a young man and James is used to having women's attention."

"That much was clear to me. Please don't think anything more of it. I was annoyed but it is of no consequence."

Miss Bell did not reply. Then Emma was surprised by the brief light pressure of Miss Bell's hand on her arm. She looked down into the brown-flecked green eyes. Miss Bell withdrew her hand and turned hurriedly away, saying a little breathlessly, "Good night, Dr. Wycliffe."

*   *   *

December arrived with cold, blustery weather. Emma, busy at the Medical School and in the public wards of the hospital, found herself also acquiring some private patients. Her reputation was spreading so that, at first tentatively and then more confidently, several of Miss Bell's friends consulted her for various female ills. Miss Bell reported to her that Mrs. Vickers and Mrs. McHugh and one or two others of the matrons who made up her circle had voiced conjectures about whether Emma would take up a permanent post in a local institution or start private practice in Baltimore. Emma, busy with day-to-day concerns, postponed thinking about the end of the year and the conclusion of her instructorship.

Of course soon she would have to come to some decision. It was unreasonable that she should continue to give all her energies to the work she was now doing if she did not intend to settle in Baltimore. On the other hand, her attachment there was the

flimsiest. It amounted only to her temporary dependence on Miss
Bell, on Miss Bell's influence. In odd moments when she
considered the matter she wondered if, without being fully aware
of the fact, she was reluctant to leave the cushioned ease of life in
Miss Bell's house. She had after all to earn her living. She was
scarcely doing so under the present circumstances.

As Christmas drew near she admitted to herself that she was
dodging the issue, that she did not want to reach a decision
because she knew that common sense said she must decide to
leave, to go back north, to the surroundings with which she was
more familiar, where she would be closer to her parents. She was
a stranger in Baltimore. Her only real income was the small pay
she got from the Medical School and the hospital. She ought not
to go on enjoying the luxuries provided by Miss Bell. Otherwise
her self-reliance would be undermined, her determination to
succeed against odds as a physician would be undercut by too
much physical ease. She might even fail to achieve the things she
had set out to do.

The more she thought about it the more clearly she began to see
the origin of her reluctance. It was Miss Bell herself she did not
want to leave. It was not Miss Bell's house, the luxury of Miss
Bell's mode of life, the freedom from worry about food and
lodging. She was still capable of making do with dingy lodgings
and commonplace food and no servants. What she shrank from
was the idea of leaving Miss Bell, not having Miss Bell to come
home to in the evenings, to talk to when her professional burdens
grew heavy.

She put it bluntly to herself. She feared loneliness, the special
kind of loneliness she had suffered when she had parted from
Alison. For such a brief while Alison had been everything to her.
Alison had filled and lighted all the corners of her inner world.
Emma remembered her own struggle while traveling in Europe to
seal off in her heart the devastation caused by the loss of Alison.
She had thought, by the time she arrived in Baltimore, that she
had succeeded, that memories of Alison were buried too deeply to
come to the surface. She thought she had reached the point where
she could look at everything and everyone with a dispassionate
and tolerant eye, untroubled by any involvement of herself. Now
it was apparent that this was not the case.

Now she knew that, unbeknownst to herself, Miss Bell had
taken up a place in her inner world. She had grown dependent,

not on Miss Bell's money, but on Miss Bell herself. Before reaching Baltimore she had had a dim awareness that Miss Bell had come to seem a refuge, a haven for her, that Miss Bell's existence created a little private space free from the intrusion of other people. This feeling, only half-realized, had come to her on the ship coming back across the Atlantic, as she sat in a secluded corner re-reading the letters she had received at each stopping place in her travels.

So perhaps she should leave Baltimore at the New Year. Perhaps it would be wiser to keep Miss Bell only as a friend who wrote letters and gave encouragement from a distance. So far their dealings, when they were alone together, were always on a certain plane of decorum. Miss Bell never delved beneath the surface of their circumspect conversations, even when Emma, in an outburst of vexation or indignation, spoke her mind more plainly. She does not really know me, thought Emma. She does not know the wild, unruly feelings I sometimes have under this skin of cool, calm professional detachment. If she ever learned of them, she would be shocked and chagrined. I should not visit that sort of disappointment on her as a reward for her kindness.

A week before Christmas she arrived home late one evening after an exhausting day of struggling with the effects of an influenza epidemic in the hospital wards. A freezing rain was beginning to accumulate as slush on the pavement as she got out of the cab. Dorcas, opening the door, gave her a sympathetic look.

"Miss Margaret is waiting for you in the drawingroom, Miss Emma."

"I'll be right down as soon as I've changed, Dorcas," she replied, hurrying up the wide staircase.

When she came downstairs she found a fire burning in the fireplace at one end of the room. Miss Bell sat close to it, the firelight flickering on her skirt. They greeted one another and Emma sat down opposite her. Dorcas handed them the glasses of sherry.

After a moment, since Emma said nothing, Miss Bell said, "I thought a fire would be cheerful this evening. The weather is so nasty."

"Yes."

After another silence Miss Bell said, "You must be very tired this evening."

Emma roused herself. "I haven't much to say for myself, have I? I'm sorry to be poor company."

"Oh, no!"

They sat silent again for a while. Presently Miss Bell asked, "Are you too tired to consider a proposal I have in mind?"

"Why, no. What is it?"

"Have you any firm plans for the coming year?"

Emma, startled out of her lethargy, glanced at her and saw a slight frown on her face. Miss Bell seemed nervous, as if she had spent some time bringing herself up to the pitch of speaking. "I have been offered some openings. One is for a post in the New York City Infirmary."

"You are considering it, of course. It would be advantageous to you, wouldn't it? Especially in New York, where there are greater opportunities for women."

Emma answered carefully. "I have been weighing it in my mind. It is the most promising of the suggestions that have been made to me."

"I see that it must be very tempting. You would like to live in New York? I imagine it may well offer greater interest than Baltimore, since this is not your home."

Emma, with a little laugh of uncertainty, said lightly, "Why, Miss Bell, are you tired of having me here?"

Miss Bell, startled, glanced anxiously at her. "Oh, no! Certainly not! Please do not think such a thing! No, no, I should never wish you to leave."

"Never?" Emma's voice was now full of laughter. "You've been beating about the bush so that I thought it must be what you meant."

"Oh, yes, of course! You are right to laugh at me." She hesitated and then went on, in a serious voice once more. "I should be very sorry indeed for you to leave. But I cannot expect you to put aside a promising offer in order to please me."

"Well, then, why don't you tell me what you have in mind, so that we may have it out? I see you have something definite in your mind."

"Yes. I have been aware that the end of your appointment here in the Medical School is in sight and yet you have said nothing about what your plans are. So, in case you haven't decided, I want to tell you of something I have very much wanted to do for some time — something I have very much wanted to do but for which I need a special person, a special sort of person I must have to help me."

She stopped. Emma waited patiently for her to go on.

"Dr. Wycliffe, I am not a doer. I am not an innovator. I have no confidence in my own ability to put a scheme into action."

"And yet everyone says what a remarkable gift for management you have, how resourceful you are and dependable in getting the best results from any enterprise with which you are connected."

"I do well enough in managing funds for projects that others have set going. I have never undertaken anything of importance on my own."

"Very well. Tell me what you have in mind."

"What I wish to do — " Miss Bell began, paused and then went on, "what I wish to do is to set up a place for refuge, with my own money — not involving anyone else, except, perhaps, as advisors, supervisors —Martha McHugh, for instance, would be interested in helping in this way, I know — in case there are financial losses that would otherwise have to be accounted for if the scheme should fail — "

Emma, listening to the words pour forth, knew she was hearing some of Miss Bell's most inner thoughts. She said gently, "A place of refuge? For whom?"

"For women in need — in need of everything, — food, shelter, care for themselves, for their children, protection from brutal husbands, from rough treatment by the police. Modern times have brought many changes here as they have everywhere. You do not know the details of the changes here in Baltimore because you are a newcomer. But this is no longer a quiet, old-fashioned city where the problems of the poor and helpless meant chiefly those of the Negroes who had once been our slaves. We have large industries here now. You know, of course, of the steel mill at Sparrows Point. And we have many foreign immigrants. You have seen some of the problems these have created, through your work in the hospital."

"Yes, I have. Well, what do you want to do now? A shelter, you say."

"Yes. But this is where I need your help. Of course, it cannot be you if you have other plans. But I know of no one else whom I could depend upon to understand what I want to do."

"Certainly an outpatient clinic would have to be part of such a scheme. There are places in existence now where women can seek help — the emergency wards of our hospitals. But you have in mind something specifically for women and their children."

"That is it! I know there are many poor and ignorant women who are too timid, too fearful to seek help in a large, impersonal public hospital."

"And you have been thinking that I could administer such a place for you."

"Yes. It is an idea I have nursed for a long time and it just seemed that perhaps —" She stopped, her burst of eloquence spent.

Emma was silent for a long while. What can I say? she wondered. I'm not ready to speak my mind. I am not even sure I know my own mind.

At last, noticing the little restless gestures of Miss Bell's hands, she said, "I'll think about it. Let me think about it while I am with my parents for the Christmas holidays. You know that I am leaving tomorrow. I shall make up my mind while I am gone. But please don't be too disappointed if I have to tell you I can't do this. I must be honest — with you, with myself."

Miss Bell rushed breathlessly to answer her. "Oh, yes, yes. I understand. In that case, I shall have to think of something else."

Emma said nothing further. Her ear had picked up the note of disappointment in Miss Bell's voice.

*   *   *

PART III

Emma waited on the station platform for the southbound train.
A cold wind whistled past her skirt and made her hunch her
shoulders under the short cape of her winter coat. The Boston
train had been delayed by snow and ice on the track. The trip by
horse cab across Manhattan and by ferry across the river to Jersey
City had been chilling and tiring. From here south, she had been
told, service would improve, but even so she would be hours late
reaching Baltimore. She had taken the opportunity offered by the
wait to send a telegram to Miss Bell, telling her of the delay.

She wondered once more, as she had in odd moments of leisure
during the past ten days, why she had not heard from Miss Bell.
One letter from her had come just at Christmas time, a brief note
enclosed in a Christmas card, sending greetings to all of Emma's
family. After that there had been nothing and Emma, used to
receiving two letters from her for every one she herself wrote in
reply, was uneasy. Had Miss Bell in fact jumped to the conclusion
that she had already made up her mind to leave Baltimore, not to
take up the shelter scheme? And having come to this conclusion,
did Miss Bell mean to let her know that matters were coming to
and end between them?

Emma shook herself. Out here on the cold platform her spirits
were low. There was no reason to suppose that Miss Bell's
interest would not continue. She herself had not written, except
for a hurried Christmas greeting. The time with her parents had
been crowded, lively, overflowing with people and Christmas
revelry — her parents overjoyed at having her home once more,
her vigorous brothers cheerful and energetic. There had been few
moments for worrying about the problem of her own future.

Emma had always known that she was both her father's and her
mother's favorite child. Sometimes she had teased her mother,
saying that she knew she was their love child, that love children
could be born in wedlock as well as out of it. But now she was
aware of constraint with her mother. As a young child, as a
growing girl, even as a young woman on her way through college
and medical school, she had never felt the need to hide from her

mother any of her innermost thoughts, any of her sudden, fleeting love impulses. But now athwart this intimacy lay the shadow of Alison. Of course her mother knew nothing of Alison, yet she seemed to suspect some romantic attachment in London. Emma found her looking at her sometimes with a watchful, anxious expression, and once she had made a tentative reference to Sir Maurice Colburn.

She explained, "Your father's friends, the Andersons, remarked several times that he seemed very much struck by you, Emma. I'm afraid he does not have a very good reputation where women are concerned."

"So I've been told," Emma answered shortly. "However, I owe him quite a debt for all the help he gave me professionally. And he does not like women physicians!"

They had gone no further there.

Her mother did not approve of her easy acceptance of Miss Bell's generosity. "Surely, Emma, it would be more suitable if you had your own lodging and were not always underfoot with her. Naturally, she feels constrained to include you in her social activities, since you are staying in her house."

How, Emma wondered, am I to make Mother understand what Baltimore is like, how Southerners look upon such things. Lamely she replied, "She likes having me a part of her circle of friends. I don't think she feels constrained."

"Considering her age —"

"She is not elderly. She simply gives the impression of being so, on first acquaintance. She is always surrounded by those older than herself," Emma explained hastily.

She hestitated for some time before telling her mother about Miss Bell's scheme for her to remain in Baltimore. When she did so, her mother listened in silence and in the end merely said, "Do you think such a scheme will be useful to you in your professional career?"

"Oh, yes. Any project Miss Bell is concerned with has the greatest respect from the people in Baltimore."

Standing now on the station platform, bracing herself against the keen wind, Emma wished she felt as confident as she had tried to appear to her mother. It was not greater money obligation to Miss Bell that troubled her. She thought she knew how Miss Bell thought about that. It was this insidious yearning for the comfort of Miss Bell's presence, Miss Bell's sympathy —

The train backed up to the platform with loud crashing sounds, wreathed in swirling clouds of steam, amid the cries of trainmen. It came to a jolting halt and Emma climbed quickly up the steps into the car that had stopped in front of her. Yes, she was very eager to get to Baltimore and find out why she had not heard from Miss Bell.

When she got out of the train at the Mount Royal Station she found Thomas waiting in the rainy night with Miss Bell's carriage. As she greeted him she said, with some relief, "Miss Bell did get my message, then?"

The soft-spoken black man replied laconically, "Dorcas sent me, Miss Emma."

Emma, getting into the carriage while he loaded her luggage, wondered briefly at this statement. But the fact that she was being met dispelled some of her uneasiness. Thank goodness, she thought, the heavy snow that had made travel so difficult in New England was only a cold, misty rain here in Baltimore. At the end of the short drive she got out and ran quickly up the steps, to find the door opened instantly by Dorcas.

"Oh, Miss Emma," Dorcas said, almost breathless, "I'm so glad you've come!"

Alert to the note of fright in the black woman's voice, Emma demanded, as she shed her wrap, "What is it, Dorcas? What is the matter?"

"Miss Margaret, ma'am, she ain't no better. I'll swear she's worse."

"Worse! What do you mean, Dorcas?"

"She got the influenza, Miss Emma. She's as hot as fire."

Even as Dorcas finished speaking, Emma was halfway up the stairs, unfastening the pins in her hat as she ran. She checked herself at the door of Miss Bell's room, to open it quietly and without alarm. A small shaded lamp was alight by the bed, only half-dispelling the gloom of the big room. As she stepped through the doorway her practiced ear caught the sound of labored breathing. She strode to the bed and leaned over the small hump in the bedclothes. She turned back the bedcovers to see Miss Bell's face.

At the touch of Emma's hand on her forehead Miss Bell moved her head to look up at her with fever-glazed eyes. Her lips moved but no sound came.

"Don't try to talk. You must save your breath." Emma turned

to Dorcas, who had followed her into the room. "Dorcas, fetch my doctor's bag from Thomas. And get some more pillows."

She put her arms around Miss Bell's body and raised her in the bed and held her until Dorcas returned with the pillows. Propping her up on them she examined her under Dorcas's anxious eyes.

Finally she asked, "Dorcas, who is her doctor and how long is it since he has seen her?"

"Miss Margaret don't have a doctor, Miss Emma."

Emma stared at her in surprise. "Then she has had no medical attention?"

"No, ma'am. There hasn't been no doctor here and she said she didn't want to let you know she was sick."

"How about Mrs. Harms? Doesn't she know?"

"Miss Susanna's been sick, too. She don't know Miss Margaret is sick in bed."

"How long has Miss Bell been ill?"

"It was before Christmas, Miss Emma. Miss Margaret wasn't feeling well when she had the dinner party on Christmas Eve. And she was worse when she sent to dinner on Christmas Day with Miss Susanna. But she didn't go to bed till a couple of days ago. She's right sick now, ain't she, Miss Emma?"

Emma gazed absently into Dorcas's worried eyes and nodded. "There is congestion in both lungs. Dorcas, who is Mrs. Harms' physician?"

"Dr. Lightfoot. He's an old man and don't make calls at night. He's never been to see Miss Margaret."

"You mean she doesn't want him?"

But Dorcas looked down and did not answer.

"Nevertheless," said Emma, "she must have medical attention. I don't think her sister will like it if I don't call in another physician. How about Dr. Richards? Isn't he the doctor who treated her for the burns she got rescuing Flora?"

"Yes, ma'am. He lives around the corner. That's why she called him that time."

"Well, send Thomas around there and see if he will come."

But Thomas came back to say that Dr. Richards was out on a call. Thomas had left a message and had been told that the doctor would come when he got back home.

"I cannot wait on him," Emma said aloud to herself. "Dorcas, bring me a basin of water and some towels. We'll try to break the fever."

Throughout the next few hours she worked steadily, until at last Miss Bell was resting more comfortably and finally fell into a light sleep. It was already daybreak when Richards arrived at the house and Dorcas brought him upstairs.

He was a man in his forties, bluff and easy in his manner.

"How do you do, ma'am?" he said as Emma stepped out of the bedroom and closed the door behind her. "Miss Bell sent for me?"

"I did. She is too ill to do anything for herself. I came back from Boston last night. She has pneumonia and since she has apparently no regular physician, I sent Thomas to ask you to come. You have treated her before."

His questioning gaze told her that he did not know who she was. She answered it by adding, "I am Emma Wycliffe. I am staying with Miss Bell while I teach at the Medical School."

His face cleared at once. "Ah, yes. You're Dr. Wycliffe. I have heard of you. But you're a physician, then. Why did you send for me?"

"Because I have never treated Miss Bell and I think it wiser to seek advice from someone who has known her longer. I would have called Dr. Lightfoot but I understand he does not visit patients on night calls."

Richards nodded. "He is half-retired. Besides, I don't think Miss Bell would have thought of calling him."

He was looking at her directly as he said this and Emma caught the sense of something unsaid. "Miss Bell is sleeping now. Will you step in and look at her?"

He shook his head. "There's no point to disturbing her, since you're here."

"Well, would you be so kind as to see if you can arrange a consultation between yourself and Dr. Lightfoot and myself sometime later this morning?"

Emma saw that he was tired. He sighed. He has probably been up night and day with influenza patients, she thought.

"Do you think it is really necessary?" he protested.

"Yes, because I don't believe Mrs. Harms would be satisfied if only I treat Miss Bell."

Richards' weary face brightened. "Oh, yes, I see. Well, in that case, yes. I'll call Lightfoot."

He arrived back at Cushman Terrace about ten o'clock, accompanied by an elderly, white-haired man dressed in black broadcloth, whom he introduced as Dr. Lightfoot. Lightfoot bowed in acknowledgement of the introduction and then turned away, ignoring Emma thereafter, even when she described the care she had given the patient and her own recommendations for further treatment. Emma realized at once that he had no intention of recognizing her as a fellow physician. Richards, visibly embarrassed, grew more jovial in his manner to compensate for the old man's behavior.

At last, when they had both examined Miss Bell, the interview came to an end. Emma said, "Dr. Lightfoot, I asked Dr. Richards to bring you here because I understand that you are Miss Bell's sister's physician. Since Miss Bell has no regular medical attendant and her condition is so grave, I thought Mrs. Harms would be better satisfied if you were to see her."

Lightfoot looked up at the tall, golden-haired young woman in the black wool traveling dress. He said in a dry voice, "I am not accepting any new patients. However, I shall always be ready to consult with Dr. Richards whenever he wishes me to."

He bowed again and left the house without a further remark to her.

Richards, left standing in the hall with Emma, laughed deprecatingly. "I'm sorry, Dr. Wycliffe. Old Lightfoot is pretty well fossilized. I don't see why on earth you shouldn't treat Miss Bell. I'm sure she'd prefer it. And I'm just overloaded right now. We are having a real epidemic of influenza cases and some of them are turning into pneumonia. Just go ahead and don't pay any attention to Lightfoot."

He was looking at her with kindly eyes and a coaxing smile. Emma, too tired and anxious to respond to his friendliness, said shortly, "I assure you, Dr. Richards, Miss Bell's life means a great deal more to me than professional protocol. Under the circumstances, I shall certainly undertake her treatment." Having made this outburst, she softened her tone to add, "Though I hope you will give me the benefit of your own advice when I feel the need for consultation."

"Oh, yes, yes, of course! You can count on me." As he went out of the front door, she heard him mutter to himself, "A damned fine-looking woman. Old Lightfoot couldn't forgive her that."

*   *   *

For the next few days Emma's undivided attention was on Miss Bell. She did not try to find an available nurse, unwilling to trust anyone to give Miss Bell the moment-by-moment care that would save her life. The few hours when it was absolutely necessary for her to sleep Dorcas watched, ready to call her at the slightest alarm.

Miss Bell was a docile patient in Emma's hands, willing to give herself up to Emma's attentions even when she was obviously in acute discomfort, calling for her whenever she awoke from an uneasy sleep. A touch of Emma's hands and the terror that came with delirium dissipated. In her weakness she could not disguise the completeness with which she trusted to Emma's care, to Emma's authority.

Dorcas had made up a couch for Emma in the big room. The bedroom, Dorcas said, had been Miss Bell's mother's and Miss Bell had been born in that bed and Mrs. Bell had died in it. Emma, aware that the spacious house, with its ample rooms and wide corridors, created the danger of isolation for someone as ill as Miss Bell, continued to sleep near her in her convalescence. Attending to her bodily needs, patiently spooning food and drink into her reluctant mouth, Emma discovered that she no longer thought of her as Miss Bell. The Miss Bell she had first met so many months ago had vanished, first in the intellectual intimacy of her letters and now in this closer physical intimacy of the sickroom. Examining her each day as she bathed her, Emma saw that her body was not that of the middle-aged woman whom the world knew as Miss Bell. It was a soft, white body, with muscles undeveloped by any regular exercise except walking, pallid from always having been swathed in heavy garments. But still it had some of the fresh firmness of youth.

As each day passed Emma was aware of a curious feeling of peace and contentment — a sort of harmony surrounding the two of them alone in the bedroom. Dorcas' presence did not seem to disturb this tranquility. Emma felt no impatience at the interruption in her normal concerns. They could wait, the hospital could wait, her few patients could wait. Miss Bell — no, she could not go on calling her that to herself. Meg — yes, that is how she thought of her now — Meg needed her undivided attention and she should have it.

Richards stopped by once or twice and congratulated her on Miss Bell's progress. "She's been very lucky to have you here to look after her. I believe you've saved her life.''

There was no pomposity in Richards. Emma was grateful for the matter-of-fact way in which he took her professional competence for granted, as if, in fact, she were a male colleague.

It was a week later, when Miss Bell was out of danger and sleeping tranquilly most of the time, that her sister came to Cushman Terrace. Dorcas came softly into the bedroom where Emma sat reading by the window, to whisper in her ear that Miss Susanna was downstairs.

When Emma went downstairs she found Mrs. Harms sitting in the drawingroom, still wrapped in her black fur-trimmed winter coat. She asked at once, as Emma came into the room, ''Miss Wycliffe, how is my sister?''

''She is very much better — out of danger, in fact. But there is always the possibility of a relapse in cases of pneumonia. She will have a long convalescence and we must exercise considerable care.''

Mrs. Harms said, after a pause, ''I would have come to see her earlier but Dr. Lightfoot said it would be foolhardy of me to venture into her room while I am not well myself.''

''Yes. I understand you also have been ill. You are recovered now?''

''I was not very ill. But I have a predisposition to such things. I had no idea that Margaret was so ill. Dr. Richards tells me that she owes her life in large measure to your nursing.''

''Perhaps. One can never tell. Dorcas has been very faithful.''

''I do not suppose that I should try to see her now.''

''I should advise against it, both for your own sake and for hers. She should not have any visitors yet.''

Mrs. Harms rose from her chair. Emma could not tell whether she looked in any way unusual. She held her thin, tall body as rigidly as ever and her normally pale face was set in its usual severely impassive lines.

''Very well, then, until Dr. Richards says she may have visitors, I shall content myself with sending to inquire after her.''

For a long moment Emma pondered and then said in a gentle voice, ''Dr. Richards is not in attendance on your sister.''

Mrs. Harms, about to walk out of the room, stopped abruptly. ''What do you mean? She is not Dr. Lightfoot's patient.''

''Oh, no. She is mine.''

Mrs. Harms opened her mouth, closed it and then opened it

again to say, in an icy voice, "I don't understand you, Miss Wycliffe. Dr. Richards has certainly been to see Margaret."

"Mrs. Harms, I am a physician, licensed to practice. When I returned from Boston and found Miss Bell ill, I summoned both Dr. Richards and Dr. Lightfoot to see her. Dr. Lightfoot declined to attend her. Dr. Richards declared that he himself was overwhelmed with patients and that it would be better if I attended her myself. I have been doing so and intend to continue until she is strong enough to decide if she wishes another physician. Dr. Richards has been in consultation with me."

Mrs. Harms seemed about to make a sharp reply, but after staring at Emma for a few moments and failing to force her to shift her gaze, she turned away and left without saying anything further.

Dorcas, closing the front door after her, looked at Emma, her black eyes bright. "She's right angry with you, Miss Emma."

"Well, that's too bad, Dorcas." Emma answered tartly. But a certain uneasiness dwelt in her heart as she climbed the stairs back to Miss Bell's bedroom.

As she closed the bedroom door softly behind her she heard Miss Bell's weak voice, "Is it you?" Going over to the bed she leaned over to brush a strand of hair from Miss Bell's forehead. "I'm here. Would you like something to drink?"

As she held her in her arms while she drank, Miss Bell asked, between sips, "How long have I been in bed?"

"Two weeks. You should have sent for me. You would not have got so ill if I had been here."

"I wanted to, but it seemed so selfish."

"Selfish! Nonsense."

Miss Bell lay quiet in her arms. Emma, sensing that she drew comfort from her touch, sat still, holding her lightly. Presently Miss Bell said, "It is such a joy to have you with me, Dr. —"

Emma interrupted her gently, smiling at her. "Say 'Emma'."

"Emma," Miss Bell repeated obediently.

"And you will be Meg. I think of you as Meg."

The brown-flecked green eyes looked up at her full of undisguised love. "Emma, Emma," she whispered and turned her face again into Emma's shoulder.

*   *   *

In the days that followed Meg grew quickly stronger. Though

not a robust woman, she had a tenacious will and she seemed now cheerfully determined to get well as soon as possible. Emma began to pick up the threads of her professional life, plunging into the work at the hospital, visiting the women, friends of Mrs. McHugh and Mrs. Vickers, who asked her to attend them and their children. Sometimes, in the press of her new activities she did not return to Cushman Terrace at noon before going to her later appointments. Meg was strong enough to sit up for an hour or two at a time. Emma did not think that, with Dorcas to look after her, she would greatly notice her absence.

One evening she returned too late for supper with Meg. She was aware of the fact with an undercurrent of uneasiness. But as she mounted the front steps of Meg's house in the chill early dark her thoughts were principally on the problem of a consulting room. If she only had a place where her private patients could come to see her! Without such a convenience she was compelled to use up such a lot of time and energy going to their houses, even then there was no real illness to warrant it.

She opened the front door with her latchkey and, still preoccupied, stepped into the vestibule and began to remove her hat and coat. While she stood there she heard Dorcas' voice, coming from the upper landing.

"Miss Emma, you there?"

"Yes, Dorcas. What is the matter?"

The maid came down the stairs carrying a tray with an almost untouched meal on it. Observing that Emma noted the fact, Dorcas did not answer.

Emma said, "She has not eaten her supper."

"No, ma'am." Still standing with the tray in her hands, Dorcas waited another moment and then said, "Miss Emma, Miss Margaret sure do miss you."

"I'm sorry I'm late this evening, Dorcas. But I could not avoid it. I had an unexpected call at the end of the afternoon."

"She didn't eat her lunch either. And she wanted to come downstairs this evening and wait for you, in the drawingroom. I was scared, Miss Emma. I told her I didn't think she should do anything like that till you said she could."

"Did she?"

"She gave up when she tried to get dressed. She's too weak."

"Of course she's too weak!" Emma stared purposefully up the stairs.

The tone of Dorcas' voice made her pause. "Miss Emma."
Emma looked down into the black, anxious eyes. "Miss
Emma, Miss Margaret needs a lot of mothering. She never did get
enough."
Emma stood for another moment with her hand on the
bannister, looking down at her. Then she said, "All right,
Dorcas. I'll remember."
Emma opened the bedroom door carefully, wanting to get a
glimpse of Meg before Meg saw her. But Meg, standing by the
fire, in her light wool dressing gown, her hair caught back from
her face, turned quickly around.
"Emma!" Her voice was a gasp.
"Meg." Emma strode across the room to steady her, for she
was off-balance from her sudden move. "Meg, sit down." She
eased her gently but firmly into the armchair drawn near the fire.
"Meg, you must take care. If you don't, you'll be ill all over
again."
"It makes me so impatient," said Meg fretfully. "My body
won't obey me."
Emma pulled up a small chair close to her and sat down. "You
must wait till you're strong enough. Dorcas says you tried to go
downstairs this evening. Meg, you must not leave your room for a
while yet." As she spoke she took Meg's wrist in her fingers to
check her pulse. She was surprised to notice a certain resistance
on Meg's part. Emma raised her eyes to look at her, but Meg
lowered hers to avoid her glance.
Emma asked, "Has something upset you?"
Meg, half-sulky, said, "I'm so sorry, Emma. I don't mean to
be a nuisance. But you've been gone all day."
Emma, because she was alarmed, was short. "I am not
neglecting you, Meg. Dorcas is here to watch over you. I have my
hands full. It takes me a great deal of time to get through all my
day's duties."
Meg said in a shaking voice, "Forgive me, Emma. I'm being
silly. It must be because I have been ill." She seemed unable to
go on speaking and dropped her face in her hands.
Emma, disconcerted, sat for a moment undecided. Then,
obeying a strong impulse, she leaned over and took Meg in her
arms. Meg's stiffness melted and putting her arms around Emma's
neck, she wept into her shoulder. After a while she grew quiet but
Emma sat still, waiting for her to make the first move. Presently

she raised her head and looked at Emma through tear-swollen eyes and then looked away, as if ashamed. When she straightened up and sat back in her chair, Emma got up and, fetching a wet towel, sponged her face.

"That will make you feel better."

"Yes." Meg was docile again, accepting her attentions. "I cannot bear the thought of you not being here. I am frightened sometimes, when you are not with me, that you have gone away, that I will not see you again."

Emma, feeling the tremor in her body, said quickly, "Why should I not be here? You must not frighten yourself like that. Of course I am here. Of course I shall always come back to you when I've finished my work."

Meg accepted her chiding silently. The she said, "It has been very kind of you to stay and look after me. It must be a great inconvenience to you."

Emma said in exasperation, "Meg, what are you talking about? I have no intention of leaving you while you are ill."

"I know, I know. You've shown me that. But, Emma —"

"But what?"

Meg looked up at her suddenly with tragic eyes. "Emma, when I am well — oh, Emma, I can't bear it!"

Emma, sensing the climax of hours of nervous apprehension, said gently, "Meg, what is it that you've been fretting about?"

"I cannot expect you to stay here indefinitely. When I am well, you perhaps will be going away from Baltimore —"

"Oh." Sudden comprehension kept Emma from saying anything more.

"I am very grateful to you for interrupting your plans to stay here with me these last few weeks. I know — I realize —" Meg in her agitation stumbled over the words. "You have not told me but I can only suppose that that means you intend to leave, that your other plans are already made —"

Emma, astonished at herself, exclaimed, "Why, Meg, I have no other plans. I came back here to you, to Baltimore, without any other plans. I have made no effort to find other opportunities. I was waiting till you got better. In fact, I've given it no thought."

And having said all this she realized that even before she had left New England she had decided to stay in Baltimore, that in returning to Miss Bell's house she had indeed intended to stay.

She was roused to action by finding that Meg had fainted in her arms.

*   *   *

The next day when Emma came home in the early afternoon Dorcas said that Mrs. McHugh was waiting for her in the drawingroom. Emma was very glad to see her. There was something about the portly, mildly bustling woman that spoke of amiability, good feeling, friendliness. She walked quickly across the room to take both of Mrs. McHugh's hands in her own.

Mrs. McHugh's soft rosy face beamed. "Oh, my, Dr. Emma! I'm so glad to hear Margaret is better. I've been in New York with my daughter and I've been just petrified to hear she's been ill. But when they told me you were here with her, I gave a sigh of relief. I knew she would get well then."

Emma laughed. "You're very kind, as always, Mrs. McHugh. I'm just sorry I wasn't here sooner. But Meg would not send for me."

Obviously Mrs. McHugh's ears picked up the familiar "Meg". But she said, "Well, I'm thankful it wasn't too late when you did get here. Margaret can be stubborn like that. No, I haven't had that horrible disease. I was terrified when I got home and found everybody prostrated, the whole town just laid waste."

Emma, growing accustomed to the hyperbole of Southern speech, nevertheless smiled a little. "I think the worst is over. I'm told there are not nearly so many admissions to the poor wards in the hospital."

"Well, Lord have mercy. Now, Dr. Emma, I'd like to see Margaret if you think I should. That was another reason I came to call."

"Let me see if she is sleeping."

Docas, hovering in the hall, said, "Miss Margaret went to sleep after she ate her lunch. She's still sleeping."

"So," said Mrs McHugh, settling back in her chair, "let me tell *you* what I want. It's a question of the funds of the Poor Women's Benevolent Society. I know Margaret is in no condition to be consulted on financial matters but we've just got to get that ledger."

"A ledger?"

"Yes. It is normally in her possession. Of course, since she is treasurer, she keeps it. So I presume it is somewhere in her office.''

"And you want to look for it? Why, I see no reason why you shouldn't.''

"Yes, but you see, the door to that room is always kept locked. Margaret has a lot of records she keeps under lock and key — and even money. There is a safe in there.''

"I have no idea where it would be, Mrs. McHugh. I think Dorcas would be more help to you.''

"Perhaps we could ask her where Margaret keeps her keys. I know she does not allow even the cleaning woman in there unless Dorcas stays with her.''

"Dorcas is upstairs with Meg now. If you will wait, I'll go up and ask her.''

Emma entered the darkened bedroom quietly. She saw Dorcas' white apron come towards her. She murmured, "Dorcas, where are Miss Bell's keys? Mrs. McHugh wants the key to her office.''

Dorcas stepped lightly to the small table beside the bed and pointed to the shallow drawer in the top. Emma, glancing at the sleeping Meg to see that she had not roused, opened it quietly and took out the ring of keys lying in it. Nodding to Dorcas she went downstairs once more.

She had never been in the big room that Meg used as an office. She knew that it was the room Meg's father had used for his business affairs. It was gloomy now, with the heavy curtains half drawn, keeping out what little winter daylight filtered down between the house and the wall of the carriage house.

"I'm sure you will have a better idea of where to look for what you want than I, Mrs. McHugh,'' said Ema, switching on the big table lamp.

"Margaret keeps everything so tidy all the time, I do declare she could put her hands on anything in the dark.''

Mrs. McHugh gathered up her rustling silk skirts and sat down in the armchair drawn up to the big businessman's desk. As she busied herself with the keys, seeking the one in the ring that would fit the lock, Emma glanced around the room. It was somber with polished dark wood trim and heavy dark red brocaded wallpaper, thick turkey carpet. She was surprised to see a door open to another room.

"Why, there is more than one room here!''

Mrs. McHugh, glancing up preoccupied, explained. "That was Mr. Bell's smoking room. Now, Dr. Emma, stay here while I find that thing. I think it is just as well there are two of us present."

Emma laughed. "I'm quite sure Meg would never accuse either of us of pilfering."

"Not Margaret, no. But I'd like to have you to back me up if anything is found missing. You know how folks are about money."

Listening with half an ear to Mrs. McHugh's rich Southern Maryland vowels, Emma stepped into the further room. It was smaller than the office. The furniture had a more comfortable look. And the walls — she gazed about in surprise — the walls were lined with bookshelves full of books. This must be where Meg liked to sit. A woolen wrap of hers hung on the back of the armchair. There were two books lying on the table as if Meg had laid them down the last time she had been in the room, expecting to return to them at another time.

Intrigued, Emma walked over to a book case and examined the backs of the books. She had not thought of Mr. Bell as a bookish man. She was further surprised to find that all the books in the bookcase were in Latin and Greek. The Latin she had learned with her father and refurbished later in preparing for medical school was enough to tell her that all the classical authors were represented — Cicero, Lucretius, Catullus, Virgil, Livy. There were commentaries, treatises, histories, plays and poetry. Emma walked over to the table and picked up the two volumes lying there. Her vague recollection of the Greek alphabet made it possible for her to recognize Pindar's *Odes*. She remembered the letters she had received from Meg abroad, the allusions to the ancient writers. She glanced at the shelves on the other wall. They were filled with French books and some Italian. The Elizabethan poets had a section to themselves. She took down a volume of Spencer. It had Meg's name inside the cover. These were presumably Meg's contribution to the collection.

Emma walked back into the office. "Do you know, Mrs. McHugh, I never thought of Mr. Bell as a classical scholar."

Mrs. McHugh, buried in the ledger which she had at last found, was startled. "Oh, no, he wasn't."

"Well, then, did Meg acquire this whole library herself?"

Mrs. McHugh looked blank for a moment and then exclaimed, "Oh, I understand you now! No, it was her grandfather, her

Guyon grandfather. He was bishop of St. Mary's, you know. I believe he taught Margaret to read Latin and Greek. My, what a predilection for a girl! Susanna never did approve." She turned back to the ledger. "Now, Dr. Emma, I have made a note about what we have to know. It's better to leave this ledger right here. It's safer. You tell Margaret, as soon as she can take notice, what I've done. And lock the door behind me, if you please."

Smiling, Emma followed her out of the room and locked the door.

"So it was her grandfather."

"Poor man. He was like a lost soul when he came here to live with the Bells after his wife died. And of course his daughter, Margaret's mother, was already dead. He brought his library with him and that room was the only place to put it. I remember Margaret as a child, you know, and I used to wonder how she could bear to spend so much time pouring over such dusty old books. But it was her nature — still is, for that matter."

"Yes," said Emma, thoughtfully tossing the keyring in her hand.

*   *   *

Whenever she could Emma came back to the house for lunch. Meg did not break down again. She seemed to have reached a turning point in her recovery. At least outwardly she regained the unfailing self-control that had formerly always been hers. Even when Emma could not come home at midday and was late arriving in the evening, Meg was cheerful, ready to talk or listen. But Emma, wary now, sensed that this poise was delicately balanced.

Occasionally she surprised Emma by spontaneously putting her hand on Emma's arm as she greeted her. Emma, intrigued, watched her covertly. Before this Meg had always drawn back from the most casual touch. She has got used to my hands, thought Emma. She no longer shrinks away from contact with me.

Dorcas had told her that Miss Margaret had never been seriously ill since she was a little girl — never sick enough to keep to her bed and require nursing. Probably, thought Emma, with that strain of asceticism in her character, she did not give in at times when a more self-indulgent woman would have taken to her bed. It is a change, thought Emma, for her to learn dependence on someone else's care.

One evening as Emma was taking off her wraps in the vestibule Dorcas hovered around her.

"What is it, Dorcas?"

"Miss Susanna was here this afternoon, Miss Emma."

Emma paused in taking off her hat. "Did she go upstairs to see Miss Bell?"

"Yes, ma'am."

Emma waited but Dorcas did not go on.

"Did she upset her?"

Dorcas said, with a noncommittal air, "Miss Margaret's lying down. She says she has a headache."

But when Emma quietly entered Meg's bedroom, Meg was seated by the fire and smiled when she saw her. Emma waited for her to mention her sister but Meg said nothing about a visitor. Emma toyed with the idea of speaking of Mrs. Harms herself but, noticing Meg's manner, did not.

Instead, the next morning, when she looked in on Meg, she said, "I think you could receive some of your visitors now, Meg. Mrs. McHugh, for instance, or Mrs. Vickers."

"Dorcas says they come by every few days to inquire. May I go downstairs to receive them?"

"Not yet. Next week, perhaps. You can see those you know well here in your room."

Meg nodded but still she made no reference to her sister's visit.

That afternoon, when Emma arrived home, she found Mrs. McHugh about to leave. She had come to see how Margaret was, she said, and had found her full of energy and talking about a shelter for women who needed a temporary refuge for themselves and their children, safe from abusive husbands and fathers. Meg had explained that it was to be her own venture. The expense would be entirely her own. She intended to be responsible for it herself. But she thought it would be wiser if she had a board of lady visitors, made up of women in whom she had confidence, friends who sympathized with her intentions, who could help guide the policies and methods to be adopted.

"She said, Dr. Emma, that of course you would be the physician in charge. Naturally she could not hope for success without you. You are to choose the place where the shelter is to be housed and how it is to be fitted up and so on."

"Meg has talked to me about this, Mrs. McHugh, but only in

general terms. I have agreed to do whatever she wants me to. That is as far as we have gone."

"Well, I have promised her that I will try to find a suitable place. You must help me in that. You must tell me more or less what you think would be suitable."

"Do you have some locations in mind?"

Mrs. McHugh looked doubtful. "I'm not sure. Of course, I understand it must be somewhere that would be easy for poor people to come to, which means somewhere downtown, I suppose."

Emma gazed at her for a moment before saying, in a decided tone of voice, "Not simply downtown. It must be in a poor neighborhood, among the tenements where these women live. I have in mind several streets where I've gone on emergency calls." She watched Mrs. McHugh's face as she named some of them.

Mrs. McHugh's face showed her chagrin and dismay, "Oh, Dr. Emma, those are very rough neighborhoods! They are not fit for a decent woman to go into unescorted and even then —"

Emma took a long breath. "Mrs. McHugh, I'm not going into such places as a woman but as a physician. A physician must go where she is needed. Besides, there would be no purpose to creating such a shelter if it is not accessible to those who most need it."

It took several minutes of argument before Mrs. McHugh could be brought to agree with Emma's ideas. In the end she said soberly, gathering up her gloves and handbag, that she would have to consult her husband about properties that might be available for their purpose. When she heard of something she would be in touch with Emma again.

When Mrs. McHugh had left, Emma went upstairs to see Meg. She found her alert and waiting.

"Did you talk to Martha McHugh?" Meg's voice was eager.

"Yes."

"She must have told you of my conversation with her."

"She said that you had told her of the shelter you want to establish and that you want her to find a suitable building for it."

"Ah, then, things are underway!" Meg's eager eyes were scanning Emma's face. The reserve she saw there made her ask, "What is the trouble, Emma?"

"There is none, really. We've simply hit a snag."

"A snag?"

"It is the question of where to set up the shelter. Mrs. McHugh — and she says your other friends will agree with her — does not like the idea of setting it up in a really poor neighborhood. The sort of neighborhood I think suitable she believes would be too rough and dangerous for us to work in. I pointed out that the shelter cannot serve its purpose if it is not right where the women live who will come to it. The women we want to help cannot go traveling across the city, dragging a swarm of children with them. They do not have the money for streetcar fare. They do not have the energy to walk long distances even if their need is desperate. Like those wretched women who work in the canning factories, getting up at four in the morning to go to work, carrying their babies and small children with them. And the oyster shuckers, so poorly paid that the men don't want the work, even the immigrants, so that their women and children are hired instead."

"Oh, Emma!" Meg paused for a moment. "But the decision is yours. I told Martha that you must have the determining voice in everything!"

"Now, don't get upset, Meg. We did not arrive at any real dispute. She had some suggestions, but I thought they would not do. We left it that she was to consult her husband about other possible sites."

Meg sat back in her chair. The eagerness in her manner had changed to a determined thoughtfulness. She said presently, "I think I can settle that question. I shall talk to Preston."

Surprised, Emma asked, "Your brother-in-law?"

There was an odd gleam of cynicism in Meg's eyes. "My brother-in-law — indeed I am sorry to say it — owns quite a lot of property in the rougher parts of town. I think it would be only just that he should let me have a house or a portion of one in any such neighborhood as you should select. I shall broach the matter to him."

Emma said warningly, "You must take care, Meg. You're really not strong enough yet to engage in business dealings."

"But I may go downstairs to see him, Emma, if I arrange for him to come here?" Before Emma could answer, she added, "I shall feel very thwarted if you do not let me get our plans underway. I am sure I shall be much longer recovering if you do not let me act now."

"Oh, I see. You're threatening me now." Emma smiled. "How will your sister take this?"

"Susanna must know nothing about it — at least until I have concluded the matter with Preston."

"Won't she know of it from him?"

"No. There are many things that Prestion does not tell Susanna. I don't believe their married life would be nearly as harmonious if he did not make sure that she does not know much of what takes place in his business and political affairs."

"Really!"

"Oh, he does not actually deceive her. I think Susanna is too intelligent for that. But he always arranges things so that she can ignore what is inconvenient."

"Why, Meg —!" Emma's first response was to laugh. But a glance at Meg's face made her stop. She was silent, watching Meg sitting absorbed in her own thoughts.

*   *   *

The shelter opened its doors on a Monday in February and by the following Saturday morning a long line of women, all drably dressed and some ragged, carrying babies and holding older children by the hand, waited patiently in the damp cold to see Emma. By the end of another week Emma's day had become fixed in an endless battle to outrun the demands of each hour. Even though she arrived at the shelter before the day was fully light, there were huddled, shivering women waiting for her, their children crying with hunger and cold. She learned to contend not only with drunken husbands who sought to disrupt the work of the shelter, with the police who uneasily saw the crowd gathered on the sidewalk as a danger to the precarious peace of the neighborhood, with the hostile curiosity of the pimps, the drug peddlers, the casual thieves, the tramps attracted by the novelty of a beautiful, golden-haired, well-dressed woman in such surroundings. Very shortly the shelter was a focus for other young women — young medical women eager for practical experience, students pursuing careers in the social services opened to them by the Johns Hopkins University and the other local colleges.

Emma's private practice was squeezed into the last two or three hours of the afternoon. She was often very late in getting back to Cushman Terrace. Meg was now fully recovered and had resumed all her own usual activities. But she refused to sit down to dinner alone. Emma, she said, was gone in the mornings almost before she herself was up. She caught a bare glimpse of her before Emma left the house. And even at night Emma was sometimes called for emergencies. Richards had found that she was a willing and capable assistant when he had an especially difficult case.

One evening, however, Meg ate early, for she was going to the Peabody Institute, for a recital by a visiting European pianist. Emma, arriving very late, found a meal keeping hot for her over spirit lamps on the sideboard. There was no sign of Dorcas and she supposed Meg had sent her to her quarters to await her own return at midnight or later.

Relieved that she had caused no disruption of routine, Emma served herself in a desultory fashion. She carried her plate to the place set at the table and ate a few mouthfuls. Then overpowered by her own fatigue and the muffled stillness of the big room lit only by a great lamp at the farther end, she leaned back and rested her head on the tall chairback.

She was startled by the touch on her arm. Through the habit of professional training, she was instantly awake. She looked up to see Meg still in her opera cloak and gloves, bending over her, with Dorcas' face appearing over her shoulder.

"Emma! Are you ill?" Meg's voice was full of alarm and her eyes were wide.

"No, of course not! Good heavens, I must have fallen asleep. Oh, my neck!" She sat up and rubbed the back of her neck.

"Emma, how long have you been sitting here?"

Emma gave a little laugh. "I don't know, since I don't know what time it is."

"It is one o'clock. Surely you've been here all evening!"

Emma yawned. "I expect so."

"Come upstairs at once. Dorcas, bring Miss Emma something hot to her room."

Meg took hold of her hand and urged her to her feet. Heavy with unfinished sleep she docilely followed the slight figure up the stairs and into her own room. She was vaguely aware that Meg pushed her down on the bed and that presently Dorcas' hands were unfastening her dress. She heard Meg's voice admonishing her. But the waves of sleep once more overcame her and she felt herself sinking luxuriously into warm, soft oblivion.

The next morning when Emma came down to breakfast she

found Meg sitting at the breakfast table, awaiting her. Meg said at once,

"Emma, you must cut your day shorter. You cannot work like this, at all hours of the day and night."

Emma said cheerfully, "It is part of a doctor's life, Meg. I shall get more used to it."

"Nevertheless, something must be done. This schedule will undermine your health, Emma."

Emma did not answer. She sat down at the place set for her and began to eat the breakfast Dorcas set before her.

Meg went on. "You must heed me, Emma. When I asked you to run the shelter I did not mean that you were to sacrifice yourself in this way."

Emma took a sip of coffee. "It is no sacrifice, Meg. I enjoy it. I enjoy having more to do than I have time for. I am very strong, you know. I can outlast most of the men I work with."

"But obviously you are using up your reserve of strength. You must have fallen asleep as soon as you got in the house last night."

"That is only one occasion," said Emma equably, buttering a biscuit.

"It is the first, shall we say."

Emma sat back in her chair. "Meg, I confess I am tired. And there is indeed one change that would help very much. It is something I have been thinking of mentioning to you. I have hesitated because —"

She stopped and Meg watched her expectantly, finally prompting her, "Why, Emma?"

Emma's smile was diffident. "As usual, it means asking you for money." As the words left her mouth she saw her mistake. Meg's body stiffened and her face grew stony. She turned away as if to avoid Emma's eyes. Emma, understanding and yet surprised, thought, Now I've offended her. She said hastily, "Meg, you've been so generous with me that I do really hesitate —"

She did not finish her sentence, because Meg, without a word, walked out of the room.

Emma's day was too full of demands for her to brood over this breakfast-time interchange. But at odd moments the recollection of Meg's face came to her and she felt an uneasy compunction. Why had Meg responded in this way? Her remark had been no more than the truth. Why had Meg been so touchy? And how would she be this evening? How were they to arrive once more at the delicate balance of intimacy and reserve that had become so natural? Something in her own manner, the tone of her voice, rather than her words, had touched Meg on the raw.

She could not explain to Meg that her own nerves had been wrought upon by her mother's most recent letter. Her mother did not harp on the question of her dependence on Miss Bell in so many words. But there was always an undertone of uneasy disapproval that Emma never failed to detect. I cannot tell her, thought Emma, why it is that I trust Meg so much. I cannot tell her that there is something unique in our dealings with one another, something that makes this different from the usual patroness and protegee situation. I cannot tell her because I don't know how to explain it to myself. And yet this morning —

It was late when Emma finally arrived home. She was half-dismayed to find that the drawing room was lighted and ready, that Meg was obviously sitting in the drawing room waiting for her. As she changed her dress she found she shrank from coming into Meg's presence. A heavy silence, a meal eaten in stiff formality, was more than she could bear. She girded herself for the encounter and walked into the drawing room.

Meg was seated as usual by the big lamp. She put down the book she was reading and said, as Emma came in, "Good evening."

Emma, listening, could hear nothing unusual in her voice. "Good evening, Meg."

"You have had another long day."

"I'm afraid I've kept you waiting. My last call was out beyond the Park."

Dorcas appeared with the glasses of sherry on the silver tray. When she had left the room, Emma said, aware that there was a trace of defensiveness in her own voice, "I really believe, Meg, that I should find myself somewhere to live — oh, nearby, hopefully! — where I could come and go without being a nuisance to you. I know I disrupt your household. Flora and Dorcas both must feel annoyed at dinner being held so long in the evenings. And then the telephone calls in the night."

Emma felt rather than saw Meg grow stiff. She said drily, "My servants are here to serve me. I consider them, of course. But their business is to suit me."

This statement, unusual in its forthrightness and yet said in Meg's most characteristic voice, silenced Emma. They sat for a moment without speaking, sipping their wine.

Presently Meg said, "I believe I understand what you were going to say this morning, Emma. I have given some thought as to how it must be accomplished."

Emma thought wrily, Grasp the nettle of adversity. That is Meg. What gives you pain must be met at once and without flinching.

"Meg, I had no intention of hurting your feelings this morning —" Emma began.

Meg swept her words aside. "What is necessary is that you should have a consulting room where your private patients can come and see you. You exhaust yourself in going all over Baltimore to see them."

So she has understood, thought Emma. "Yes. But I cannot afford to rent a consulting room, especially in the sort of neighborhood that would be expected by the women who seek me out. That is what I meant, Meg, by saying that I should have to ask you to advance me money, until my income makes it possible for me to repay you. That is all I meant, Meg."

Meg, as if annoyed by her eagerness, made a quick, dismissive gesture. "That would not be necessary under the plan I have in mind." She paused and then went on. "This is a very large house, Emma, ridiculously large for one woman and her servants. I propose to turn my office into a consulting room for you. It has, as you know, its own outer door. It was my father's office when he saw the people with whom he had business dealings. He did not like to bring his commercial interests into his home. There is space enough, with his old smoking room, to make a waiting room and an examination room for you. The separate entry would provide privacy for your patients. I can arrange to have the work done now and promptly."

Taken by surprise, Emma exclaimed, "But, Meg, this will entirely upset your own affairs. You use that office as your own now and the other is your private library. I cannot think of uprooting you like that."

"You are depriving me of nothing. There is plenty of space in this house. I can have the old sewing room upstairs fitted for my own use. It is never used. Habits have changed since my mother's day. And if I have visitors, I receive them here, as you know.

That is no problem, Emma. I believe this is a simple solution."

"Except," said Emma, with an edge in her voice, "that it will require quite an outlay of money."

There was a long silence, during which Dorcas came to say that dinner was ready to serve. They both got up and Emma waited for Meg to lead the way to the dining room. But Meg stood still and finally said, "Then you accept this solution, Emma?"

Emma, with a sense of rebellion, said sharply, "I don't know that I do."

Meg turned to face her fully. In the muted lamplight her face was paler than usual and set. "Emma, you cannot refuse." Her eyes, bright and piercing, searched Emma's face. What she saw made her reach out her hand and tentatively grasp Emma's arm. "Emma —"

Emma, her momentary vexation ebbing, found herself yielding. "Let me think about it, Meg. You have not considered how your sister and your friends may view this." Emma was aware that, in voicing this objection, she was hiding a deeper doubt.

"My actions are not determined by what other people may think."

"But perhaps you have not considered the fact that they may not have the same opinion of me that you do."

"That, Emma, is something I should scorn to consider for a moment." Meg's voice softened. "Emma, you did not use to hesitate to accept my help."

"The situation has changed, Meg. I was still a novice, still learning my trade. Now I should be on my own feet."

"But that is no reason to — to spurn me!"

"Spurn you! Oh, Meg, how can you —!" Emma checked herself and said in a different tone. "This is not the sort of way we should speak to each other. I am sorry, Meg. It is simply that I must maintain my own independence."

"I have no wish to encroach on it."

"No, I believe that you don't. I used to take it for granted that you would never do so."

"Why have you ceased to believe that? What have I done, Emma, to make you think otherwise?"

"You have done nothing."

"Then it is 'other people'?" There was a trace of bitterness in Meg's voice.

Emma looked at her, shocked at the revelation her words had

made. Yes, other people. Just what she had tried to make her mother understand—that between Meg and herself there was a special feeling, a special ground of dealing that had existed from the very first, when she had known Meg only as Miss Bell, formal, reserved, remote.

Emma said humbly, "Yes — other people. Forgive me, Meg." She put her arm around Meg's waist. She felt Meg yield at her touch and then stiffen.

"Then it is settled," Meg said in a suddenly brisk voice, as she turned away to walk to the dining room.

*   *   *

Mrs. McHugh was the first to know of the alterations being made to the house. Emma arrived earlier than usual one afternoon to find her standing in the vestibule taking leave of Meg, half their conversation drowned out by the noise of the workmen hammering to make new partitions in Mr. Bell's old quarters.

"Now, don't let me upset you, Margaret," Emma heard her say. "The world can't stand still just to please Susanna. Oh, Dr. Emma! Margaret says you will have your new office by next week. She will have to have a tea party as a house-warming."

Emma laughed and looked at Meg. Meg, who seemed preoccupied with some unhappy thought, tried to smile as she said goodbye to Mrs. McHugh.

After Mrs. McHugh had left she was not talkative and the shadowed mood lingered on her for the rest of the day. Her sister does not like what she is doing, thought Emma. But Emma said nothing. Meg in this mood was unapproachable, withdrawn into some past habit of solitariness.

The following day, early in the morning, when Emma had just begun to attend the women and children waiting at the Shelter, she was interrupted by the entrance of a policeman. That in itself would not have struck her as strange. The building in which the Shelter was housed had once been a warehouse. It was surrounded by saloons, pawnshops, stands where stale vegetables were sold at half price. Around the corner was a street with several brothels. Several times police had come to the Shelter looking for petty thieves and other suspicious characters. More than once Emma had had to call the policeman on the beat to help in evicting drunken men attracted by the novelty provided by the Shelter.

But this time the policeman stood impatiently by while she

finished washing out a child's sore ears. Then he said she was
wanted at the precinct station two blocks away. The sergeant had
sent him to fetch the nearest doctor and that was herself.

"Is it an emergency?" Emma demanded.

The policeman nodded. Without argument Emma took up her
bag and followed him out into the street. Though she asked him,
as they walked along, the nature of the emergency, he shook his
head glumly and said only, "The sergeant'll tell you."

At the stationhouse the sergeant got up from his desk the
moment he saw her coming in through the door. "Come this way,
doctor," was all he said and led her down a corridor past several
empty cells to one at the back. The door was open and Emma, in
the gloomy light, made out the form of a woman lying on the
floor. The sergeant and the policeman stood silently by as she
knelt and gently lifted the woman's head. In the dim light she
could see that the woman's eyes, half-open, were glazed and that
there was blood at the corners of her mouth.

Still holding the woman's head Emma asked, "Can you get me
something to put under her? And a blanket to cover her till the
ambulance comes."

"The ambulance?" demanded the sergeant.

"Haven't you sent for one? You know as well as I do that her
skull is probably fractured. She is in shock. Call the hospital at
once. There is nothing I can do here."

Reluctantly the sergeant withdrew. Emma waited as the
patrolman brought two army blankets, one to fold under the
woman's head and the other to wrap around her. Emma sat
silently on the stool that the cell was furnished with, while the
policeman stood sullenly beside her, listening to the woman's
stertorous breathing. When the ambulance crew arrived with their
stretcher she helped them shift the woman carefully onto it and
walked out of the cell and down the corridor behind them. She
was vaguely aware of faces peering curiously at her from dark
corners.

As she walked across the charging room the sergeant stopped
her. He said grimly, "You understand, ma'am, there won't be
any statement made about this. You can report it as an accident.
We just found her that way."

Emma stared at him. "Where? Under what circumstances? Why
was she in that cell? What did you arrest her for?"

"She was in there because we didn't have anywhere else to put her. She was picked up in the street, in the gutter. She's a street-walker. Some john beat her up — probably because he caught her trying to shake him down. You don't have to go to the hospital with her. The ambulance boys can just tell the admissions clerk what I said. The hospital will take care of the rest.''

For a moment Emma was silent with indignation. Then she said, ''I shall do nothing of the kind. Since I was called to examine her, I shall go to the hospital with her and see that she gets prompt treatment. It can mean the difference between life and death.''

There was a flare of anger in the sergeant's eyes. ''The sooner that sort dies the better for everybody, instead of spreading disease and misery among decent families.''

Emma, too angry to speak, walked past him out of the station.

*   *   *

Emma stepped through the door that led from her consulting room into the main part of the house. She had come in by the side entrance in order to see what progress had been made by the workmen. The alterations were almost finished. The room smelled strongly of the white paint that had been used to banish the gloom of Mr. Bell's smoking room, now her examination room. The new furniture was already in place in the waiting room. In another day or so she could move in.

She heard the sound of voices coming from the drawing room as she walked quickly to the stairs. Dorcas suddenly emerged from the half-light under the stairwell.

''Miss Emma, Miss Margaret wants you to come to the drawing room.''

''Now?''

''Yes, ma'am.''

Emma turned and went slowly across the hall, puzzled. She recognized James West's as one of the voices. He was getting to his feet at sight of her. They had met a number of times since the Thanksgiving dinner at the Harms' and he had called often to press her to go out some evening to dinner with him. She had always refused. This was the first time she had seen him at Meg's without Mrs. Harms.

As they greeted each other, Meg said, ''Emma, James has been waiting to see you.''

Something in her tone caught Emma's ear as meant as a

warning. She looked at James. "Me? Whatever for?"

He said jocularly, "Well, I've been waiting on the doorstep for sometime now for you to say you'll let me take you to dinner."

"But that is not what you're here for now."

At her abruptness he said drily, "Always to the point, Dr. Emma, aren't you? No, that's not why I'm here now. It is something not so pleasant."

Again Meg spoke. "James has something to say to you about the woman you were called to see in the police station."

James looked annoyed at her intrusion. "Well, yes. I'll be brief. I believe you were called yesterday to see a woman who was being held in a cell at the precinct station near the Shelter."

"Yes," said Emma.

"She was injured in a brawl."

"She died at two o'clock this morning. There was very little that could be done for her. I don't know how she was injured, but I don't think it was in a brawl."

"How do you know it wasn't?" His tone was almost hostile.

"I was told she had been beaten by a man she picked up on the street. I think she was injured in the police station, when they tried to subdue her."

"That is what was reported in this afternoon's paper. In fact, that newspaper account is what I came to see you about. It was foolish of you to tell the newspaper reporter that story."

Emma retorted angrily, "If I thought it was the truth, I see no reason why I should not."

"Because it gives a distorted version of the case. It throws a bad light on the administration of the police here in Baltimore. The police are justified in resenting that sort of publicity."

Emma's temper flared. "If you have come here to defend the police, you are wasting your time. The woman is dead, from a beating in which her skull was fractured. No doubt whoever was responsible did not intend that. Nevertheless, she was killed and I believe the beating took place in the police station."

"Did she accuse someone?"

"She never fully recovered consciousness. But she made some statements — which were heard by several of those attending her in the hospital — that were highly suggestive, under the circumstances."

"That's a serious charge to make. That woman was the dregs of the gutter. Nobody would believe any statement she made, even if she was in her right mind."

"Especially since she has a long record of arrests not only for soliciting but for drunken and disorderly conduct."

James began to agree heartily with what she said, but the cool tone of her voice made him pause.

"Well, then, why did you give that reporter the impression you believed her story?"

"Because I do believe it."

James was exasperated. "Even if there was some truth to it, don't you realize that policemen can't handle criminals with kid gloves? If she resisted, they had to use force to subdue her."

"In other words, she brought about her own death."

They were both silent for a few moments. Then James said, as another mode of attack occurred to him, "You know, you've got to consider your own interests in a case like this. This kind of publicity doesn't do you any good professionally. And I doubt if Cousin Margaret appreciates having her affairs brought into this sort of notoriety. Everybody in Baltimore knows she supports that Shelter."

Emma's temper flared again. "I'm sure if Miss Bell has any complaint to make, she'll make it to me." She glanced at Meg and saw that she sat stiff and straight in her chair, her hands clasped tightly in her lap, her eyes intently on them.

James, noticing her glance, also looked at Meg. He said, in a milder tone, "Just the same, I'd be careful how you talk to newspaper reporters. I'd be careful about making irresponsible statements."

Emma, fighting to control her temper, replied, "I'm not in the habit of making irresponsible statements."

Afraid that her own efforts to control her temper would be overwhelmed by the sight of his face, she turned away, to stand at the window. He came to stand behind her.

He said placatingly, "Now, look here, Dr. Emma, I know you naturally get upset when you see something like this. You're a woman and you aren't used to dealing with vicious people. You're tenderhearted. But let me tell you, that sort of woman isn't worth your sympathy. I blame that sergeant for sending for you. He had no business bringing a lady into that place."

Emma whirled around. "He sent for the nearest doctor. I was the nearest doctor. His mistake was in supposing that I could be intimidated into keeping my mouth shut. All he wanted was a

doctor to sign a death certificate when the woman finally died —
in that cell, without care."

James was obviously going to retort, but he checked himself
and said, still trying to mollify her, "I'm not defending him. But
take my advice and stay out of that sort of situation." He turned
away to speak to Meg.

The turmoil of indignation that gripped Emma closed her ears
to the meaning of the words that he exchanged with Meg.
Vaguely she was aware that he was taking leave. The room
became silent.

Presently she felt a light touch on her arm and looked down to
see Meg gazing anxiously up into her face. Emma exclaimed, "I
will not be silenced when I know I am right!"

"Emma, I am sorry. Of course you must do what you think
right."

Emma, disarmed by her gentle voice, replied in vexation,
"Yes. But I should not have brought such a thing into your
house."

The rare color came into Meg's face and her clear, green-
brown eyes suddenly sparked. "It was not you, but James.
Emma, I am not blind and deaf to the miseries that afflict people
less fortunate than myself. But I do want to warn you. James is
right. You are a stranger in Baltimore. You have a reputation to
build as a physician, a difficult thing for a woman under the best
of circumstances. I am sorry that James could not be more
courteous but it is his manner."

"So I must walk softly and look the other way!"

"No, I do not mean that. Emma, I will stand by you under any
circumstances. I know that you have important and valuable work
to do. It is time that we have a woman trained as you are to deal
with the injustices all women suffer from here as everywhere. But
you must be prepared for unexpected opposition. And besides —"
Meg seemed to weigh her words — "James is very well disposed
to you now. I can see that you have captured his attention. But,
Emma, I must warn you. He is not a man to let anyone stand in
his way. That is why, I think, he made such an effort to persuade
you. He does not want to find himself at odds with you. Emma,
he is very much taken with you."

Emma retorted angrily, "I'm very much obliged to him!"

*   *   *

Obviously James' influence prevailed. The newspapers dropped
all further mention of the woman who had died. No mention of
Emma or the Shelter appeared, nor any reference to a coroner's
verdict on the cause of death.

But James himself was much more often in her orbit. One
afternoon as she stood on the street corner waiting for the streetcar
to take her into the center of town Emma was surprised to see him
get out of a cab across the street. Telling the cab driver to wait he
came over to greet her.

"Ah, Dr. Emma. Let me take you home."

Emma hesitated. It would save her valuable time if she
accepted. Reluctantly she followed him across the street and got
into the cab.

As the horse started up, James said, "Don't you have any free
time at all? You never come with Cousin Margaret to my aunt's to
dinner."

"Well, I imagine Mrs. Harms hasn't told Meg that I am
invited."

He looked at her sideways but saw only good temper in her
face. "How about coming with me to dinner some evening? Do
you like oysters?"

"Meg expects me to dine with her when she is at home."

"Then some evening when she goes out."

"Perhaps," said Emma.

He was tenacious and after several more refusals, Emma agreed
to go out with him. She found he was an agreeable man when he
wanted to be. He amused her with his running commentary on
their friends, his relatives, the political world of Baltimore and
Annapolis, the hidebound customs of Maryland society. I really
should like him very much, thought Emma. He is quite broad-
minded when it comes to women's rights. And I can't complain of
the way he treats me.

But there was some other quality about him that made her
uneasy. She noticed a certain watchfulness in him. Often she
would, in the midst of lively talk, glance at him to find that his
eyes were fixed on her in a veiled sort of way. Perhaps, she
thought, it is only a mannerism, picked up from his uncle. But she
could not convince herself that it was only a mannerism. He
seemed to be biding his time, as if he had a goal in mind and was
prepared to use endless patience in waiting for the opportunity to
press forward towards it, an opportunity that must inevitably

come. Her uneasiness, she decided, came from the fact that she
sensed in him an implacability, that he would not brook any
opposition to his own will. Any concessions he made were made
at his desire only, not because of anyone else's claims.

As the warmer days of spring arrived and with them the longer
daylight, he came to join her at the tennis club for a game when-
ever she could snatch a respite at the end of her working day.
Often he came to the Shelter at a time when he knew she might be
leaving and took her wherever she wanted to go by cab. He talked
about getting Mrs. Harms to invite her to the horse farm near
Annapolis, but she avoided giving him a definite answer.

*   *   *

It was in the early part of May that the newspapers began to
give a good deal of space to the activities of the League for Urban
Purity. There were detailed stories about crime syndicates, about
the interweaving of the operations of crooked gamblers, dealers in
illegal whiskey, pimps, brothel-keepers and prostitutes, habitual
criminals. Emma, with little time to read the papers, was chiefly
aware of these happenings through the women who came to the
Shelter. They told her of police raids, of their men made more
violent than usual by the visits of public health investigators come
to survey the lack of sanitation in the tenements.

One morning the paper announced that the public prosecutor's
office was to make a special effort to clean up the redlight
districts. This was at the urging, it was said, of the League for
Urban Purity and there was a good deal of rhetoric by politicians
on the need to "rid our fair city of this shame." Emma, glancing
at the front page of the paper as she ate her breakfast, noticed the
prominence given to James West. He, as a specially appointed
assistant in the prosecutor's office, was to be in charge of these
clean-up operations.

Emma, looking up from the paper, saw Dorcas lingering at her
elbow. Dorcas pointed to the paper. "Miss Susanna is on her high
horse again."

"Mrs. Harms?"

Dorcas nodded and put a thin black finger on the phrase, "the
President of the League for Urban Purity."

"Is this a special interest of hers, Dorcas?"

"Miss Susanna don't hold with people being scandalous."

Emma laughed, "Well, I don't suppose any of us approve of
that, except those who like it."

"You can't change the men. If they don't find women one place, they'll go looking somewhere else."

"That, Dorcas, is a profound statement. So Mrs. Harms, every so often, tries to clean up Baltimore."

"That's right. Don't do no good that I can see. But every so often she gets on her high horse."

"I see. And what does Miss Margaret think of this?"

"She don't say. Least, I've never heard her say."

"But she doesn't belong to —" Emma glanced at the paper again — "to the League for Urban Purity?"

"I don't think so, Miss Emma. But she does their accounts for them." Dorcas seemed to consider and then added, "Miss Margaret ain't eager to join anything Miss Susanna runs."

"Oh. Well, I imagine they are both better off in their own affairs."

"Yes, ma'am," said Dorcas, taking away Emma's empty plate.

That afternoon Emma returned to Cushman Terrace early and since no patients were yet waiting for her in her new consulting room, she went into the main part of the house to see if Meg was home. She found her in her private sitting room. It had amused Emma to note how, when Mr. Bell's former office had been made into her consulting room, the old sewing room had been transformed into an intimate nest for Meg. The walls were lined with book shelves into which the library of Latin and Greek authors had been moved. Meg's desk and the cabinets with the financial records of the organizations for which she served as treasurer were neatly confined to one corner. Meg was no longer, thought Emma, a homeless bird perching in an abandoned nest, a mere interloper in her grandfather's old sanctuary. There was a quality to the newly fitted-up room that spoke of Meg.

Coming into it Emma found Meg sitting thoughtful, her hands folded in her lap. A newspaper was folded back and lay on the desk before her. Emma's eye lit on the headline for a long column.

"James seems quite prominent in the news these days," said Emma.

Meg glanced down at the paper. "Yes. This is, I am afraid, a perennial thing." Noting the inquiry on Emma's face, she added, "I mean, these campaigns against vice in the city. I'm sorry to say that I can't see them as anything but a political maneuver."

"Nothing is really done?"

"Oh, for the moment, of course. They have raids and arrests

and the newspapers give much space to the officials involved, to portray them as public benefactors.''

Emma laughed. "Why, Meg! Such cynicism!"

"No, no! I don't mean it quite that way! I am sure some of them have the best of intentions. But it all seems so useless.''

"Dorcas tells me that your sister is the president of the group of women who demanded some sort of action."

"The League for Urban Purity. Yes, Susanna is very active in this. And of course she has Preston's support.''

"Then there should be some real success.''

Meg looked at her as if to see whether there was some hidden meaning in her remark. "I believe Preston is quite sincere in backing these attempts to suppress organized criminals who enrich themselves through vice. Perhaps it is simply that the problem is too great to be solved by such methods. After all, Baltimore is a port and it is now an industrial city besides, and unfortunately it has a history of corrupt politics. Preston is not to blame if his efforts are not more fruitful.''

"And James also. Perhaps he will have more success.''

"James is Preston's protege. He is grooming him for a political career. That is something that Susana wishes also. She places great value on James. I only hope he will never disappoint her. Susanna's feelings are deeply buried but they are very strong.''

Emma prudently made no reply.

*　　*　　*

The woman was shouting as she pushed her way through the throng in the Shelter.

"Where's the doctor! Where's the doctor!''

Emma looked up from the bandage she was fastening. "What do you want?''

"If you don't come right now, she'll bleed to death. Come on.'' The woman laid hold of her arm.

Emma stood still and looked at her. She was young, there was a remnant of freshness in her face, but her eyes were bloodshot and her breath was foul.

"Who are you talking about? Where is she? What has happened to her?'' Emma's voice was stern and she did not budge.

"At the station house! She was bleeding when they picked her up. I told them to let her alone, that she was sick. The sons-abitches never listened.''

As the woman continued to rave at her, with strings of curses, Emma recalled vividly the woman who had lain in the cell with a fractured skull. All through the preceding night Emma knew, the police wagons had been rounding up women from the streets and brothels. The women who had come early to the Shelter had told her of the raids, the street fights, of the uproar in the tenement flats.

The woman began to plead and Emma, with a word to her assistant, followed her out into the street.

Emma entered the door of the station house alone. The woman who had brought her stopped half a block away and stammered, "You go on, doctor, I'm afraid to go in there. It's Lena that's sick. They had no business picking her up." And she had run away down the street.

The outer room of the precinct station was jammed with policemen and newspaper reporters. The noise was clamorous, compounded of the babble of voices and the yells and cursing of the women in the cells beyond. The crowd of men parted at once for her to pass. The sergeant jumped up from his seat behind the desk. His manner was belligerent, but he waited for her to speak.

Emma said, "You've got a woman here who needs medical attention."

He said defensively, "I've already sent for a doctor."

Emma, not believing him, said, "But he's not here and I understand she is bleeding to death."

The sergeant obviously was aware of the sudden concentrated attention of the newspaper reporters in the room. He turned abruptly and began to elbow his way through the crowd, saying to Emma over his shoulder, "I warn you. If you go in there, they'll tear you to pieces. And I'm not responsible."

Emma, clutching her doctor's bag to her chest, made no effort to respond. They passed one cell, crowded with shouting women who reached through the bars to snatch at her. When they arrived at the door of the second cell, the sergeant paused before turning the key in the lock. "Remember what I said. Rosy Shanahan is in there and you know what they call her — the Maneater."

"I'm not a man," said Emma sharply, and the policeman just behind her burst into a guffaw.

When the sergeant opened the cell door a dozen hands seized hold of her arms and her clothes and dragged her into the midst of a press of bodies. For a moment she thought the sergeant's forecast would come true and that the women snatching at her garments and cursing in her face would tear her apart. She made no effort to resist them but said as calmly as she could, "If I'm to do anything, you're going to have to stand back."

As she spoke she wondered whether it was in fact possible for them to do so, since the small space was so jammed by their numbers. It was a cell intended at most for two or three prisoners and now it must hold five times that number of women.

But though in the press she could not see their faces clearly, she had been recognized, especially when one tall woman snatched off her hat and clutched at her hair. "It's Goldilocks," the woman yelled. "We're in luck. Come on. Move back."

The woman who spoke was black-haired and brawny with long arms and she used them now to push the others aside to allow Emma to reach the center of the crowd. A woman lay in the small space in the center of the cell. Emma knelt down, conscious of the close, heavy air saturated with body smells and stale, cheap perfume. She began to check the unconscious woman's breathing, when someone yelled into her ear, "It's the other end! She's bleeding from her cunt."

Pushing aside the wall of skirts that hemmed her in, Emma was able to reach the woman's legs, drawn up against her body. Pulling up her dress, Emma saw that her undergarments were soaked in blood and a rivulet was seeping onto the floor. In frantic haste, in the sudden silence, filled only with the heavy breathing of the women watching avidly, she packed the woman's vagina with cotton plugs and gave her an injection. Then wiping her bloody hands she straightened up and pushed her way to the cell door. The sergeant and several other men, fascinated by the total calm in the hitherto seething mass of women, stood watchfully in the corridor.

"You'll have to get an ambulance as quickly as possible," said Emma. "I cannot keep her from bleeding to death here, without help."

"I've already sent for one," said the sergeant. His eyes and those of the men with him traveled over her, taking in her disordered clothes and the bright gold hair hanging about her ears. The sergeant made as if to unlock the cell door again to let her out. But Emma, as the women once more began to clamor and curse, stopped him.

"I'll stay here," she said, "till they come to get her."

She leaned her back against the bars of the cell door and tried to put her hair back up on her head.

"Here, dearie," said the woman closest to her, reaching up to help her.

Two or three of the women nearest her began to squabble in an attempt to do it for her, dragging at the thick coils until a golden flood fell down her back.

The tall, black-haired woman reached over their heads and plucked the pins out of their grasp. "Leave Goldilocks alone," she ordered. Intimidated, the other women watched while she expertly dressed Emma's hair into a high bun on top of her head.

The sergeant said drily, "That's a good job, Rosy. You a lady's maid now?"

He grinned as his remark brought a rush of curses and taunting yells from the women in the cell and started up the clamor all down the corridor. The uproar continued until the ambulance crew arrived, and after a brief pause while the unconscious woman was carried away, broke out again.

As Emma came out of the cell on the heels of the stretcher-bearers, trying to straighten the jacket of her costume, she found herself face to face with James West. He was smiling.

"Daniel in the lion's den? The sergeant said you weren't even afraid of them."

"Why should I be?"

"*I* would have been," he said jocularly.

"I've treated several of them in the hospital wards. They recognized me."

"Oh, so that's it. Just the same, I admire you." He paused and seemed to consider for a moment. "Are you going to have another newspaper story out of this?"

Emma glanced at the reporters clustered around. "You will not be able to hold me responsible this time, if there is." She paused for a moment and then added, "But I do think that the public should know that fifteen women are being held in cells intended for one or two prisoners, without food and no water to drink."

James frowned angrily. "You're eager to pamper this scum, aren't you?"

Emma flushed but spoke calmly. "They are women — degraded and abused, but women nevertheless."

He was about to make a sharp rejoinder, but stopped himself. Instead he turned away to say to the sergeant, "I'd like to have a word with you." He watched as Emma stepped past him and out of the station house.

*   *   *

Mrs. Vickers set down her teacup and said, with a troubled note in her voice, "I don't altogether understand it. You would think that these poor women who come to the Shelter would resent her—her independence, her good clothes, especially her glorious beauty. It is extraordinary that they don't."

"They adore her," said Mrs. McHugh. "I've been there with Margaret —" she glanced across the teatable at Meg — "and this is not an exaggeration. I think it is that she satisfies something of an ideal for them, a vision of what a woman can be, unattainable for them but nevertheless reassuring. You know, Margaret, it must be akin to the way poor miserable women in foreign countries worship the Madonna — Oh, I know, we're told the Madonna is not worshipped but there is no other word for it — a glorious someone of their own, that the men have nothing to do with. She is theirs and yet she is desirable by everyone. But the men can only covet and envy."

Meg laughed. "Emma would indeed be astonished if she could hear you, Martha, comparing her to the Virgin Mary."

"Oh, Margaret, you know what I mean! I have heard how wretched people in Asia, for instance, try to touch the garments of a saintly person. Well, there is something of that kind in the way these women besiege Dr. Emma at the Shelter—as if they were trying to reach a divinity."

Meg's soft laugh was gay. "How very lyrical you are, Martha! Yes, of course I understand you. I think it is pathetic that they should have so little resource to ease their miseries. After all, what the Shelter can do is only a drop in the bucket. But they are fortunate to have Emma."

"Indeed they are," said Mrs. Vickers. Her voice deepened to a lower tone. "And what is this about those women in the prison, Margaret? I must say I have wondered at her championing these women who stand in the street and solicit men."

"You have seen the newspaper accounts," said Meg, speaking in a suddenly severe voice. "Not in prison, merely in jail cells, rounded up arbitrarily by the police. Regardless of what they are they should have medical attention when they need it and female attendants in the jails. They should not be left to the mercies of men who have long since lost respect for them. Such men have a life and death power over these women. You must realize that.''

"Well, yes. But how can Dr. Emma go right into that cell with them? How can she touch them?'' A visible shiver went through Mrs. Vickers' florid bulk.

Meg said grimly, "Emma does not feel that way. And as a physician it is fortunate that she does not have your squeamishness.''

"But you feel it yourself, Margaret, I know you do.''

Meg, aware that she was right, merely shook her head.

Mrs. McHugh said, as a diversion, "I don't think Susanna is pleased about all this publicity.''

Meg ignored the remark as she poured tea into the transparent bone-china cup. Mrs. Vickers giggled. "But there is not much she can say if James comes to Emma's defense, is there?''

"Does he?'' Meg demanded sharply.

"Oh, yes. Why, Margaret, you must have seen the statement he made to the press about the League's adopting a resolution to seek ways to implement Dr. Wycliffe's suggestions.''

"Yes, that, certainly,'' said Meg. "After all, she has public opinion on her side.''

"Susanna plainly thinks that James has a personal interest in Emma,'' said Mrs. McHugh. "They're seen together in public places. I doubt that Susanna is pleased. Has she said anything to you, Margaret?''

"It is not something that Susanna would discuss with me, Martha.''

"Well, perhaps not.''

                    *   *   *

Emma yawned and opened her eyes. The curtains in her bedroom were still drawn, but there were streaks of bright sunlight visible now and then as the mild breeze moved them. It must be afternoon, Sunday afternoon. The bitter sense of frustration with which she had struggled all yesterday, ever since the final defeat of the early hours of Friday morning, came flooding back to her. Sheer exhaustion had brought deep sleep, after a whole night of useless struggle to save the woman's life, followed by a day during which, in spite of all the demands of her usual activities, she could not shake this mood of angry rebellion. Oh, God in your mercy, why cannot I find a way to spread the knowledge I possess? If no means existed to prevent this sort of tragic misery, I should have to accept it, with everyone else. But the means do exist, I know what they are, and yet I am forbidden to speak.

She went over once more in her mind the details of the battle, hopeless from the start, the fatal hemorrhage that would not be staunched—the result of one conception too many for a woman who had never been meant to bear eight children—taking this last child with her and leaving behind two little ones who almost certainly already had the tubercular infection that had sapped their mother's strength. It had been six o'clock in the morning before Emma had closed the woman's eyes and left the basement flat to which she had been called the evening before, in the middle of dinner.

It was good of Meg never to show annoyance at such a disruption of her household. It is as if, thought Emma — yes, as if she has accepted not only the responsibility for the success of my professional career but also the task of overseeing my welfare, to watch over me as her personal duty. Dear Meg.

She broke off her musing to yawn again and sit up and stretch. That must have been the longest sleep she had had for weeks. She flung off the covers and got out of bed. Going over to the windows she opened the curtains and gazed out for a few minutes into the garden at the back of the house, walled round to keep it private from the surrounding dwellings. The daffodils had gone but the scent of early summer flowers came to her. It was Flora the cook who tended the beds of petunias and geraniums and roses that edged the small square of lawn. Just as it was Flora who owned the big marmalade cat that dozed much of the day on the kitchen window sill. Miss Margaret, Dorcas said, did not care for pets and it was Miss Susanna who was the gardener in the family. Miss Margaret, Dorcas explained, was too tenderhearted. She couldn't bear to see anything go wrong, like a cat who got too old and sick or a flower eaten by insects or wilted by disease. She had always been that way, ever since she was a little girl.

Emma smiled now at the recollection of Dorcas' words. She supposed Dorcas understood the concept if not the word perfectionist, for that was what Meg was. Much earlier in their friendship Emma had asked Meg why, since music seemed so necessary to her, she did not play the big concert grand piano that stood at one end of the drawing room. Meg had replied, "I cannot play well enough to suit myself." And instead she had insisted, on evenings when Emma was fresh and full of energy, that Emma should play for her.

"Of course, Meg," Emma agreed. "I can play well enough. But I do make mistakes. I am not a professionally trained pianist. I should think that would be equally distressing to you."

But Meg had said No. She did not mind Emma's mistakes, only her own.

Standing now by the open window Emma let the soft air of late May blow through the thin stuff of her nightgown. Then she stepped back and drawing the nightgown over her head threw it on the bed. She stretched her arms above her head and drew her body up to its full length in a gesture of luxurious ease.

*   *   *

Meg stood motionless in the shadowy stillness of the upstairs hall, her gaze on the door of Emma's bedroom. Several times in the last few hours she had quietly opened it, to listen for a moment to Emma's regular breathing. How tired she must have been! thought Meg.

Saturday morning she had returned from church to find Emma still seated at the breakfast table. She had been struck by the stern look on Emma's usually cheerful face, by her paleness, by the hasty, mechanical gestures with which she ate the breakfast Dorcas set before her. Emma had been taciturn, abrupt in the few remarks she had made. When she left the house, Dorcas had explained to Meg that she had been out all night on the call that had come for her during dinner the evening before, that she had returned only a few minutes ahead of Meg's return from church.

She had not seen Emma again until Saturday evening, when she had appeared as usual in the drawing room before dinner, and after dinner they had gone together to a concert at the Peabody Conservatory. But Emma had been almost silent. If she were anyone else, thought Meg, I should have said that she was morose. And she dwelt for a few moments on the usual sunniness of Emma's disposition, her ability to cast aside the effects of the unhappy things with which her professional life must be filled. Emma had once said to her, "I cannot be much use in my profession if I allow the tragedies I witness to overwhelm me." But occasionally Meg noticed beneath the blithe exterior a mood of anger, of brooding. On this occasion it had come frankly to the surface, as if Emma, perhaps simply from fatigue, was making no effort to hide it. I wish, thought Meg, I could see into her mind, understand what lies there, what fills the gaps in what she tells me about her life, about her stay abroad.

As usual, when she got to this point in her musing, Meg shied away from her own thoughts. She remembered Martha McHugh's veiled comments when Emma first returned from London. "You know, Margaret, she received the most flattering attention from Sir Maurice Colburn. I am told he is a very famous surgeon, that he is even called in for consultation for members of the royal family."

Meg's answer had been that, then, he must have had the sense to see Emma's gifts as a physician. Mrs. McHugh's soft face had crinkled in a smile. "But, of course, Margaret, we know Emma is a strikingly beautiful young woman. Sir Maurice, I understand, is often involved with beautiful women. He is a fashionable society doctor as well as a famous surgeon."

Meg, vexed, had not argued the point with her. The vexation returned now and she walked the length of the landing and back to the stairhead. Dorcas was somewhere downstairs at the back of the house, but she felt completely alone, except for Emma sleeping beyond the bedroom door. Yes, of course, Emma must be a magnet for a man's desire. And perhaps the undercurrent of sadness that she sometimes seemed to sense beneath Emma's cheerfulness came from a disappointment in love. Did she shrink from accepting James' attentions because of an earlier, unhappy affair?

But Emma had once denied to her that there had been anything of that sort, and Emma was always truthful. Nevertheless, if only I could prompt her to speak of her inner self. Or perhaps I should not, if it is something too intimate.

A slight sound on the other side of Emma's bedroom door caught her ear. Had she really heard anything? Emma had gone to bed exhausted. Was she all right? Self-upbraiding and a tender anxiety warred in Meg. At last the anxiety won and she stepped quickly to the door and turned the handle as softly as she could.

*   *   *

Emma was warned that the door had opened by the window curtain, which swelled out into the room. She turned to see Meg's startled face in the crack of the door.

"Why, Meg, come in!"

Automatically Meg stepped into the room, closing the door carefully behind her. She stood mute, transfixed, unable to take her eyes away from Emma's naked body, flawless—the firm round, rose-tipped breasts, the soft upcurve of the stomach from the bush of blonde silky hair between the round white thighs.

Emma laughed. "What is the matter, Meg?"

Meg turned away abruptly. "I'm so sorry, Emma. I just thought to look in and see if you were still sleeping."

As you have done many times in the last few hours, I'm sure, thought Emma. "I've certainly been lazy today. It must be almost teatime."

"And you must be hungry." Meg started for the door, but Emma caught her arm.

"You need not bustle off that way. Dorcas can get me something when we go downstairs. Wait while I dress. We've not seen much of each other in the last few days—weeks, it seems."

Meg, still dazzled, looked at her and Emma saw the tears in her eyes. "Why, Meg, what is it?"

Meg dropped her eyes and fumbled for a handkerchief. "Oh, Emma, I've never seen anything so beautiful!"

Startled, Emma exclaimed, "Good heavens! Meg dear!" Emma flung a dressing gown around her shoulders. "Sit down there while I go to the bathroom." She gave Meg a gentle shove into the armchair. On her way down the hall to the bathroom she thought, I've made her nervous and apprehensive with all this strain. She watches over me every moment, worries about me when I'm out at night. Oh, Meg!

When she returned from the bathroom she found Meg sitting in the deep armchair, her elbows resting on its arm, her fingers intertwined. She looked up quickly as Emma came into the room.

Emma threw off her robe, watching as Meg's eyes lost their abstraction and widened with the same startled, avid gaze as when she had first come into the room. Then, shy once more, she looked away. Emma, moving about the room choosing her garments, stopped by Meg's chair and on impulse leaned over her, and catching her face between her hands, lifted it to her own.

"You love me, don't you?" she asked softly as she kissed Meg on the lips. She saw the tears start again in Meg's eyes. She could feel the contraction of Meg's throat as she swallowed.

Meg, looking up into Emma's eyes, did not move or speak.

Under the touch of Emma's hands she was helpless yet struggling silently to withstand the attraction in the nearness of Emma's body. She felt Emma's grasp loosen and with returning clarity saw the tender look in Emma's face change subtly to an expression of disappointment. In her heart she cried, "No! No! Don't turn away from me!"

But it was several moments before she found her voice to say, "Oh, my dear! I do love you, of course." She winced at the resentment in Emma's answering glance. Dismayed she sat silent as Emma began to dress. Emma said suddenly, "Do sit back, Meg. You look very uncomfortable." The peremptory tone of her voice dispelled the tension in the room.

In the long silence that followed, as Emma dressed, Meg finally said, "Emma, you are working much too hard. You have taken on so much besides the Shelter."

Emma, putting on her petticoat, said sharply, "It is better for me than idleness. You know what I think of idleness as a cause of so much ill-health in women. Thank God, the younger mothers are ready to see this. I tell those who bring their girls to me to give them as much physical freedom as possible, not to put corsets on them—neither on their bodies nor their minds."

"But, Emma, you are never idle. You've had no proper rest for weeks—only the sleep that overcomes you through sheer fatigue. You must cut down."

"Well, one thing leads to another. Where would I begin? Not with the Shelter, not with all the things that need to be done for the poor women here, nor the girls who want a decent education, nor my private patients, surely."

Meg watched Emma brush her hair and put it up. "It is difficult to choose, of course. But I sometimes think that there is another reason why you drive yourself so. Has something happened— perhaps in London—that has made you unhappy, so that you seek to forget yourself in overwork?"

Emma, amazed, stopped short in fastening her skirt. "Why do you suppose that, Meg?"

Meg cried to herself, Ah, there is, then! Someone has disappointed you, someone has cut you to the heart. She said aloud, "I suppose it is because you are dissatisfied with your own greatest efforts, as if nothing you achieve can make you content. Emma, I would not speak of this except that you are working yourself to death and I cannot stand by without a protest."

Emma looked at her. Watching her anxious face she said, "Shall I be plain with you, Meg? It is because of my nature. My mother knows my nature. She worries that, in following my compulsion to be a doctor, I must sacrifice my need as a woman—that I shall in the end feel the lack of what a woman always needs, a husband and children. She thinks that without the physical satisfactions of married life, I shall become warped and soured."

"But, Emma, is this necessarily so? Must you forego a husband and children? Some of us must put good works in the place of more intimate satisfactions. But not you!"

"And why do you think so?"

"You are young, Emma, and very beautiful. There must be many men who would want you for a wife —"

"And my professional preoccupations, my long hours, the demands of my patients, the constant interruptions of an orderly household routine? No man would accept all that, Meg, and certainly I know of no man for whom I'd give it all up."

Meg got up to help her fasten the buttons at the back of her shirtwaist. "But perhaps in London you found one who nevertheless claimed your love."

Emma turned around to face her. "You have been listening to gossip. No. There is no truth in that."

The silence hung between them, full of half-formulated meaning. Meg moved away. Then, as if deliberately changing the course of their conversation, she said, "James West has a more than ordinary interest in you." When Emma made no reply, she went on, "I think I should tell you that my sister Susanna does not like the attention he pays you."

"I'm quite aware that Mrs. Harms does not approve of me or of what you have done for me. She objected, didn't she, when you had your father's old office made into a consulting room for me?"

Color came into Meg's face. "I reminded her that the house is mine. My father left it to me alone, not to the three of us to divide."

"Meg, I should greatly regret being the cause of a quarrel between you and your sister."

"You could not be. If Susanna wishes to quarrel with me, she must do it without my help. But I cannot let her rule me. I must resist her when I feel she is being too exigent. I must be myself."

"I see that she is a difficult opponent for you."

"Opponent? That is a good word. Yes. I owe her too much — that I never chose to owe."

They were both silent until Meg said, "Shall we go downstairs?"

*   *   *

"It is, of course," said Susanna, "an age of change. I do not welcome all of these changes."

She sat erect in the tall-backed chair facing Meg seated by the teatable. Dorcas silently handed her the cup Meg had just filled with tea.

"I am aware," said Meg, "that Preston does not favor a good deal of the legislation that Roosevelt forced through Congress. He should be better satisfied with Taft, who is after all not so much Roosevelt's man as we thought."

Susanna nodded. "Yes. Preston considers it hopeful that Roosevelt may succeed in splitting the Republican Party with his liberal ideas. That certainly would be a boon to the Democrats, when the next national election comes up."

"And Preston himself? I've often wondered why he did not try for a seat in the Senate."

"Preston prefers to sit in the wings," said Susanna shortly.

Where he wields much more power at every level of state and national politics, thought Meg. "You would not enjoy Washington, would you, Susanna?"

"I've no wish to leave Baltimore, even temporarily."

No, thought Meg. Her stately sister would not like the social round with a lot of strangers that was the life of a Senator's wife in Washington.

They talked on, in a desultory way, of family matters, of the comings and goings of friends. Presently Susanna asked, "Are you going abroad this year, Margaret?"

Yes. In June. I shall stay till September."

"You missed your trip abroad last year."

"You remember, financial affairs were not in very good shape last year."

"And you have had much larger outlays this year."

Ah, we come around to Emma again, thought Meg. "Nothing that I cannot easily afford."

"I question the propriety of your undertaking, alone, a project that brings you in such close contact with depraved people."

"You mean the Shelter. But I? I have nothing to do with its operation."

"But this young woman who is living in your house —"

"Emma is a physician. She cannot isolate herself from the people she treats."

Susanna made no answer to this. Presently she said, "It must be costing you a pretty penny."

Meg snapped back. "We should not begrudge spending for others what we are fortunate enough to have in too great abundance."

"That is not something you need say to me, Margaret."

"I beg your pardon, Susanna."

Their conversation lapsed again. At last Meg asked, "Do you want Thomas to take you home? You came on foot from Preston's office."

"James said he would come and fetch me."

As she spoke the knocker on the front door sounded.

"Perhaps that is James, now," said Meg and the two women listened to the soft sound of Dorcas' steps crossing the hall and then the voices of a man and a woman. Emma, thought Meg. She is home early this afternoon.

"That is James, I do believe," said Susanna.

Emma's tall figure appeared in the wide doorway. James stood behind her, his head a little higher than hers.

"Emma, do come and have some tea," Meg invited her. "How do you do, James?"

Emma, putting her doctor's bag down in an out-of-the-way spot, sat down in the chair nearest Meg. "Good afternoon, Mrs. Harms."

Susanna bowed her head slightly. "How do you do, Miss Wycliffe? How are you, James?"

He answered and sat down on the other side of the teatable. Dorcas handed him a cup of tea and he took it and at once put it down on the table.

"James," said Susanna, "have you heard from Preston?"

"He is coming home tomorrow. Most of Congress has gone home to get ready for the campaign. Washington is practically empty. T.R. is left with an empty legislative bag."

Meg asked, "Will Roosevelt really be drafted at the Convention in Chicago, James?"

James shrugged his heavy shoulders. "That's anybody's guess,

Cousin Margaret. He keeps saying that he won't accept the nomination and he's certainly plugging for Taft. But nobody knows what may happen in Chicago. There are at least five other contenders, you know, including Hughes and LaFollette."

"And how about the Democrats?"

"They'll wind up with Bryan again, I guess."

Susanna made a slight sound of disgust. "Then any Republican can win — even Taft."

Emma looked at her with interest. She had, during the last few months, come to realize that Susanna, though she rarely made a remark on political personages or events, had an innate political shrewdness that had nothing to do with her husband's views. "Why do you say so, Mrs. Harms?"

Susanna glanced at her as if just reminded of her presence. "Mr. Bryan has no ammunition left. Mr. Roosevelt has appropriated all his platforms—the income tax, the regulation of the railroads, and the control of large corporations. He has only free coinage of silver left and I scarcely think that that will elect him."

"But Mr. Taft will not be popular with labor. He did not show himself very friendly to labor in the disputes that came before him as a judge," said Emma. "Perhaps the ordinary working man does not dislike him as much as he does Mr. Root, but it is only a question of degree."

A strange smile appeared on Susanna's face. "I did not know that you included the political scene amongst your numerous interests, Miss Wycliffe."

Emma, stung by the undertone in her voice, retorted, "I am not a student of political affairs, Mrs. Harms, but my daily work takes me amongst the least advantaged people, those who have no reason to admire or trust men who have a great deal of money and the power it brings."

James, watching Emma closely, said, "You probably do have some unusual opportunities to hear what the subversives have to say. D'you know any Wobblies, Emma?"

Meg saw Susanna's head give the smallest jerk and her cold grey eyes flash briefly at the sound of James' "Emma."

Emma, unaware, protested eagerly. "James, you know I don't discuss politics with anyone. But I do have ears and I can tell you that a lot of poor people have not forgotten the business about Heywood and the parade on Fifth Avenue a year ago."

James laughed. "Well, I don't suppose J.P. Morgan and his friends have forgotten it, either. It scared them almost out of their wits."

"I wish it had done more than that," said Emma. "I wish it had convinced them that they have no divine authority to make enormous fortunes at the expense of their fellow citizens."

Susanna's voice cut in like a blade of chilled steel. "Are you a socialist, Miss Wycliffe?"

Emma flushed in sudden anger. "If you mean, am I a supporter of Eugene Debs, no, I am not. I have no political ties."

Susanna said haughtily, "That is just as well. In our society here, Miss Wycliffe, politics is not a suitable field of activity for a woman."

James interposed, smiling, "But you are for women's suffrage, aren't you, Emma?"

"Certainly. I cannot see how any woman would not be."

"Indeed," Susanna glanced at Meg.

Meg said promptly, "You know I am, Susanna."

"Well, well," said James in good humor. "It's bound to come, sooner or later—votes for women, I mean. I say we might as well get used to the idea. It would liven things up, I guess, if we had some lady delegates to the party conventions."

He glanced at Susanna and then looked away at the disdain in her face. "I cannot imagine a woman of good character and breeding engaging in such things."

"But you do have here in Baltimore an organization of women who are dedicated to the ideal of good government," said Emma. "I know, because Meg belongs to it."

Susanna ignored her statement and instead asked, "What else do you advocate, Miss Wycliffe?"

Emma, goaded by her tone, rashly declared, "Better education for girls, better opportunities for women to earn their own livings without dependence on men, family limitation so that women may seek their own salvation —"

She stopped abruptly, aware that her last words had fallen like a stone into the deep silence of Meg's drawing room. She felt James' eyes on her. Regretting her own ardor, she waited for Susanna to speak. But Susanna turned away from her. When she spoke again it was to Meg, and for the rest of the visit she retreated into her usual cold taciturnity.

*   *   *

"I'm sorry, Meg, to have been so outspoken," said Emma, as the front door closed behind James, following Susanna out.

"I cannot expect you to be silent in such circumstances."

"But I should not have gone so far. I am afraid I have offended your sister."

"Emma, you offend her by being alive and in my house."

Surprised at the sharpness of her voice, Emma looked at her and saw that she was angry and unhappy. Emma smiled at her coaxingly. "Well, I shan't leave, Meg, until you tell me to." But Meg paid no attention to her and Emma picked up another of Flora's little watercress sandwiches and ate it slowly.

Meg's voice reached her. "Susanna mistrusts poor people, uneducated people, whether they are black or white. In fact, I think she favors the black, since she thinks there is more excuse for them. She cannot overcome the feeling that someone is poor and miserable because of some failing of his own."

There was so much bitterness in her voice that Emma said softly, "She merely wishes a static world. She dislikes change."

Meg did not answer immediately. "She has a very rigid belief in the divinely ordained, Emma."

"That which is, is what God intends. But I cannot believe that God does not intend us to seek something better, does not intend for us to overcome the evil we find in our lives and those of our fellow creatures."

"If you put it that way, of course Susanna would have to agree with you, Emma. But she has a great distrust of the means that may be adopted by men to that end."

"By *men* — I would agree with her there!"

At last Meg laughed. "It is probably the only point on which you would." She grew grave again. "Susanna is not alone in believing that politics is too nasty a business for women. Give the men their due, they don't want to see their wives and daughters involved in the sort of dirty dealings they're only too well acquainted with themselves. We're all taught, you know, that a woman must be chaste, since she is the one who must maintain purity in the family — chaste and innocent. You cannot imagine, Emma, how abhorrent it is to Susanna to be even reminded that there are women who walk the streets in search of men. She thinks they have sunk to something far lower than any man."

Emma interrupted her. "Being innocent does not mean being ignorant, Meg. And if, in dispelling ignorance, you also dispel the illusion of security and purity, that is necessary. You know perfectly well, Meg, that if a woman's husband fails to protect her and her children, she then becomes the victim of this hypocritical society. She is forced to find what means she can to feed and nurture her children, without training and in the face of the resentment of men who don't want her in the labor market. If the task becomes too great for her and she takes to the streets, she is accused of having a natural propensity for vice, of being a deliberate menace to the health and morals of the community. She is shunned as no other creature is shunned. Meg, I cannot believe that women must inevitably be mere appendages of men. There are women who have as independent spirits as any man, who have no need for a man."

"Yes, yes. Some of us are all that and we are able to maintain our independence."

"Like yourself. Like me. But we are among the fortunate few. We have not been forced to marry, by social and economic pressure. And some of us, like your sister, can marry and still decline to be saddled by the burden of unwanted children. Meg, that is the supreme luxury to some women. It is one that is denied to the weakest and most wretched women — to choose to have children, when they want them and how many."

"Emma, you've spoken of this before. You have told me that the women in the tenements you visit crowd around you, asking for the secret that wealthy women must possess, to prevent the conception of children."

"Meg, what these poor women say is true. Well-to-do women, because of their money, their place in society, the fact that they have cooperative, sympathetic husbands, do have access to the means of preventing conception. Their doctors discreetly enlighten them and their husbands. But what happens to poor women, the ones who really need this help? I have heard such women plead with doctors for such information, and the only response they get is the advice to refuse to have intercourse with their men. Tell me, how is a woman to escape the sexual demands of a man on whom she is dependent? The women hoot in derision when I suggest such a thing. Their men have only one pleasure that is always within their reach—sexual satisfaction through the use of their women's bodies. Even drink must be paid for in ready cash. But a woman who is entirely within a man's grasp, tied down by children and with no other means of support but the man on whom she is dependent — don't you see, Meg?"

"Yes, of course."

"It is heartbreaking to see a woman, already wretchedly ill and unable to feed and clothe several children, compelled to carry and give birth to yet another. Do you wonder that such women so often destroy themselves in seeking to get rid of a coming child?"

Overcome by the revival of her own feelings of frustration, Emma stopped and looked at Meg. She was surprised to see that Meg's eyes were on her with a shrewd, cool gaze.

"Emma, this is a perilous subject for anyone, but especially for a physician."

"I'm well aware of it. Even the bravest of us are forced to be cowardly."

For a while they were both silent and then Meg said, "There are laws, are there not, that provide severe penalties—imprisonment and loss of the right to practice—for those who disseminate information about contraception and contraceptive devices?"

She is always surprising me, thought Emma. I should not have expected her to know that. "Yes. The Comstock Laws. They are downright devilish."

The faintest smile appeared on Meg's face but it vanished quickly. "I can only urge you to be as cautious as possible, in spite of your feelings. Emma, is there anywhere where such information may be freely given out?"

"Nowhere is it absolutely unhampered, except —"

"Somewhere abroad?"

Emma hesitated, abashed. At last she confessed. "You have guessed, haven't you? When I wrote from London and asked you for money to go to the Continent, I was not frank with you. I had a specific purpose."

"You said only that you were eager to round off your professional training with visits to the great medical centers of Europe. That seemed quite reasonable to me."

"But I had another goal besides the general one of seeing Europe and visiting its medical centers. I wanted to go to Holland and see the clinics founded by Dr. Adele Jacobs. They are clinics for the distribution of information about and the means of contraception."

"Ah, I see now. I have wondered why you never have had much to say about your stay in Holland—except to tell me that you had seen Rembrandt's 'Night Watch' in Amsterdam." Meg smiled at the chagrin in Emma's face. "Of course I noticed that you never explained why you spent four weeks at The Hague when you had so little time for the rest of Europe. But why did you not want to be frank with me?"

"For the obvious reason — I did not think you would approve. Even in England a physician must be circumspect on this subject. I was warned against taking any special interest in the matter by one of the most eminent women's doctors in London."

"Sir Maurice Colburn?"

"Yes."

"Then I add my voice to his. Emma, please don't endanger yourself. It must gall you terribly to see in your daily work the consequences of such narrowmindedness as these laws represent. But it would forward nothing for you to jeopardize your standing as a physician."

"Narrowminded! They are vicious! They force physicians to retreat from giving any help to the women who most need it."

"Yes. But until the laws can be changed —"

"We must remain cowards."

Meg's voice was brisk. "Emma, how much worse it would be for you to deny some of these women the care and skill you can bring them, simply by making it impossible for you to treat them. Is it not more praiseworthy to sacrifice your own indignation to that greater good?"

"*Is* it the greater good, Meg? What I can do is a mere palliative. It is treating symptoms instead of the disease. What real good is done if I can snatch one woman from the edge of the grave, when within a year she may die of the same cause and a hundred more like her?"

"Yes, yes. I know what you must feel. Nevertheless, Emma, you must be careful —"

"Meg, I will do nothing to bring the Shelter or you into any scandal or notoriety. But I have learned that with you I must be open and aboveboard. I've not succeeded very well in deceiving you, have I?"

Meg, answering her sudden smile, put her hand on Emma's arm. The rare gesture awakened in Emma a quick rush of tenderness but, afraid to alarm Meg, she remained still.

"Emma, I shall always know when you try to hide something from me." Emma felt Meg's hand tighten on her arm. "But there is something further that I must warn you against. Whatever you do, Emma, don't on any account give Susanna any weapon to use against you.''

''She already knows I favor family limitation. I've just told her.''

''That is bad enough.''

''Yet you tell me that she has never wanted children.''

''Yes. She has always expressed thankfulness when, once or twice, she has conceived and miscarried. Emma, I find it very difficult to speak of Susanna. I am sure she has always loved me, in spite of the disruption I caused in her life. She was engaged to be married, you know, when I was born and my mother died. She set everything aside to look after me, as her sense of duty required. And when she did marry, it was not to the man she had loved. It was too late for that. She married Preston because he wanted her and he offered her the status of a married woman. I am always conscious of the fact that she might have been a happier woman if it were not for me. Oh, Emma, I am expressing myself so badly!''

Emma made no move. The strength of Meg's distress communicated itself to her through the grip of Meg's hand on her arm. She said gently, ''She has a will of iron which she uses against herself as well as others. But why are you so concerned about your sister's attitude to me?''

''I want to warn you to be on your guard with her, Emma. If you give her the opportunity, she will use any means to discredit you, to undermine your standing here in Baltimore.''

Emma felt the strong tremor in Meg's hand. ''How can she do that? What makes you so frightened? Has she threatened to do this?''

''Oh, no. She would never speak directly to me about it.'' Meg faltered and then added. ''She disapproves of my — affection for you.'' Meg raised her eyes in a brief, sharp glance. ''She will find justifications for destroying your reputation —''

''Destroying my reputation!''

''So as to put an end to your work here in Baltimore, in order to drive you away from me, from my house.'' Overcome by her own forthrightness, Meg took her hand away from Emma's arm and turned away to hide her face.

Emma stood still, astonished. That Meg should have put so much in words —! ''Your sister must dislike me very much.''

Meg said over her shoulder, "She does not think of it in terms of a personal dislike. She thinks of it as for my protection, my well-being."

"Your well-being!" Emma stared at her back. "But how am I dangerous?"

Meg turned halfway towards her. "Because you inspire me to do things she does not approve of. You make me act as if I were younger — and impulsive. She thinks that for me this is dangerous."

Emma, baffled, only stared at her.

*   *   *

With the coming of early summer Emma found a little more time for tennis. When she first suggested to Meg that it would be an enjoyable form of exercise for her, Meg had demurred.

"Why, Emma, I've never played any sort of game like that!"

"Not even as a little girl?"

"Well, sometimes when I went to stay with Cordelia in the school holidays I played things like croquet and — well, Cordelia was very good at inventing games for us to play."

"Cordelia?"

"A childhood friend. I have mentioned her to you before, I think."

"And she doesn't play tennis?"

"Why, as a matter of fact, she does. She learned to play in England, before it became a popular game for women here."

"And she never persuaded you to learn?"

"The opportunity never seemed to arise."

"Well, if Cordelia can play, I can't see why you can't. Come with me and try, Meg."

With a little more coaxing, Emma got her onto the courts, and then, since Meg could never undertake to do anything less than well, to a coach with whom she practiced when Emma was too busy to play.

James knew of this new venture, and Dorcas. Dorcas, watching Emma and Meg arrive home from an hour on the courts, grinned at Meg's appearance. Meg, red-faced from the unusual exertion, the collar of her white blouse limp from perspiration, her hat held in her lap since her hair refused to stay confined under it, noticed the grin. Half-annoyed and yet half-exhilerated, she challenged her maid.

"You think I'm too old for this sort of thing, don't you, Dorcas?"

But Dorcas, with a cheerful glance at Emma, said, "You ain't all that old, Miss Margaret. But I wonder what Miss Susanna's going to say."

Meg gave her a half-angry glance and walked by without an answer.

The next evening when Meg and Emma sat together before dinner, Meg said, "Susanna came to see me this afternoon. She has heard about my tennis lessons — from James, no doubt."

"And what did she say?"

A wry little smile twitched at the corners of Meg's mouth. "She thinks I am foolish. She thinks it is a childish pastime for a woman of my age, and dangerous. She thinks I would never have thought of doing such a thing, if I had not been persuaded against my better judgment."

"There are a lot of women your age and older who play tennis. Didn't you tell me that your friend Cordelia plays?"

"Yes, but nothing that Cordelia does would be a recommendation to Susanna."

"Then what did you say to her?"

"I said I was doing it on the advice of my physician and that I had benefited from it already."

Emma laughed. Meg, after a moment's hesitation, joined her.

*   *   *

The day of the Preakness was sunny and hazy, with the sudden warmth of coming summer. The stands of the Pimlico track were gay with the colors of the women's dresses. The brief moment of excitement came and went in a wave of shouting and cheering. The winning horse came up before the grandstand to be weighed in, the collar of daisies around his neck, the jockey was congratulated, and the governor of Maryland presented the owner with the trophy. The stands quickly emptied as the people began milling around the grounds.

Emma, wearing a wide-brimmed straw hat, sat in the stands with Meg and her sister. She had come with James, who had insisted on stopping by Cushman Terrace to pick her up. But the filly he had been grooming for the last year at the Harms' horse farm near Annapolis was entered in the main event and he and his uncle had been occupied with their entry. As soon as the race was

over he came back to join them. The race results had been
announced and there was a lot of talking and comparing by those
who had placed bets. Meg had won quite a bit of money and
Emma was amused at Mrs. Harms' equivocal manner when the
men in their party chaffed her. It seemed that Meg often won
money at horse races.

James escorted them all to the clubhouse. His uncle, he said,
was occupied in watching over their filly. She had not won this
time but there were other races to come. Walking with Emma
behind the other women he said, "My uncle doesn't trust anybody
when it comes to a horse." Horse racing was a passion with
Preston Harms. It was the one thing for which he would lay aside
any serious business.

Emma joked, "It sounds as if he considers horse racing a
serious business in itself."

"I suppose he does. I do."

"What does that mean, James? Would you give up politics for
the horse farm?"

"That choice doesn't arise. I wouldn't disappoint my uncle. He
expects me to carry on his political interests."

They had reached the steps of the wide porch of the ornate
Victorian clubhouse and he busied himself seating Meg and her
sister with a large party of friends. But then he insisted that Emma
come with him to another part of the verandah where they would
be alone. "Wait here," he said, seating her. "I'll fetch us some
refreshments."

While he was gone she tried to keep her attention on the scene
before her, full of novelty as it was. But the thought of James kept
obtruding itself. His persistence irked her. Whenever he wanted
her to do something, he never left off until she gave in and did
what he wanted. It seemed to her that he was now constantly
underfoot. Sometimes he came to the Shelter when he thought it
was about the time she would leave. Sometimes he lingered in
Meg's drawing room, waiting till she finished with her private
patients. Nothing she said or did seemed to discourage him.

He was coming towards her now, his hands full of the ice
cream dish and beer he was bringing. He handed her the ice cream
and sat down beside her on the wicker seat.

"I don't get many chances to see you alone, Emma. You put a
good many obstacles in my way. You never have time."

"The last is certainly true. I rarely have time for myself."

"Then we have to make a change."

Emma gave him a sharp glance at the "we." He went on, "I've something to say to you."

Emma looked at him again but said nothing. She had got used to this manner of his now. She saw his jaw set and there was a slight twitch in the muscle of his cheek. This was James determined to have his own way. She had come to recognize in this and other small movements of his eyes and hands that he was entirely absorbed in what he was about to say, in some plan he was intent upon. She had seen him like this when he had opposed her over the women held in jail in the vice raids, over her insistence on campaigning for police matrons — this deceptively still and calm exterior that covered his determination to wage war without quarter.

What he said was, "Emma, I want you to marry me."

For a long moment Emma did not reply. She had really not expected this. How odd, she thought. He might as well be speaking to someone else. He cannot really be thinking of me. He doesn't know me.

What she said was, "That is not possible."

"What do you mean?" The undercover blaze lit up for a moment in his eyes.

"I've no intention of marrying anyone."

"I can change that — if I know your reason."

"I do not have to give you a reason. Besides, you can't really want it."

"Why not?"

Emma was suddenly impatient. "James, you must see it is impossible. I do not intend to marry. And from your point of view, I'd be a most unsuitable wife. Our habits would never fit. To say nothing of how Mrs. Harms would dislike it."

"Keep her out of this. It's not true we couldn't make a go of it. Other women with careers marry. If you were my wife, you could do what you liked with your free time. A regular practice is out, I suppose. And I wouldn't allow you to get involved with politics. Come on, Emma, you have a good thing in me. Nobody could stop you doing what you wanted to —"

"Except you!" Emma's anger blazed out. "My free time! James, you are completely off the track. Medicine is my life, not something I do in my free time. I know it would not work, trying to be a wife such as you or any man would expect and carry out my own intentions. So I shall not marry. And nobody—neither you nor anyone else—is going to tell me when and how I do anything!''

He eyed her steadily. ''You're not going to find any other man who'd put up with all that.''

''I've told you that I do not expect to. And, James, I don't want to. Won't you believe me when I tell you that?''

There was disbelief in his voice. ''No, I don't. You'll get married sooner or later. It might as well be now and to me.''

Emma cried out with a desperate feeling that she could not make him hear her. ''James, can't you understand me? I don't want to marry! I've never wanted to marry. I have chosen what I want to do with my life, and it will take all my time and energy. I don't want — I don't need a husband —''

He cut in. ''You don't strike me as being made to be a nun.''

Infuriated, Emma retorted, ''That's not your affair. And I don't like your tone. If I should ever change my mind, the only sort of man I could marry would be one who would go halves with me, who would not expect to dictate to me what I should do and when.''

''A man's got to be master in his own house. Otherwise, I don't want to stand in your way. With me you'll always know how far you can go.''

With a great effort Emma kept her voice calm. ''Certainly you are being honest. You've made it perfectly plain what you expect of a wife. I'm quite sure you won't have to look far for a woman who will meet your requirements. But I am not she.''

''I don't take No for an answer when I want something.''

''You'll have to take No from me.'' She got up from the seat. The crowd had thinned out as people scattered across the grass, drifting in groups toward the enclosure where the carriages stood.

''Where are you going?'' James demanded, also getting up.

''I shall go home with Meg.''

James smiled complacently. ''You'll have to come with me. They have already gone.''

''I don't think they have.''

She began to walk along the now empty stretch of porch, toward the corner that hid Mrs. Harms' party from their view. But he suddenly gripped her hand hard and compelled her to stand still.

He said, into her ear, ''You're the first woman I've ever asked to marry me.''

Emma's instant reaction was to snatch her hand away, to drive him away from her with a hail of blows. But the strength of his grip made her powerless. She remembered in a sudden vivid flash the instinctive fury with which she had freed herself from Colburn's grasp when he had tried to kiss her in London. She remembered also the chagrin she had felt afterwards. She made herself stand still and try to release herself by less violent means.

"Let go of me, James. You've no right to do this." She knew her body was rigid with the effort not to struggle against him. He must release her very soon, her inner revolt told her, or she would not be able to prevent herself from tearing her hand out of his grip with all her strength. His nearness, his breath on her cheek, his closeness, produced a sick feeling that she could not control. She began to shiver with the strain.

James felt it. He drew his head back a little to look at her. "I knew you didn't mean it."

This time she could no longer restrain herself. Blindly, wildly, she struck him in the face. "Let me go! Take your hands off me!"

He released her at once. Her blow had glanced off his cheekbone. There was a red spot where it had landed. She was too undone herself to see the fury in her eyes. It faded so quickly that by the time she had gathered herself together she saw only the usual faintly arrogant smile on his face.

She said angrily, "James, I've never given you any invitation to do that."

His smile grew broader. "I don't wait for invitations. And you don't have to give them. They're there all the same. All right. I'll take my time. You'll get used to the idea."

He seemed pleased with himself as he courteously took her elbow in his hand and began to walk with her along the deserted porch. When they turned the corner they found Mrs. Harms and Meg standing at the top of the flight of steps to the ground. The black gleaming bulk of the Harms' touring car stood at the foot of the steps.

"Oh, there you are, Emma!" Meg exclaimed. "Susanna thought you would be returning with James. But I thought James would be too busy with the horses."

Ignoring her, Mrs. Harms said, displeased, "James, your uncle has been looking for you."

"All right," said James. "I'll go and find him. Emma can go back with you."

He handed them all into the car and said Goodbye. Emma obeyed Meg's gesture to get in. She knew that Meg had noticed both her manner and James'.

*   *   *

Meg was to sail for Europe at the end of June. She seemed suddenly to have made up her mind. What decided her, she told Emma, was a letter from her old school friend Cordelia, now the wife of a man who had for several years served as American Minister in a number of the smaller European capitals.

"Cordelia was a Lightfoot—a niece of Dr. Lightfoot's. I have told you that she was my closest friend in boarding school. We've always kept up, even though Cordelia has been away from Baltimore a good deal. Her husband is much older than she. He has decided to retire now and they are returning to Baltimore, to stay, Cordelia says, for a while. I know she is unhappy about that, because she complains that Baltimore is so staid. She prefers the excitement of New York. Cordelia is very anxious for me to spend a few weeks with her in Paris. I think she feels that this is the last she sees of Europe for some time."

Meg had made this announcement in the middle of May and in the normal course of events it would have been something that both of them would set aside in their minds as shortly to take place but unregarded till the moment of departure came. Meg had gone abroad too many times to bother much about preparations. There would be a difference this time, she said, because she would not close the house, since Emma would be there. Flora and Thomas would have a month's holiday. The horses would be boarded at a neighboring stable. But Dorcas would be there to look after her. Dorcas never left the house for more than a day or two, to visit her sister who lived in St. Mary's County. Dorcas preferred to stay in Cushman Terrace, mistress of her own time and inclinations.

"She is an excellent cook, Emma. She always cooks for me when Flora is ill or away."

Emma laughed. "I'm quite sure I'll suffer no deprivation with Dorcas here." They sat in the drawing room sipping their sherry. Emma lay back in the big armchair, her long legs stretched out before her, her feet crossed on the hassock. It was the moment of the day when they were entirely free of intrusion, the moment they both had come to count upon as the time when they unburdened their minds and spirits to each other. Does Meg, Emma wondered, feel this as I do? And as she wondered she knew that it was Meg who had brought this about, who had created this moment of privacy, who saw to it that there was no intrusion at this hour, except for Dorcas' discreet presence in serving them. And undoubtedly Meg missed it even more than she did, when the demands of her patients or emergencies robbed Emma of this short respite.

Meg said now, "We've had very little time together lately, Emma. You are more and more in demand."

Emma smiled across the patch of lamplight at her. The long summer evening's light had only just left the room and Dorcas had lit the lamp when she brought their sherry.

"Meg, you've succeeded only too well in forwarding my medical career."

"Oh, of course, I cannot complain! But I hope, while I am away that you will take care of yourself. Three evenings this week you have been busy beyond the usual hour and twice you have been out on night calls. That leaves you little time for rest."

"Or for visiting with you, which is more important."

"Oh, Emma, I don't mean to be selfish!"

"Certainly not," said Emma, smiling at her. "But I am selfish. I shall miss you, Meg, more than I can say. It is delightful to know that, when I can shake free of an evening, you are here, ready to listen to my complaints or bolster my self-confidence." She watched as Meg cast down her eyes, sitting forward in the high-backed chair, her hands loosely clasped. On an impulse Emma got up and in one swift movement crossed the space between them and knelt by Meg's chair. There was no banter in her voice when she said, "Meg, you mean much more to me than simply a good friend. Do you understand that?"

Meg's brown-flecked eyes lifted to look into hers but only for an instant, as if she dared not let Emma see what spoke in them. She did not answer. Emma waited, her arms around the slight figure, so stiffly unyielding. After a while, Meg lifted her hand and thrust her fingers into Emma's thickly piled golden hair. Emma could feel the nervous tension in their touch on her scalp.

Emma caught her other hand and kissed the palm. "Do you remember, Meg, the first time I came here to your house?"

Meg's voice was choked. "I shall never forget it."

"Why, Meg, did it make such an impression?"

"I have never been so affected by anyone as I was with you that afternoon."

"And you wrote me such charming letters all the time I was in London. I was so surprised by them at first. Each time I received an envelope addressed in your handwriting I expected to find inside some businesslike communication discussing my outlays and asking for an accounting. After all, you were the treasurer of my funds."

"Oh, Emma!"

Emma laughed softly. "I lost that idea by the time I had the third letter. But for a long time I wondered why you gave so much time and thought to me, to write so often and in so sympathetic a way. And when you began to send me presents of money I wondered even more. If it had been anyone else, I would not have accepted them so readily. But by that time I had begun to think of you as someone in a special relationship to me, someone who stood on a very special footing, as no one else had ever done. At first it was merely gratitude and surprise that someone like you would be so understanding about what a little extra money could mean to someone like me. Young people can be very selfish, Meg, can take a great deal of what is done for them for granted, merely as what is due them. And I had carried away from that first meeting with you the idea that you were much older than I, like those kind, matronly women who surrounded you—someone ready to help a younger woman, as you would help a child. How blind I was!"

"Blind, Emma?" In her astonishment Meg looked directly into her eyes again.

"Yes, blind. I became less blind by the time I left London, less ready to take such a friend for granted. Meg, I shall never be able to tell you what your letters meant to me when I was traveling about Europe. I became so used to thinking of you as my confidant, the sharer of all my trials, that I had to remind myself that you knew nothing of what was going on in my heart and mind. By the time I started home you had become my lodestar, the one person to whom, in imagination, I would be able to unburden myself, who would know just what I needed in understanding and sympathy."

Through the touch of her fingers Emma could feel the sudden stillness in Meg's body. After a moment Meg said, "You speak of trials. Emma, I've often thought that you had an unhappy experience while you were in London. You have denied it or tried to.''

Emma tightened her embrace. "You're always surprising me by the way you can look into me—even across the ocean!''

"Then you do not deny it. I know that there is something in the bottom of your heart that saddens you.''

"A certain discontent is always a spur to greater effort. It would be terrible to have no more worlds to conquer. And that, at least, will never be the danger in a medical career. The millenium is very far away.''

"Yes, but this is not something of that sort. It troubles me to see you unhappy, Emma.''

"I am not, really, now. I think I have got over it. Only at times, when I am discouraged, it comes back to me.''

"Someone disappointed you, severely. You have tried to lose the memory of it by keeping yourself constantly occupied. Forgive me, Emma, but I don't think you have succeeded.''

"Perhaps not, by that means. I tried to kill all that sort of feeling—all that sort of softness—so that no one else could ever hurt me again. But, Meg, I counted without you. It is you who have got in under my guard. Oh, Meg, I love you with all of me!''

Meg, caught fast in her arms, made no effort to free herself. Her voice was quiet and loving, "Emma, Emma." After a while she strove to push Emma away.

Emma, resisting, frowned up at her.

Meg said, "I do love you, as I have never loved anyone else, even — But, Emma, you must seek someone else — a — a man who can give you all the satisfactions of life you need, which I cannot.''

Instantly Emma relaxed her hold and withdrew her arms. Her frown had grown angry and she stared at Meg with her lips firmly closed.

Meg put her hand on her shoulder and seemed about to say something more but in the end did not. Instead she leaned forward and softly kissed Emma on the lips. Emma, at first drawing back, relented and accepted the kiss in resignation.

In the time that elapsed between that evening and Meg's departure they were in a mood with each other different from anything that had gone before. It was as if, thought Emma, one more curtain of reserve had been drawn away between them, leaving them far more visible to one another. This difference was apparent in little ways. Meg was readier to respond when Emma wanted to kiss her. She no longer made any effort to disguise the look of love in her eyes when she gazed at Emma when they were alone. She no longer pulled back when Emma put her arms around her.

But beyond this new softness Emma felt a stronger, higher wall, which she had suspected but never before encountered. Meg seemed to say, So far but no further. But it was said with a gentle fondness that held none of the tense rejection of her response in the past. Sometimes, rebelliously, Emma wished for a return to that more passionate mood. But she found in herself a fund of slightly bitter resignation. At least, now Meg and she knew and acknowledged how they felt towards each other, even though they hung together in a never-never land.

This new mood added a strange quality to the last few weeks before Meg's departure. To Emma it was an elegiac quality, as if they mourned in anticipation their separation. As the final day drew close she wondered, vaguely and irrationally, whether Meg would change her mind and cancel her passage. She realized that this was in fact what she wished for, because she had come to dread Meg's absence. Watching Meg's face covertly she looked for some sign that Meg also was visited by this same regret. But though Meg's normally pale face was a little whiter than usual, set in somewhat grim lines when she was unaware of Emma's scrutiny, there was no indication that she was any less resolved to carry out her plans.

There were a good many farewell teas and dinners. On the few occasions when she could arrange to be free, Emma begrudged the time spent in these social gatherings. On several evenings, when James wanted her to go out with him, she refused, even when she knew Meg was otherwise engaged, hopeful that Meg would come home early and they could spend an hour or so together.

The afternoon came when at last they took leave of each other in the vestibule of Meg's house. Thomas waited at the door, the carriage loaded with Meg's trunks and boxes. Dorcas hovered in the shadows of the stairwell. But Meg in the midst of saying Goodbye suddenly broke down and flung herself into Emma's arms, unable to speak. Emma, feeling the wetness of Meg's tears on her own cheek, held her for a long moment in a fierce grip. At last, when Meg pulled away and, straightening her hat, almost ran out of the front door, Emma, without a backward glance, strode across the vestibule and through the door that led to her consulting room.

*   *   *

The last of June was gone and the humid heat of July enveloped Baltimore. Emma, her white cotton dresses damp and limp in the ninety-degree temperatures and sodden air of the dirty streets surrounding the Shelter, found her hours of work lengthened by the diseases that flourished among the slum-dwellers. Her private patients, escaping to their houses on the Bay, on the Eastern Shore, or down on the lower reaches of the Patuxent River, gave her greater leisure in the afternoons but she found even that free time absorbed. She declined Mrs. McHugh's invitation to come for a holiday down in the seventeenth century calm of St. Mary's County. She even resisted her mother's plea that she join her parents in the cottage they had taken on Cape Cod. Especially she could not do that. Her mother would see at once that there was something gnawing at her beneath the professional success.

Eagerly she waited for Meg's letters. They were the only oases, she thought wrily, in the dreadful desert of her life alone in Baltimore. The first was a long one, posted in Liverpool as Meg left the ship. Emma, examining the postmark, saw that it was two weeks old. Obviously the letter had come by a slower vessel than that which had taken Meg to England. Meg would have been those two weeks in London. The letter reminded Emma that she intended to spend three weeks in London, before going on to France.

Every afternoon, as she entered the house, Emma's eyes went at once to the small hall table where Dorcas placed her mail. She knew that when another letter from Meg arrived, Dorcas would put it on the top of the pile. Another two weeks passed without it.

One Saturday night, late in July, she arrived home exhausted from a long series of medical crises and went at once to her room. Dorcas was nowhere in sight and she was unable to do more than take off her clothes and fall into bed. In the middle of Sunday afternoon she got up and dressed and went down to sit in the shadowy quiet of the dining room to eat the meal that Dorcas put in front of her. On the table, by her napkin, she saw two letters, both with English stamps. They must have come the day before and she had not noticed them. One, she saw at once, was from Meg. The other — She picked it up and held it in her hand for a

long while before she turned it over to read the return address and
confirm what she already knew. It was from Alison.

She put them both down unopened and ate the food on her
plate, stopping between bites to stare again at the two envelopes.
When she had finished eating, she picked them up and carried
them into the drawing room, to the big chair drawn close to the
window. There was a hushed stillness in the house. Any sound
that Dorcas might make was deadened by the door that closed off
the kitchen quarters. For some minutes she gazed out at the street,
empty in the hazy, shimmering July sun, the unopened letters in
her hand.

Suddenly, with a swift motion, she opened Alison's letter and
spread the sheet out to read the small, tidy script.

"Emma dear. I know you will be surprised to receive a letter
from me, since we agreed that we should not try to keep in touch
once you had left London. But something has happened that I
must tell you about. I have met your Miss Bell! You remember
how we used to talk about her — how intrigued I was by her
generosity to you and how little you really could tell me about
her. Well, I shall begin at the beginning. As you know, Angela
has a lot of American friends, and she is always being called upon
by new visitors to London with letters of introduction from those
who have returned home. A good many American women have
been coming to see her this year, intent on learning how effective
our suffragettes have been. Miss Bell is one of them, brought by
another friend to a gathering at Angela's digs after a street rally.
In their talk Angela discovered that Miss Bell is especially
interested in the position of women in the medical profession. So
of course your name came up and Angela mentioned me, that you
and I had shared lodgings while you were here. Angela, full of
this—you know how impulsive she can be—said at once that we
must meet, Miss Bell and I, since we were both such friends of
yours. I could not say No and besides I was most curious to see at
last in the flesh the Miss Bell who provided so handsomely for
you!

"Angela arranged for us to have tea together at her flat the next
day. My dear Emma! What an absolute character she is! I arrived
at Angela's first. I don't know what I expected her to be, how I
expected her to look. But when Angela opened the door for her I
knew instantly who it must be—this meager little spinster dressed
all in brown—excellent quality in her clothes but no particular
fashion, old or new. I was surprised by one thing. I expected her

to be elderly. I remember you always said you could not describe her to me but you thought she was middle-aged. While she was listening intently to my description of your stay in London, I noticed her eyes, how steady and clear they are, the eyes of someone whom it is not easy to deceive. I had thought of her as someone very reserved, puritanical, who must be frightened if she knew of the ideas you really hold. But I do believe she must be quite aware of your iconoclastic view of things. I was very careful, Emma, not to make too much of our friendship, of our closeness. In fact, I must have sounded as if I was talking about a schoolmate in boarding school! She told me that you are having a most gratifying success in the private practice you have established in Baltimore and how much respected you are for your medical work among the unfortunate. And I gather that you must be living in the lap of luxury, in her house, with a fine consulting room! Oh, Emma, I am very pleased to hear this! But how clever of you to have found such a benefactress! She obviously looks upon you as a paragon of all the virtues.

"When she was about to leave she looked at me in a very penetrating way and asked where it was that we had had our lodging together. She knows London well and was able to identify the street. Then she remarked that I was married, now, wasn't I? and I said Yes, that Arthur and I married shortly after you left London, while you were traveling on the Continent and that when you stopped in England before taking ship for America we had not been able to meet. She seemed to have something on the tip of her tongue to ask me, but did not and then merely remarked, 'I see.' She did not stay long after that, but said she had another engagement to which she must hurry on."

Emma laid the letter down on the table. There was nothing more in it, except a comment that Alison hoped that Miss Bell would continue to see in Emma the ideal channel for her philanthropy. She added, "Emma dear, you deserve everything she has done for you."

For some while Emma sat still. She was aware now that, before she had opened the letter, she had had a sudden wild yearning to find in it something of the Alison she had first known, something of the Alison who had first accepted her with the same happy abandon she had brought to their early days together. But that was impossible. That Alison was gone forever. If it had not been so, it would mean that Alison was troubled by memories, by regrets that would reflect on her present marriage to Arthur. And I don't want that, thought Emma. I don't want her unhappy. She told herself that she was glad that Alison was too sensible, too self-protective to allow that. Alison obviously believed that Emma had come into a safe harbor with someone well-armored against the dangers of a too-close relationship.

With a rush of anger at her own moment of weakness, Emma pushed Alison's letter aside and picked up Meg's. It was, as she remembered Meg's letters always to have been, several pages long, the familiar script moving smoothly on over the heavy linen paper.

"My dear Emma. I have had a most interesting few days in London. Americans are here in force and I have even encountered several Baltimore friends, who tell me that summer there is extremely hot and that typhoid has broken out in the poorer parts of town, something that happens every year but is stoutly denied by those who do not need to deal with it. I do hope, Emma, that you will take every precaution and not overwork yourself."

It was when she reached the back of the second sheet that Emma saw Alison's name.

"A Mrs. Melton, who is an ardent supporter of Mrs. Pankhurst's, took me to tea with a young woman who is secretary for one of the women's organizations, Angela Bigwood. In the course of conversation, we discovered that we both knew you. Miss Bigwood said enthusiastically how much impressed everyone was with you when you were here last year. She could not speak more highly of you and said that everyone here who knew you whom I might meet would sing your praises to me. And no one more, she said, than Alison Clifton. She looked at me expectantly, as she mentioned this young woman, as if she took it for granted that I would recognize her name. She seemed a little disconcerted when I said I knew nothing of her. So Miss Bigwood explained that Mrs. Clifton—as she now is—had shared lodgings with you, before she married, and she thought must have been your closest friend while you were here. She said I must certainly meet Mrs. Clifton and she arranged for me to come to her flat the next afternoon. Mrs. Clifton—as you undoubtedly know—is the wife of a young lawyer who is making quite a name for himself as an advocate for liberal causes, chief amongst them votes for women. But you know all that better than anyone, I'm sure. I met her. We had a very pleasant cup of tea together. She was full of her remembrance of her few months of living with you. It is plain that this period of her life will always have a special place in her memory. I am not surprised. You have a remarkable effect on people, Emma.''

Do I? thought Emma, putting the letter down for a moment. Oh, Meg, how like you! She took up the letter again.

"She told me how much she wanted to meet me, when she learned that I was in London. She said that you had often spoken of me and of the help I was able to give you, and how grateful you were. She was quite flattering. I had the impression that she did not want to speak too much of you and yet could not restrain herself. She said she had not had a chance of seeing you again when you returned to England on your way back to the States. Emma, she is a very pretty girl, so fresh and animated. It seems to me that, though she has fond memories of you, she is quite satisfied with her present life. She made a remark, at the end of our visit, that she hoped you had found, in your medical work in Baltimore, the right outlet for the ardent feelings that so govern you.''

Meg's letter broke off there, as if she had been interrupted by her own thoughts or by someone else's intrusion. The next paragraph, which obviously had been written after an interval, was quite different in its tone and described a visit to the Royal Academy. Emma scanned it with half her mind. She returned to the preceding passage. Meg, dear Meg, had tried to fathom the depth of Alison's feelings and had been disappointed. Emma read again the phrases, "She is quite satisfied with her present life," "she hopes you have found the right outlet for the ardent feelings that so govern you." Yes, Meg had guessed and probably had guessed quite accurately.

Emma, her lips pressed into a straight line, picked up Alison's letter and held it for a moment. Then slowly and firmly she tore it into a hundred small pieces. Meg's she folded and sat holding it in her hand for a long pensive hour.

* * *

When August came Emma, alone in the house with Dorcas, saw her only in the morning and evening. She was aware that Dorcas, who regularly received letters from Meg, watched her closely. The black woman was always on the alert for her return and while she was in the house. Meg would not have had to tell

Dorcas to do this. Dorcas, intuitive, intelligent, very readily grasped what passed in Meg's heart and mind. Sometimes Emma had the feeling that Dorcas was on the point of saying something but she never did. The cause of her watchfulness was left unnamed, hanging in the air.

Except for Dorcas she felt very much alone. It did not seem possible that she could miss Meg so much. She longed to be able to go into Meg's sitting room and see her there, seated at her desk, her head resting on her hand, reading, till the sound of Emma's entrance caused her to look up. There was always a flash of pleasure on Meg's sharpcut, delicate features as she turned towards her at once. Meg's straight-backed, slender body, her prim dresses, opulent in fabric and simple in cut, the exquisite grace of her narrow, long-fingered hands — The vivid recollection of her presence went through Emma like a sword.

The only remedy was to keep herself busy. There was little she could do in the way of recreation. The weather was too hot for tennis and in any case there was a dearth of partners. James was in Baltimore frequently, coming up from the horse farm or from visiting on the Eastern shore. He spent a few days at a time in town, always seeking her out and trying to persuade her to return with him for a weekend, a couple of days, in the cooler air of shore or country. She would enjoy sailing, he said, and he kept a boat in the Severn River, near the outlet to the Bay. She always refused and each time she did so she saw the expression of resentment cross his face. Once he again took hold of her arm with a grip strong enough to leave bruises. It told her plainly of his inner rage of frustration, of the effort he made to restrain himself. Their dealings with one another had become a trial of wills, at least in his view. He must conquer. Perhaps, she thought with a wry smile, that was her value for him—a woman to be conquered. He knew in his bones that if she agreed to marry him, she would never be an acquiescent wife. She would always provide him with a contest.

She knew she was not the only reason he kept coming back to Baltimore. Politically, she was vaguely aware, he had irons in the fire and he came to tend to them, and to look after his uncle's business interests. She supposed that he believed that they could settle down to the sort of tacit agreement that existed between Preston and Susanna. James would be careful to disguise from her any aspects of his affairs that she would not like and she would return the compliment by looking the other way. James would see nothing amiss in that. Politics, he said, was a dirty business, but he and his uncle saw no reason why that should persuade them to leave the control of city affairs in the hands of the completely corrupt. Sometimes it was necessary to set a thief to catch a thief and Preston Harms did not hesitate to do so.

"As long as you can control your thief," said Emma.

"That's it," James agreed. "That's where we have to be careful." She saw a light in his eyes that said he enjoyed this sort of battle.

What really annoyed her was the continual struggle to convince him that she would never marry him. She thought that perhaps she was making some progress in this when he began to hint that her outlook and scientific background would make an alliance outside of marriage more agreeable to her. She laughed outright the first time this occurred to her as the meaning of his latest remarks, one afternoon after he had left her. Next time he was bolder and more explicit, confirming to her what had until then been a tentative idea.

She said, amused, "James, I'm not any more ready to have an affair with you than I am to marry you. That is what you're suggesting, isn't it? You're really wasting your time with me, you know. I'm sure you could find somebody more willing with very little effort."

He scowled at her laugh, when she brought it out into the open like that. She offended him, he said, by supposing that any other woman would do. She laughed again, even more heartily. When he said Goodbye that evening, she knew she would not see him for a while, at least.

*   *   *

It was the end of a hot, silent Saturday afternoon. Emma, who had spent an hour or so alone in her empty office, studying medical journals, was just on the point of closing her door when a woman came into her waiting room, a young woman, fashionably dressed, pretty and hurried.

"Oh, Dr. Wycliffe, I hope you can see me now!" she said eagerly. "This is the only opportunity I have had to come and consult you."

Emma noted briefly the oddness of the statement, but passed it by in her habit of professionally observing her visitor. A young matron, she guessed, obviously well-to-do, the sort who would typically have left the city for a cooler, fresher place to spend August. She was Mrs. Frederick Minton—Clara Minton—she said, and she had heard of Emma through her aunt, Mrs. McHugh.

"I must leave Baltimore tomorrow morning," she added, "but I must see you before I go."

She was smiling brightly but Emma caught a glimpse of the desperation behind the outward cheerfulness. "Very well. Will you come into my examination room?"

Emma ushered the woman through the door and indicated the chair beside her desk.

"I am so glad I was able to catch you," her visitor said, breathlessly, as she sat down and drew off her gloves. "Oh, I might as well be frank with you, doctor. I have waited till the end of your office hours in hope that everyone else would have gone."

Emma, alert to every nuance of her manner, said encouragingly, "Well, you have chosen a good moment, then. Do you wish me to examine you?"

"Yes. I cannot tell you how thankful I am that I heard of you from Aunt Martha. There is absolutely no one else I could go to. I am almost beside myself with worry!"

Emma waited for her to go on but when she said no more, she pointed to the screen behind which she could undress. Emma noted the bright, fair hair, the fresh, young skin, the fragrant daintiness of a well-cared-for body. But she noted also the tautness of her muscles, the tremor in her hands as she began to unfasten her garments, the jerkiness of her movements.

Half an hour later Emma stood washing her hands at the hand basin, her back turned to her patient, whom she had helped off the examination table. "You are pregnant and I should judge in your third month."

The utter silence that greeted her statement caused her to turn around. Clara Minton was staring at her white-faced, despair in her eyes.

Emma said quickly, "But you must have been almost certain when you came to see me!"

The woman dropped her face in her hands. "Oh, I hoped — I thought you must be able to tell me it isn't true. Can — can there be any doubt?"

"None whatever." Wiping her hands, Emma eyed the wedding

ring on the slender finger. "You are a married woman. But I
judge that you have not had children before this. Are you afraid of
bearing a child? You are a perfectly normal, healthy young
woman. There is no reason to fear childbirth."

Clara made no answer but Emma saw a shudder pass through
her. She put her hand on Clara's shoulder and gave her a little
shake. "Now, take hold of yourself. Tell me what it is that
frightens you so. I am sure you have worked yourself into a state
of nerves over something that can be solved."

Clara seized hold of her arm with both hands. "No, doctor, no!
You must help me get rid of this — this thing! I cannot go
through with it! I will be lost, utterly lost!"

The large blue eyes were fixed on Emma's face with a blaze of
frantic fear. Emma stood still, passive in the other woman's grip.
"That is something that it is impossible for me to do," she said
slowly. "There are no medical grounds on which I could abort
you."

Clara dropped her head against Emma's shoulder. She was
moaning incoherently. Emma made no effort to move. Presently
Clara raised her head. She licked her lips so that she could speak.
"It is not my husband's child. He will disown it. He will abandon
me."

"Is there any reason why he should suspect that it is not his
child?"

"Oh, he will know it is not! He has only just returned from an
absence of six months. He has business connections in France and
he has been gone since last January."

"And the child's father?"

"He has refused to admit that it could be his."

Emma thought for a while. "Is there any prospect that your
husband will go away again for a while — long enough for you to
have the child and provide for its adoption?"

Clara shook her head and buried her face again in Emma's
shoulder.

Emma said, "You have perhaps two more months in which you
may be able to hide your condition. Is there a possibility that you
yourself could go away somewhere for a visit until after the child
is born? Do you have a relative, a friend who would be able and
willing to help you?"

"No. No one."

"Not Mrs. McHugh?"

Clara seemed to hesitate. "Oh, I cannot burden her with this! She has always been so kind to me. And now she has gone to California for the rest of the summer. Oh, doctor, you must help me!"

Emma shook her head. "I cannot. I see nothing for it but for you to tell your husband and seek his forgiveness."

"He would never forgive me! He would throw me out of the house at once! He is a very hard man. He has no tolerance, no kindness."

"Nevertheless you should try. Perhaps you are mistaken. Sometimes such a man can show compassion."

In the midst of her despair Clara looked at her with disbelief. "You do not know him. Of course, you are a stranger in Baltimore. You have never heard of him, have you?"

"I can't say I have."

"You would not suggest the possibility if you had."

A long silence followed. After a while Clara drew herself away from Emma's support and mechanically began to dress herself. Emma helped her fasten her corset and the buttons of her dress. Clara did not say anything until she was ready to leave. Then she asked in a hopeless but dignified voice, "Then you won't help me?"

"I cannot, I cannot!" Emma cried, driven beyond her own power to speak calmly.

Clara picked up her handbag and walked out of the room.

Emma, alone, caught sight of her own face in the looking-glass over the hand-basin. In a sudden rage she flung up her hand at her own image. "Coward!" she exclaimed.

*   *   *

Emma was unable to sleep through that night, her inner debate raging through the hot hours of darkness. Of course she must not jeopardize her professional life by giving in to this appeal. She would risk the ruin of her own reputation and—worse—involve Meg in any scandal that might result. The woman had been foolish. But, then, who among us, thought Emma, is not foolish sometimes, swept into folly by the emotion of a moment? Indignation gripped her whenever she thought of the fact that it was the woman who had to face alone the consequences of an act she could not have committed by herself. And why? Because, said the world, a woman must be chaste, a woman must have the strength and the foresight to deny herself a forbidden pleasure. And I, thought Emma, *am* a coward, the sort of coward I've always scorned other doctors for being, too self-protective to give aid where it was most needed.

She could not escape the constant circle of these thoughts in the next days. Even when the emotional impact of Clara Minton's visit began to fade, her mind reverted again and again to the dilemma of what she should really have done.

It was in the middle of the night that she had the summons from Richards. Come at once, he said. I need you. And she dressed hurriedly and went in the carriage that was waiting at the door, arriving within a few minutes at the only lighted house in a long, dark street.

Richards met her in the hall, hurrying out of the bedroom to draw her quickly inside. A screen was drawn around the bed. They were alone except for the woman hidden behind it, whose weak wailing filled the air.

"Emma, I don't need to tell you what this is. You will know as soon as you see her."

His strained voice and the sight of the beads of perspiration on his forehead struck a sudden chill through Emma. She waited, fearful, for what he said next.

"She has tried to abort herself. I am afraid it is too late for anything that we can do. She is Clara Minton. She has spoken your name several times."

It was too late but she and Richards struggled through several hours in a last ditch effort to conquer the massive infection that was draining the woman's life away. It was morning by the time Emma returned to Cushman Terrace, somber and self-reproachful. "I could have prevented it," was the only clear thought that filled her exhausted brain.

Richards came to see her later in the day. Dorcas, who had hovered over her ever since she had returned to the house, lingered for a moment after she had shown him in, as if anxious about what he had to say. Emma, noting the fact with a corner of her mind, thought fleetingly, "I wonder what she has heard through the other servants."

"Emma," Richards said abruptly, "the Minton case is developing into an ugly situation."

"Can it be uglier?" Emma said bitterly. "The woman is dead, miserably dead, when she need not be."

He looked at her with kindly, worried eyes. "Yes, yes. I know how you must feel. But she is out of it now—out of her misery, of the scandal. Because I'm sure there will be a scandal. We're the ones in trouble now."

"We? You had nothing to do with her condition, I am sure."

"No, no. I don't mean that. She did not come to me before-hand. I did not see her till her husband sent for me, when she was in the condition you saw."

"Then you mean me. I am in trouble."

Richards frowned. "Emma, of course, Minton knows his wife was unfaithful. He is very bitter. He is also vindictive. I know him from the past. And he will spare no one, however innocent they may be."

"But won't he make an effort to protect his wife's reputation— or his own, for that matter?"

Richards shook his head. "You don't know the type of man he is. If people are going to talk, he will give them all the material he can. Clara Minton was delirious, before she became too weak to speak, and she raved about having been to see you, about begging you to perform an abortion, about having been driven to mistreat herself in desperation when you refused to help her. The nurses, Minton himself, heard her. He is demanding an autopsy and an investigation."

Emma grew pale. "But if she said I refused —"

"That is what I believed her to say. And I have enough confi-dence in your professional integrity—in your common sense—to know that you must have refused. But Minton is a man half-demented with rage and a thirst for revenge—against someone. His wife is no longer available. But he can vilify her character and he won't hesitate to do so. Emma, I'm afraid you are in for a bad time. I've really come to warn you—to prepare you."

Emma did not answer. A curious shaft of feeling went through her, as if she welcomed this new menace, as if this threat of disaster in some way could lessen her sense of guilt for the sin she had committed against the dead woman. For a sin it had been. The woman would not have lost her life if she had had the courage to help —

Richards had gone on speaking. "The coroner is going to hold an inquest on Clara Minton's death. I'm afraid you are going to have to give evidence of your dealings with her. She did come to you, didn't she?"

"Yes. And I refused to help her. I blame myself for her death."

"You acted correctly. That is what you must impress on the coroner."

"Correctly!" Emma's voice was full of scorn. "Correctly! Not by my standards!"

Richards frowned severely. "Emma, you can't take that attitude. As a physician you're committed to preserving life."

"So I am. And because I refused to give a woman my professional attention, she has died."

Richards' attempt to be severe faded. With a sigh he patted Emma's arm. "Now, look here. You know that every doctor must face these dilemmas, not once but often. Just remember, Emma, when you are before the coroner, that you made the right decision." He paused for a moment. "I'll have to be there, too. You'll have all the support I can give you, Emma."

Her eyes filled with tears at his kindliness and she turned away to hide them. Presently she said briskly, "There is such a thing as professional confidence. I cannot be forced to speak of something a patient has told me in confidence."

"That's quite true. You'll have to decide, when you are questioned, what you can say that is not in violation of that principle. But, Emma, let me warn you. If you are too particular about that, it may make a bad impression. You don't want them to think you have more to hide than you do. Well, I'm going now. Don't be too downhearted."

Very soon after he had left, Dorcas showed James in to see her.

"I've just got to town, Emma," he said. "What is all this about an inquest on Clara Minton?"

"Is the news that common already?" Emma countered wearily.

He gave her an alert, speculative glance. "Well, of course, I'd hear it first off. I know the Mintons. But how did you get involved?"

"I don't have to discuss my professional problems with you, James."

"You don't have to tell me. I'll tell you what I was told. Clara Minton came to see you for an abortion. One version is that you refused and she tried something else and died as a consequence. The other version is that you did help her and it didn't work and she died as a consequence."

Emma, feeling cold in spite of the hot weather, said as easily as she could, "And which do you think it was?"

"Why, that you refused and she tried something else."

"Well, that is kind of you, James."

He smiled with a trace of malice. "Yes, but the other version makes better gossip. Well, you did the sensible thing. I suppose it is Frederick Minton who is causing the trouble. He is not a reasonable man. But he can be dangerous."

Emma burst out. "Oh, James, I am sick at heart over this!"

He was looking at her as if weighing something. "Why? You did the right thing."

"And the woman died."

He shrugged. "She took a chance, with her eyes open."

Rage burned in Emma. "And how about the man? She couldn't have done it alone."

"Well, what about him? You're no innocent, Emma. You know that a woman is a fool to let a man get her into trouble. She shouldn't expect him to take the blame."

Emma was too angry to speak. James went on. "The important thing is this coroner's inquest. That's not going to be very nice for you, Emma. Even if it is an open and shut case, it doesn't help a doctor's reputation to be publicly questioned about such a thing."

"Do you suppose that I am not aware of this?"

"Well, I came by, as soon as I heard about it, to give you a hand, Emma. If you say the word, I'll see what can be done about suppressing the whole thing. Even Frederick Minton can't buck Preston Harms."

He had stepped close to her, as if ready to put his arm around her. Emma backed away. "What are you talking about?"

"You know what I want. I want you, whether you marry me or not. I'm offering you a fair deal, Emma. Say Yes and you'll hear nothing more about the inquest."

Emma stood perfectly still. The sense of outrage that seized her stopped her ears, blinded her eyes. It was as if she was being consumed in a fire too intense to be felt.

James, seeing her face, white to the lips, said in a mild voice, "It's better to have me as a friend than as an enemy."

Emma heard her own voice, strained to the breaking point, say, "I had never expected you to become my enemy."

He seemed to consider her statement and her manner and finally said, as he turned to leave, "If you change your mind, let me know."

Emma, in the tumult of her own feelings, heard distantly the sound of his leaving the house and Dorcas closing the front door after him. Her mind now was filled with the thought of Meg. Never since she had been a child had she so longed for someone's reassurance, someone's comfort. Oh, Meg, if only you were here!

She was startled by Dorcas' voice at her elbow and turned to look down into a pair of worried black eyes. "Miss Emma, what did Mr. James want?"

"He — he came to speak about the inquest on Mrs. Minton."

She was surprised at the expression of contempt she saw on the black woman's face. "Mr. James always thinks he can get what he wants if you're in trouble." Dorcas paused for a moment. "Miss Margaret shouldn't have gone away and left you."

Emma smiled wanly. "You mean I need her here to protect me?"

"You're working yourself to death, Miss Emma, and now you've got this trouble. She shouldn't have gone away. I as good as told her so. But she got that notion into her head and she can be as stubborn as a mule."

"What notion, Dorcas?"

"About you and Mr. James. She thinks you like Mr. James and you might get to like him better and she wasn't going to stand in the way, like Miss Susanna."

Emma stared in shocked silence. Dorcas' teeth showed in an indulgent smile. "You never would have guessed it, would you, Miss Emma? But that was her notion. She never would have gone to Europe otherwise."

PART IV

Meg, seated on the terrace of the Hotel d'Angleterre, gazed out across the luminous lake. There were other people about her likewise enjoying the warm summer night and the unusually clear view across the water to the moon-whitened snowy peaks in the distance. Small groups were seated at the nearby tables chatting and two or three couples strolled back and forth along the balustrade that defined the garden that lay in darkness beyond. But she had chosen a seat in a corner where the shadow cast by the wall protected her from recognition by acquaintances. She did not want company. She wanted no one to dispel the state of dreamy pleasure that had fastened on her ever since she had left London.

She had left London earlier than she had planned. In fact, right after her visit with that young woman who remembered Emma so fondly. The next day she had sought the street and house where Alison said Emma had shared lodgings with her. Alison had tried to speak only as a helpful friend, a fellow worker in the cause of women's rights, the witness of Emma's year of study and achievement in London. But in spite of herself she had said, to Meg, a great deal more. Meg, walking by the house where the two of them had lived, gazing up at the windows of the top flat now obviously occupied by someone else, knew certainly that she had discovered the source of Emma's underlying grief. Alison was Emma's lost love.

After that Meg had not wanted to stay in London. She cut short her visit, saying to her friends that she had decided to spend that remaining week before she was to join Cordelia in Paris, in Geneva, where she would consult Professor Lenoir. She did not in fact intend to consult him. She would simply pay him a courtesy call of short duration. Ten years ago she had been sent to him, a specialist in nervous disorders, when, with no obvious physical ailment, she had been unable to sleep or eat, had become alarmingly thin and subject to all sorts of fears and worries. He was a kind man, a sympathetic doctor, but he could not cure her, since she could not tell him what she knew was the cause of her

illness. How could she tell him, how could she tell anyone, that at
the age of twenty-eight, she was overwhelmed by a sense of
uselessness, of worthlessness, by the grim thought that what she
was then—a woman whose youth has passed, empty of everything
except material ease—was only too plainly what she would be for
the rest of her life? Without his help, she had in the end finally
achieved resignation. This obviously was what she was put on
earth to be—an assuager of the miseries of others less fortunate
than herself, through the use of her money. Otherwise life was
only a waiting, a long empty journey.

She knew Professor Lenoir had had his own diagnosis of the
cause of her depression. She had seen it in his eyes: a well-to-do
spinster, with no outlet for her physical energies, no husband or
children on whom to expend them, no close human relationship.
No doubt he had wondered what had once aroused her to the point
that she was aware that she had physical desires that went unsatis-
fied and certainly she would never tell him, never unearth those
terrible passages of her adolescence.

It had become a habit, over the ten years since she had
consulted him, to meet him for a social visit each time she came
to Geneva. He invariably watched her with observant eyes,
though the state of her health was never mentioned between them.
He was, she supposed, measuring the degree of contentment she
showed in this leisured life filled with impersonal pleasures—the
yearly round of visits to the centers of European culture, the
concerts, the operas, the showings of paintings, the contemplation
of ancient buildings and art objects, the stimulation of play-going
and the conversation of other similarly occupied friends. For years
she had tried to persuade herself that all this satisfied her
emotional needs, that this deliberately measured life, dependent
for warmth on her own sensitivity to sights and sounds and mental
and spiritual activity, was enough.

But now all that had receded into the background. The
interview with Alison had somehow catalysed her feelings for
Emma. She had carried away from London, locked up in her
heart, the knowledge that it was Alison who had given Emma the
greatest joy and had then destroyed it. How much did that loss
still weigh on Emma? How deeply was it buried? She had wanted
to turn these questions over again and again in solitude, without
the intrusion of anyone else. She was astonished with herself,
astonished at what was happening within herself, now that she

was alone. She dreamed of Emma at night, Emma in her arms, Emma warm and sensuous, arousing in herself the most intimate response. In the daytime the sensation that Emma was bodily with her was so strong that she had to set a guard on her tongue and manner. It was a joyous, extravagant, unbounded happiness that seemed to possess her now, one she could scarcely restrain beneath her usual quiet behavior. She amused herself at the thought that she might speak aloud to Emma and give anyone who heard her the idea that the grave Miss Bell had suddenly taken to talking to herself. She knew that she must often be smiling when there was no apparent cause.

When she lunched with Professor Lenoir and his wife she saw that he at once observed a difference in her. She saw his head cock in her direction from time to time during the hour or so she spent with them. She could imagine, when they finally left her, that he would have some discreet comment to make to his wife. She found herself laughing at the idea and stopped herself, a little perturbed at this wild feeling of — yes, freedom. For now she felt within herself free, free from a bondage that had held her for so long. She had known the cause from the very beginning. She loved Emma, she had fallen in love with the tall, golden-haired, dazzling girl the moment she had first walked into the drawing room of her Baltimore house. She loved Emma possessively, passionately, body and soul. So she dreamed at night of Emma's beautiful, naked body in her arms, awake to the touch of her hands. Her desire for Emma consumed her.

Clearly she foresaw the anguish she was preparing for herself. She was used to being solitary. She had learned the pleasures of that sort of apartness. She did not feel loneliness. And yet now she longed for Emma. She had been reckless, heedless of the eventual cost. For Emma could not always be even as much hers as she was now. Emma would not always be dependent upon her. Emma would go on, leaving her behind.

Her mind, momentarily returning to the reality of Baltimore, shied away from its contemplation. She did not want to think of James West, of her sister, of Emma beyond her reach. Yet it was to allow the normal, necessary course of events to unfold without the check of her presence that she had come abroad. For a moment she wished that Emma was a better correspondent. But then she decided she did not really want to know how things went there, across the Atlantic. Here she had Emma to herself.

One of the promenading couples passed close to her and she sat motionless, waiting for them to go by. The woman wore a dress of silver cloth which glimmered in the moonlight. She was leaning on the arm of a man whose head was bent down as he murmured in her ear. Meg, watching them stroll slowly past her and hearing the woman's soft laugh, thought, Ah, Emma, how many times I've heard you laugh like that. The silver night seemed filled with a sensual warmth, the whispers of a thousand lovers' voices. Emma, Emma, Emma. You drive me right out of my wits even at this distance. You wake me at dawn like the ray of day. You lie now out in that ghostly white light, beckoning me. Aphrodite, they say, was the beguiler, the golden goddess who laughed heartily and yet sweetly at those whom she ensnared. But you do not mock me, Emma.

Her dreaming was cut short by a current of night chill creeping under her wrap. She shivered. The silver glory of the night, however, kept her in her seat until the other guests had gone and a waiter came out on the terrace to gather up the cups and glasses from the small tables. Startled when he realized that someone still sat in the shadowed corner, he exclaimed, *"Pardon, madame,"* and added quickly, "It would be advisable, madame, for you to come inside. The night damp is harmful."

She said Yes and got up and followed him indoors.

*   *   *

Cordelia Drummond opened the big box that had come from the modiste and drew out the enormous hat covered in tulle and feathers.

"There, now, Maggie! What do you think of that?"

She lifted the hat from the box and placed it on top of the masses of glossy dark hair piled up on her head.

Meg, seated in a big armchair that swallowed up her slight body, laughed. "It certainly suits you, Cordy. And the dress does, too. You really don't look a day over thirty."

Cordelia turned her fine dark eyes on her. "And you don't look a day under fifty, Maggie. You could do better than that, you know. Nobody would ever guess that your clothes are made by the same couturier who makes mine. It's an utter waste. You might as well buy your things off the rack in a department store. You have your dresses made by the same pattern every time. You could spend five minutes with the dressmaker and get something really fashionable."

"There is no such thing as spending five minutes with a dressmaker, Cordy, and you know it. I detest wasting a whole morning sitting around in a dressmaking establishment, listening to tiresome chatter about fabrics and laces and necklines."

Cordelia's eyes sparkled. "Oh, certainly! How deadly boring! What a dreadful waste of time! Most women adore it. But not you, Maggie. I shouldn't expect it of you. Where *did* you spend this afternoon?"

"In the Louvre, of course. You know I always go there first thing when I reach Paris."

"You must be the world's authority on it by now. I suppose I've been there half a dozen times, when I couldn't escape from a visitor who had to be taken about and shown the sights. You're such a little sobersides, Maggie."

Yes, thought Meg. I can't even tell you, Cordy, what draws me there. I do go there, not once but many times whenever I'm here.

She had spent a glorious hour in the little room where the Venus de Milo stood alone. The Venus had always been a magnet for her. The splendid marble body, the serene marble face, had long ago captured her as a lover is caught. Whenever she visited the museum she enjoyed a secret, voluptuous pleasure which she never spoke of to anyone. Indeed, the hidden nature of this delight gave it a tremendous extra value. It was her one joke at the expense of those who saw only the outward Miss Bell, immune to any sensuous feeling. This afternoon she had sat and gazed for the hundredth time. The golden goddess, violet-crowned Cytherea, without whom there could be no joy or loveliness anywhere.

This visit had had a particular purpose. Whenever she recalled the glimpse she had had of Emma's body her mind's eye had conjured up the image of the marble goddess. To see the Venus once more with this comparison in her mind's eye had become a fixed idea. As each mile of ocean and each London hour had passed she grew more and more eager. By the time she reached Paris she was in a fever of impatience. At the first opportunity she had taken a cab to the Louvre and gone at once to the statue.

Yes, yes. Her heart had bounded as she saw the marble. That was Emma indeed — Emma in the guise of antiquity — Emma without the trimness of muscle and flesh that came from bicycling and tennis. She gazed at the lovely marble face, the flowing lines of shoulders and breasts. Oh, Emma, Emma!

Cordelia's voice finally penetrated to her consciousness. "Maggie, what is the matter with you? I've been talking for ten

minutes and you haven't heard a word I've said. You have a very
funny look on your face."

"Have I?" Still Meg found difficulty in returning to Cordelia.
Cordelia stepped over to her and lifted her chin in her fingers.
"Maggie, Maggie. Where have you been wandering? You really
should not go mooning about like a schoolgirl. Will you never get
over that?"

"Don't scold me, Cordy. You know I find it hard to shake off
impressions when I've been looking at paintings and sculpture
—"

"Or listening to music or reading Greek and Latin. Maggie,
you are hopeless. You should really pay more attention to the
world around you." Cordelia paused and stood looking down at
her fondly. "But you don't want to, sometimes, do you? Sweet,
you must not let that imagination of yours absorb you so."

She turned away and took off her peignoir. Drawing a dress out
of the dressmaker's box, she said, "Come and help me, Maggie. I
don't want to call the maid."

Obediently Meg helped her put on her corset. Standing close
behind her she gazed at the fine satiny skin of Cordelia's back. It
was a well-fleshed, supple back and she fell at once into a reverie,
comparing it to Emma's.

"Maggie! Don't pull those laces so tight!" Cordelia half turned
to look at her.

Meg murmured, "Oh, Cordy, I'm sorry." But she was still too
lost in thought to notice the abrupt silence as Cordelia studied her
face. She was aroused by Cordelia's voice, saying in a bantering
tone, "Maggie, have you gone and fallen in love?"

The glare of anger in Meg's eyes, the immediate whiteness of
her face, turned Cordelia aghast at what she had said. She said at
once, humbly, "Forgive me, Maggie. That was stupid."

With relief she saw vexation take the place of anger in Meg's
face, saw Meg bite her lip in the old habit of self-discipline.
Apologetically she reached over to touch Meg's cheek with her
fingertips. Meg gave no sign that she noticed the gesture.
Cordelia, knowing that this meant a tacit acceptance of her
apology, turned away reassured.

In a casual tone of voice Cordelia then asked, "Have you heard
from Baltimore lately, Maggie?"

"Not since London. Susanna is at the Eastern Shore, Martha
McHugh has gone to California. Everyone else is away. I've not
heard from Emma. She has no time to write letters."

"Emma? Oh, your young doctor friend. You know, Maggie, I've been hearing the most alarming things about her."

"Really?"

Cordelia, warned by her tone of voice, glanced at her alertly. After a moment's consideration she decided to go on. "I hear that she has all sorts of radical ideas — votes for women, women in the professions, saving fallen women, educating girls as if they were boys — Heavens! It seems there is no end to her notions."

Meg's voice was cool. "The only difference between Emma's ideas and those of mine and the women I've been working with is that she wants to attack the causes of women's disabilities, not just ease the effects."

"Maggie, don't you know, that is very dangerous, attacking causes." Cordelia was watching her out of the corner of her eye. "That's what must be upsetting Uncle John Lightfoot. Women's disabilities? Why, who says we have any?"

She smiled as Meg exploded. "Cordy, don't talk nonsense! Not even in fun. Just because you have everything your way doesn't mean that most women don't have a hard time of it. You're baiting me and you know I hate that."

Cordelia's smile broke into a laugh. "Maggie, I can't resist teasing you. Of course, of course. Your Dr. Emma is going to make over the world, beginning with Baltimore. I must say I admire her fortitude there. Fancy reforming Baltimore! There, now, Maggie, kiss me. I promise I shan't tease you any more. You know the only reason I can abide the idea of going back to Baltimore is that you're there. We haven't seen much of each other for the last few years."

She leaned over Meg and kissed her gently on the lips. Meg, in a gesture of forgiveness, touched her cheek.

Cordelia straightened up. "There's my sweet Maggie. Well, not everybody is afraid of your young doctor. Martha McHugh speaks of her as of the Second Coming whenever she mentions her in her letters."

"Cordy! Of course, no one who has known her professional care and attention would do otherwise."

"Martha said she gave you very devoted care last winter when you were so ill."

"Yes. I might have died without her."

"Oh, dear, Maggie! That's a dreadful thought. I gather that Susanna does not like her."

Meg did not reply. Cordelia, after listening carefully for her to say something, went on, "Martha also says that James West is smitten with her. That wouldn't please Susanna either."

Again Meg was silent and Cordelia said, "I find it hard to believe that James is getting serious about any woman. Do *you* think he is interested in her, Maggie?"

With an effort Meg said, "He gives every sign of it."

"But does he want to marry her?"

"He gives that impression."

"And what about her? Does she like him?"

After a long pause Meg said, "I don't know. I think she does."

Cordelia looked at her with raised eyebrows but she checked what she was about to say and said instead, "Of course, James must be much more sophisticated now than when we had our little affair. He had a great deal to learn then about how to treat a woman—unless she was a streetwalker."

"What he has learned I am sure he learned from you."

Cordelia gave her an admiring glance. "Now, Maggie, you're quick today! Of course. How else? Did Susanna ever find out about us?"

"I haven't the slightest idea. Certainly not from me."

"Of course not from you. But you don't like that sort of thing any more than Susanna does."

"Not for you, no. In any case, it is something beyond my comprehension."

"But you love me just the same. You're my sweet darling, Maggie. Well, perhaps James can provide me with a little entertainment this winter in Baltimore."

*   *   *

A week went by and Meg, still in a half-entranced state, savored the pleasure of Paris — Paris with Cordelia's spice.

Cordelia never got up before the middle of the morning and Meg made no effort to see her until her husband, a ponderous, slow-moving man, returned from the American bankers with an armful of letters and newspapers. This morning she met him in the sitting room of their suite and he handed them to her, saying, Would she like to take them to Cordelia because he wanted to attend to his own letters. They were the first to arrive since Meg had reached Paris.

Going into the bedroom she found Cordelia sitting up, her empty breakfast tray pushed aside and the counterpane strewn with dress samples and undergarments. Cordelia's fine white shoulders and bosom swelled above the low neck of her thin nightgown. Her mass of glossy dark brown hair was negligently pinned up on her head.

When she saw Meg she threw out her arms. "Maggie, where have you been? The maid says you've been out for hours."

"I've been waiting for you to wake up, Cordy. So I took a walk. You know I like to get up early."

"So you do. Well, I've been waiting for you." As Meg bent to kiss her, she reached up and drew her down onto the bed into her embrace. Meg, her face buried in Cordelia's neck, lay quiet for a few moments, breathing in the warm fragrance of Cordelia's flesh. Then she commanded, "Let me go, Cordy." For a second she felt Cordelia's arms tighten and then release her. When she sat up she saw Cordelia's sidelong smile.

"Here are your letters. John fetched them. He asked me to bring them in to you."

Cordelia quickly shuffled through them. "Only one from Baltimore." She tore open the envelope. "Letitia Stoneman. She is a dreadful gossip, but she does tell me more about what goes on at home than everyone else put together."

She fell to reading the letter while Meg untied the bundle of Baltimore papers. After a moment Cordelia exclaimed, "Maggie! Clara Minton is dead! Why, she wasn't thirty years old!"

"Clara Minton! Oh, poor Martha. Clara was her favorite niece. But, Cordy, what happened?"

Cordelia was frowning. "There seems to be some mystery about her death. This is what Letitia says. 'Ugly rumors are being circulated that her death was the result of an unsuccessful attempt to treat her for a delicate condition.' Oh, shoot! What she means is a bungled abortion. Why doesn't she say so? 'Her husband is demanding an inquiry.' God! What a brute Frederick Minton always was. I never could see how she stood him."

"Well, was he responsible for her death?"

"No. On the contrary. He seems to think someone else was. Hence the inquiry. Here, read the letter while I look at the papers and see if there is anything in them."

She thrust the letter towards Meg. Meg, remembering the pretty girl that Clara Minton had been, thinking of how Martha McHugh had been as fond of her as if she were one of her own daughters, was absorbed for a while in puzzling over the unfamiliar handwriting. There was a lot of talk, said Letitia, about the cause of her death. There was a lot of conjecture as to whether her husband had known about her condition.

"Maggie." The sound of Cordelia's voice made Meg aware that for some moments the room had been quiet, that Cordelia's running commentary on what she was reading in the newspaper had been stilled.

"What is it, Cordy?"

"I'm afraid Frederick Minton is creating a scandal. There is to be a coroner's inquest into his wife's death. He wants the doctors who attended her to be questioned. And, Maggie, the doctors named are Teddy Richards and Emma Wycliffe. This is impossible!"

Meg snatched at the paper that Cordelia held out to her. She read, "Dr. Richards was called in to treat Mrs. Minton when her condition became critical. Dr. Wycliffe is to be questioned about a visit Mrs. Minton paid to her for professional advice a few days before she became ill. It is assumed that Dr. Wycliffe will be able to explain the cause of Mrs. Minton's death."

Cordelia, alarmed at the expression on Meg's face, said anxiously, "Maggie, this is very bad for your friend. Isn't James West in the prosecuting attorney's office now? Surely he could have done something to keep this out of the papers."

Meg said angrily, "Emma would never want anything like this hushed up. If she really did treat Clara Minton, you may be sure Clara would not be dead now. Someone else must have made a botch of things and Emma was unable to save her."

Still holding the paper, she stood up. Cordelia said anxiously, "What are you going to do?"

Meg, her mind running on her own thoughts, did not answer. She put the paper down on the bed and, turning away, began to walk rapidly to the door.

Cordelia sat up straight in bed. "Maggie, where are you going?"

"To book passage for New York. The Mauretania leaves Southampton tomorrow. If I can get a berth and I leave Paris now, I shall be able to sail on her."

"But, Maggie, what about our visit here? You're sailing with us in two weeks' time!"

"I'm sorry, Cordy. I cannot wait. You'll have to do without me," said Meg, disappearing through the door.

*   *   *

The night was dark, warm and close. It must be well past one o'clock, thought Emma, as she let herself into the house. She climbed the stairs slowly, having turned off the big overhead lamp that Dorcas had left on for her. Once in her room she undressed quickly, throwing her garments across the nearest chair, too tired to give them the inspection she usually did after having spent the evening at the dispensary. Dorcas would have to attend to them in the morning. It was no use, she told herself, giving tonics to the malnourished girls who came to the evening clinic, if they had not the means to buy food to satisfy their appetites.

She put on her dressing gown and went across the landing to the bathroom. When she came out and started back to her room, still sleepily involved in her evening concerns, she was startled to see Meg's door open. Meg herself, in her nightgown with her hair in a braid, stood in the beam of bright lamplight.

"Emma!"

"Meg!"

They were in each other's arms. Emma's drowsiness fled. She held Meg's tense, eager body to her, the thin nightgown scarcely muffling the vibrancy she felt there.

Meg said, drawing her into the bedroom and closing the door, "You were very quiet. I must have dozed for a moment. Dorcas said you would not be back till very late."

Emma saw the steamer trunk standing open. "When did you get here?"

"Soon after you left the house this evening, from what Dorcas said. Emma —" She still held Emma's arm and now she looked at her carefully in the lamplight. — "You are thin and pale. You have been working much too hard and in all this heat."

Emma ignored her remark. "What are you doing here? I did not expect you until the end of the month."

"Why, I came home, of course. I did not stop in New York. I thought the train would never get here."

"But why are you here?"

Meg looked up at her. "I think you know. I saw an account of Clara Minton's death in the Baltimore Sun — of course, a week or so late."

"So you came to see for yourself."

Meg heard the ironical overtone in Emma's voice. "I knew I could not get here for the inquest. But I could not stay there and wait to hear the outcome. Emma, what has happened?"

"Nothing catastrophic. The inquest was held two days ago. The coroner decided that there were no grounds for censuring my conduct."

"Oh, thank God!"

Emma said bitterly, "That is not a verdict that will help my professional reputation much—a no-contest, shall we say."

"You should never have been questioned! You should never have been required to appear in such a proceeding! If I had been here, it would not have happened."

Emma gave her a caustic smile. "Hadn't you better hear first what I was accused of—by implication, of course?"

"Emma, don't speak to me like that! I know quite well that whatever you have done was done properly and conscientiously. I have grave doubts about the motives of the others who were concerned in the affair."

Emma sat down on the edge of the bed. Meg stood still in the center of the room. The heavy night air drifted in at the window. "Tell me what happened, Emma."

"Clara Minton came to see me late one evening. She wanted me to examine her. I did and confirmed what she already knew, that she was pregnant. She pleaded with me to abort her. I told her that there was no medical reason to justify my doing so, that it was dangerous to do this since her pregnancy was so far advanced. She still pleaded with me, telling me that the child was not her husband's and that he would know that it was not. I still refused and she left me, obviously very much upset. A week later Richards called me late at night to come and help him with her. She was dying, from a badly done abortion. She was too far gone to tell us who the abortionist was, but while she was delirious she spoke of me and of having been to see me."

"Did her husband say anything to you at that time?"

"No. He was not in the room when she died. When I left the house, Richards was trying to reason with him. I could hear him shouting. Several days after that Richards came to warn me that Minton was enraged and was demanding that an inquest be held. I believe some of his friends and relatives tried to dissuade him because of the scandal, but he is too vindictive. He seems to want to drag his wife's memory through the mud in order to revenge himself. And of course that means me too."

"I see. Yes. I know the sort of man Frederick Minton is. However, even if it was necessary to hold the inquest, it could have been done with less publicity. There was no need for it to be featured in the newspaper."

Emma's smile was a grimace. "A cloak of secrecy would scarcely improve the situation."

"Oh, Emma! I know how you must feel! It is simply that, amongst the people with whom we mingle, newspaper publicity is the one unforgiveable offense. That, surely, could have been avoided."

Yes, it could have. I had an offer that would have avoided it."

Meg, who had been moving restlessly about the room, abruptly stopped and looked at her. "What do you mean, Emma?"

"James West came to see me, almost on Richards' heels."

Meg's manner was tense. "What did he say?"

"I wonder if you will believe me."

"Why, Emma, how could you think I would not?"

Emma hesitated. "Before I tell you, there is a question I must ask you. Did you go abroad under the impression that I wanted to be left alone with James?"

The color came slowly up in Meg's face. "Who told you that?"

"There could be only one person who would know your mind that well. Dorcas. According to Dorcas, you went abroad so that James might have a clear field in persuading me to marry him."

Meg rushed to excuse herself. "Emma, I did think you were becoming interested in James. I knew he was pursuing you and, after all, he is a very good match for you. He can give you a great deal. And since Susanna —"

Emma's temper blazed. "Stop it! I won't listen to such nonsense! I have no interest in him. I have no interest in marrying any man. Meg, you should not have left me here alone for such a reason. You should not have believed me capable of such feelings."

Meg, upset by her anger, said hesitantly, "Oh, Emma, it seemed the natural thing to think —"

"Not by you, of me. I shall tell you something more about James. I have been perfectly frank with him. I at last convinced him that I would not marry him. Since then he has been hinting that we should have an affair, that something of that sort would suit both of us better."

"Emma!"

Emma's smile was angry. "As a matter of fact, he was right. I'd rather have an affair with James than marry him. It would be much less — confining."

Meg, her indignation ebbing, said, "I see. So what was it that he came to say to you after Clara Minton's death?"

"He told me plainly that if I gave in to him, he would do everything in his power to hush things up." Emma's anger flared up. "I would not have done such a thing for any reason whatever! I have done nothing that I must hide. I will not allow anyone to impute the contrary."

"So now" — Emma saw Meg's anger rising — "he has not only not helped suppress Minton's vengefulness, he has done everything he could to give the case the utmost publicity. Oh, I know that side of James! He will not be baulked and especially not by a woman."

In the little silence that followed Emma said quietly, "And you wanted me to marry him."

"Emma, no, no! Don't twist my words! No, it was simply that I could not bear the idea of being an obstacle to you."

Emma sat back against the pillows and sighed. "None of this would have happened, if I had not been such a coward. I should not have refused to help her. She would be alive now, if I had treated her. I'm no better than those selfish doctors I have scorned for refusing to place themselves in a moment's danger to save a wretched woman's life."

"Emma, you cannot defy the law, defy society."

"The law must be defied, society must be defied, sooner or later, if this sort of injustice is to be corrected. Perhaps I would have acted if — if —"

As she fell silent, Meg prompted her. "If what?"

"Meg, I can't involve you in my problems. I can't repay you for all you've done for me by dragging your name into all this sort of publicity. And yet, that's what has happened. Everyone knows that it is Miss Margaret Bell who has been harboring me, a dangerous radical, a menace —"

Meg's soft little laugh stopped her. "Indeed, they know that! Nothing could please me more."

She stepped across to Emma. Emma saw the lamplight catch the brilliance of her eyes. Meg seized hold of her head. She was breathing quickly.

"Emma, come, get into bed with me." She leaned past Emma and climbed into the bed.

Emma, astonished, turned towards her. Without a word, Meg undid the cord of her dressing gown and pushed it off her shoulders. For a moment she sat smiling at the sight of Emma's naked body. Then she sank down on the pillows, her arms held out.

Emma rolled over towards her and took her in her arms. She expected a soft, yielding Meg, half-reluctant to accept her embrace. But this was a new Meg, this was a Meg she had never suspected. This was a Meg who responded to her touch with a sudden surge of strength, who wrapped her legs around her with unchecked urgency, whose vehement mouth sought hers as someone dying of thirst drank water, who expertly, without delay, roused her body to a throbbing response, broke the long-enduring sheath of suppressed desire. Entranced, scarcely believing the reality of what was happening, Emma redoubled her own caresses. Her hand traveled over Meg's spare, vibrant body, over the small breasts, the narrow back, coming finally to the space between Meg's thighs, her fingers seeking carefully in the soft bush of Meg's hair for the moist warmth within. Almost at once Meg's body thrust against her own, wildly, uncontrollably.

Meg gasped into her ear, "Oh, my darling, hold me to you! Don't let me go! How I've longed for you!"

She lost speech again as the surge of orgasm once more stiffened her body. After what seemed to Emma a long moment, she sank back in the soft bed, passive in Emma's arms. Emma kissed her tenderly, on her lips, her cheeks, her throat. Her eyes opened into Emma's shining in the lamplight, and she moaned a little, wordlessly.

For a while they both lay still. Then Meg stirred and said softly, "Even more lovely."

Emma asked, "What did you say, Meg?"

But Meg only moved her head a bit. Emma forgot what she had said in the luxurious acceptance of Meg's renewed caresses, lost in the bliss created by Meg's expert, unavoidable fingers. She soared avidly in pursuit of Meg's bidding, no longer remembering unhappiness, fatigue, disillusionment, frustration. Only one stray thought shot through her mind — Alison. But Alison now was gone, dissolved in the delicious tumult that Meg's being, Meg's touch, the pressure of Meg's soft stomach created.

The first light of day had crept into the room by the time they fell asleep.

*   *   *

Great streaks of lightning rent the blue-black sky, followed by long, threatening rolls of thunder. Emma, jumping from the cab that brought her to the door, dashed up the steps and into the house. She laughed as Dorcas helped her off with her raincape.

The violent weather exhilerated her. The storm promised relief from the oppressive heat. All her lassitude, her moodiness, her fatigue, her discouragement, had left her. Meg was back, a wonderful new Meg and the world had changed.

That morning she had left a drowsy, contented Meg in the big bed and had gone early to her own room to prepare for the day. Meg had not got up for breakfast. Disappointed but with her gladness undiminished she had gone out to her round of hospital visits, her morning's stint at the Shelter. Even the thought of the inquest, of the possible ostracism by important people swayed by the Minton scandal, did not dampen her spirits. She felt invincible, armed for victory, ready to take on any challenge that might present itself. For Meg was here and Meg was hers.

Dorcas, at once aware of the difference in her mood, watched her with a broad smile. "Why, Miss Emma, you certainly are gay! Miss Margaret is waiting for you."

Eagerly Emma stepped across the vestibule. Few of her private patients had yet returned to Baltimore and with the storm it was unlikely that anyone was waiting for her in her consulting room. There would be time to stop and see Meg. Anxiously she looked around the big room and her eyes lit up and her heart sang when she saw only Meg's slight figure. She crossed the room to her in a bound.

Meg's face brightened when she saw her and she allowed her to embrace and kiss her. But there was a restraint in her manner that checked Emma's first exuberance. "What is the matter, Meg? We're alone."

Meg patted her cheek and gently disengaged herself. "Yes, of course. But, Emma, you're so headlong." The smile on her face sought to soften the effect of her firm little gesture of repression.

The blood rushed to Emma's face. Half-angry she said, "You're playing with me, Meg."

Meg was indignant. "No. Certainly not. We must simply be — we must use restraint. There are problems we must face. Emma, I have seen James. I went to Preston's office. James was very surprised to see me."

"Why did you do that?"

"I wanted him to know that I shall not overlook what he has done—that I think he has behaved very badly."

"Will that really have any effect on him?"

At the disbelief in Emma's voice, Meg gave a little sigh. "Oh, yes. There is one person whom James will never offend in the slightest degree—my brother-in-law. Preston, you know, is quite fond of me. He will always listen, sympathetically, to anything I have to say.''

"I see."

"There is another thing that you must realize. James will let my sister know at once that I am back in Baltimore. She will know why I have returned. She no doubt approved of James' not helping to suppress the scandal. She will be angry because she knows that my being back here will change things considerably for you. She knows that it means that I am giving you all my support and she knows that everyone else amongst our circle also will recognize that fact.''

"I am very grateful, of course, Meg. But what does all this mean—beyond the fact that you can require Baltimore to take me at your own valuation, regardless of events?''

Meg hesitated. "It means that I shall be under very close scrutiny by Susanna. Oh, Emma, I can't explain it all to you! There is so much that must stay —'' She had put her hands on Emma's arms. Now she broke off and looked beyond Emma and said, "What is it, Dorcas?''

Dorcas stood in the doorway. "Ma'am, there's somebody waiting for Miss Emma.''

"Thank you, Dorcas.''

They stood looking at each other for a moment and then Emma went away to her consulting room.

When they were once more together, Emma was wary, her new happiness tempered by uncertainty. As Dorcas served them at dinner, Meg was charmingly talkative, full of anecdotes of her travels, smiling, and succeeded in making Emma laugh. Emma thought, watching her across the table, this was the Meg of the letters, witty, sophisticated, assured. Even her appearance bore out this new character. The gown she wore, a cream-colored silk trimmed with deep flounces of lace, the single strand of pearls catching the lamplight, her hair dressed higher than usual on her head — yes, it must have been the day or so in Paris that had made the difference. Emma, entranced, gazed at her with an overflowing heart.

Afterwards they sat briefly in the drawingroom under Dorcas' hovering presence. Meg made no further reference to the Minton scandal, to her sister, to James. Presently they went upstairs together. On the landing they stood for a moment, saying Good night as if parting for the night. It was Meg who stepped to the stair rail and looked down, mindful of Dorcas. They both knew that later, when Dorcas had seen Meg into bed, Emma would come to join her.

When she did so, it was not the same as it had been the night before. Emma, tentative now, knocked softly before she opened the door. Meg stood in the middle of the room, in her nightgown, which stirred a little in the coolness of the night air, freshened by the afternoon storm. The light of the lamp shone through its folds and revealed the outlines of Meg's body. In a rush of returning confidence Emma caught her in her arms.

Again there was that baffling withdrawal after the first acceptance. Emma protested, "Meg, why do you pull away from me?"

Meg tried to move away from her. "Emma, you're too impetuous. We must not give in to these feelings."

"You did not think that last night. You were as eager as I."

"I was overwrought last night — I could not prevent myself. Oh, Emma, I have been so stretched, so driven to the limit of my power to control myself! Every moment I was abroad you were with me. Even when I slept I dreamt of you, of the sight of your beautiful body, of your laugh, of your dear presence."

"You wanted me, as I have wanted you. You have not admitted this, until last night. Before that you pushed me away."

Meg said desperately, "Emma, I love you beyond anything I ever imagined. You're my heart, my soul, my being. I cannot bear to be away from you. I was beside myself all the while I was abroad."

"Then why are you standing off from me now?"

"Because we should not — We have been very good friends —"

"We are more than that now. You can not put boundaries to what we are to each other now."

As if giving up the struggle that was taking place within her, Meg moved away and got into bed. When Emma joined her, for a moment her body was tense, withheld. But then she yielded and they sank together into a quiet tenderness. When Emma slept, it was to carry with her into her dreams a sense of sadness, of dismay.

Emma was awakened in the morning by the sound of a tap on

the door. Dorcas' voice said through the panel, "Miss Margaret, are you awake? It's gone seven o'clock."

Meg, already awake, replied promptly, "Yes, Dorcas. I'm getting dressed. Don't disturb Dr. Emma. She needs a little more sleep."

"Yes, ma'am," said Dorcas.

*   *   *

Emma, in the next few days, felt caught in this odd mood of Meg's. Their oneness seemed so complete that Meg's sudden, momentary withdrawals, so subtle, so unexpected, were more shattering than if their closeness had been flawed. Emma was conscious of bewilderment. She realized that she knew very little about Meg. It was obvious that Meg was no novice in the art of love. Meg knew how to cajole, entice, command. Yet who would have supposed her mistress of so much experience? With whom had Meg learned to please and demand pleasure from a beloved? The Meg of beneath the surface, the Meg of infinite resource — what *was* the explanation?

Emma knew she could not ask. Something about Meg's manner told her that Meg would not tolerate questioning. And this in itself added to Emma's bewilderment. Meg, alone with her, had acquired an air of absolute authority that astounded her. She was used to the Meg who was the Miss Bell of various women's organizations, the Miss Bell who wielded a certain power in her circle of Baltimore society. But that was a Meg who softened her demands with diffidence, who could never be thought commanding. This was a Meg who made it plain to Emma that she was in control.

As the days went by their dealings with each other ebbed and flowed in a closed pattern. To Emma it seemed that they lived in a sealed glass sphere, visible to others as they had always appeared but inside it, to each other, different. They were no longer outside each other's consciousness to any degree. They were alive to each other's states of mind, even during the portions of the day when they were not together. August was still not at an end and many of Meg's friends and relatives had not yet returned, nor had most of Emma's private patients. They saw, therefore, more of each other during the daylight hours than usual.

This was both a boon and a vexation. When they were together, the conflict between them, even when unvoiced, lent a sharpness to their manner that disturbed their ease. Yet separation, even for a short while, seemed intolerable, as if it postponed a solution. This was not the same as her experience with Alison, thought Emma. Here there was no fading of the intensity of communication between them. In fact, the conflict seemed to increase their sensitivity to each other, so that each would wince at the slightest sharpness. Sometimes Meg seemed to yield altogether, to grow softer, as if wearied by her own intransigeance and ready to cede. On these occasions they spent the night together. But on the morning after she seemed for a while more obdurate.

Emma, made nervous by the strain, saw that Dorcas was aware of the tension between them. As always she was watchful of Meg and noticed her unusual impatience, her occasional irascibility. Emma was certain that she had learned that sometimes they spent the night together in Meg's room. She wondered if Meg realized this.

They sat together of an evening before dinner, as they always had. One evening Meg asked, "Emma, have you heard anything more about Clara Minton's death?"

"No. Why should I? The case is closed."

"As a matter of law, yes. But there are family problems that remain." After a moment's pause, she asked, "Emma, did she say anything to you that would indicate who the man was?"

"No. If she had, I could not repeat what she told me in confidence. Have you heard any gossip?"

"Martha McHugh was here today. She is just back from California. She was not able to get back in time for Clara's funeral. But she is greatly distressed. She was very fond of Clara and she is appalled at Frederick Minton's behavior, at the way he has exposed his wife's reputation to publc scandal. I'm afraid Clara's family will suffer from this disgrace for some time."

"Did she say anything about the man who might be suspected?"

"She reported to me that she had heard James West's name linked with Clara's. But I pointed out to her that was some time ago — that I did not think this rumor was of recent origin." Meg hesitated and then added, "There have been other occasions when James has been suspected of having affairs with married women. But not recently, Emma, not recently."

"It is no concern of mine, Meg, what James does. But what about your sister? How is she taking all this?"

"I have not yet seen Susanna. She is still down on the Shore. She would not refer to such things in a letter. But if any blame is to be apportioned, it will not be James she will hold responsible. She has always closed her ears to anything unfavorable about James."

"But what about Mrs. McHugh? Who does she think is to blame?"

"She reproaches herself because she was not here. She says that if she had been here, Clara would have come to her for help and she could have found some means of preventing her from doing herself harm."

"Perhaps."

"She knows, Emma, that you could not have done other than you did. But she thinks that between the two of you, you could have saved Clara."

"I have told you. I know *I* could have saved Clara."

"No, no, Emma. Please don't reproach yourself that way."

*   *   *

For a while her natural optimism bore Emma up. In due course, she told herself, Meg must come to see that nothing that took place between them could be wrong or evil. But as the days passed Meg's resistance to her seemed to grow stronger. Each time, of a night, when Emma in her nightgown and robe waited impatiently in the dimly lit upper hall until all signs of Dorcas' presence had vanished, she thought hopefully that Meg would be different. Standing for a moment at Meg's door looking down the stairwell into the dark, silent house, she remembered with grief the joy that had abounded in her heart the night of Meg's return. Yet each time she opened Meg's door softly and saw Meg in bed, propped up against the pillow with a book in her hand, she knew her optimism was unfounded, that the response she sought in Meg was becoming less and less likely.

How can you torture me like this, she cried silently as the yearning for Meg swept through her. Only to touch Meg sent a fire through her body. Only to dream of her at night made her wake to an agony of desire. I cannot stand it, she told herself. And yet each day she withstood it, drowning her feeling in the unending demands of her work.

Meg did not reject her outright. She would put her book aside and welcome her with a kiss. From then on it was the reluctance in her manner that gradually wore away Emma's enthusiasm.

Sometimes Emma could not refrain from upbraiding her.

"Emma, I cannot deny you," Meg pleaded. "I cannot. But please spare me."

"Spare you what? Do you spare me? Have you no thought, Meg, of what you do to me? The night you came home you gave me a few hours of ecstasy, of the joy of knowing that you were mine, that we are one, and now you propose to snatch it all away. I will not accept it! I will not!"

The note in her voice reached Meg deeply. But Meg could only bury her face in Emma's shoulder and weep.

Sometimes, when fatigue after an especially tiring day combined with a welling up of the resentment buried in her heart, Emma did not make the effort to go to Meg's room. The third or fourth time this happened she was astonished the next morning to find Meg looking pale and sleepless, seated at the breakfast table. Her irascibility and Dorcas' anxious glances filled Emma with a sense of guilt. I must not do that, she thought. Evidently Meg wanted her with her, if only to sleep quietly at her side. Thereafter she resigned herself to this passive role. Whatever Meg wanted of her she must supply.

A night came, however, when, returning late from an emergency call after dinner, Emma undressed and in a mood of sudden impatience, got into bed. Lying in the dark, waiting for the solace of sleep that did not come, she justified herself with the thought that after all she should not rouse an already drowsy Meg at this time of night. The sound of the door opening brought her upright in bed. Against the dim radiance from the hall showing through the crack of the door she saw Meg.

Meg's voice was almost a whisper. "Emma, are you awake?"

"Yes." She felt Meg's weight on the side of the bed and lifted the sheet for her to creep under.

"I could not sleep for wanting you." Meg's hands reached for her. With a half-sob Meg sought the comfort of her body. Emma, with a fleeting moment of amazement, took her in her arms. There was no withdrawal, no restraint in Meg's lovemaking this time.

The next morning, as Emma sat at the breakfast table, she was surprised to see Meg come into the dining room. Obviously she had not gone to church as usual. They said Good morning and then were silent until Dorcas came in with the basket of hot biscuits and exclaimed, "Why, Miss Margaret!"

Meg cast her an annoyed glance and said, "Bring me some coffee, Dorcas. No, I did not go to church. I have a headache."

Emma thought, She was sleeping quietly when I left her early this morning. But now she certainly looks pale and worried. Emma said aloud, "Perhaps I had better give you a sedative so that you can have another sleep."

Meg, drinking her coffee, replied, "No. I think I need some exercise. I shall go out when you leave."

She waited till Emma had finished her breakfast. Then getting up suddenly, she came around the table and gave Emma a brief kiss. "My darling," she murmured and walked quickly out of the room.

Emma, conscious of Dorcas standing at the sideboard, sat still for a moment, looking after her. She was roused by Dorcas' voice, in which there was a note of exasperation.

"She's all upset."

"But why, Dorcas?"

"Don't you know, Miss Emma? Miss Susanna gets back to town today. Miss Margaret is going to have lunch with her."

*   *   *

She would give a dinner party, Meg said, to welcome her sister back to Baltimore.

"That will be the easiest way," she told Emma, "to get it all over with." Wondering what "it all" was in Meg's mind, Emma murmured something noncommittal.

They were back to their uneasy state of unvoiced conflict. The sudden surprising burst of unrestrained lovemaking that Meg had initiated had not been repeated. The next night she had been even more withdrawn than before, gently but anxiously pushing Emma's hands away. Emma had not gone again to her room and Meg had made no further overture.

Meg was still speaking of the dinner party. "I shall set it for Sunday evening, Emma, and I hope you will be free. Cordelia will be here by then. The Lightfoots are giving a dinner for her and her husband on Wednesday. She is bringing the dresses I had made in Paris, which were not finished when I left. There are several for you."

"For me!"

"Meg smiled briefly. "I took one of your dresses with me, for measurements. You've not even missed it, have you?"

"Dorcas every so often takes some of my things to clean and repair. I never know what is missing."

The next day, arriving home unexpectedly early in the

afternoon, Emma found a dray standing in front of the house and Thomas helping the driver to unload several large trunks and carry them in and up the stairs. Dorcas stood on the steps watching them.

"Miss Margaret's dresses from Paris," she explained, stepping back to let Emma go into the house.

From the drawingroom came a throaty, carrying voice. "Maggie, you look as if you'de been dragged through the bushes backwards. Susanna has been giving you a bad time, hasn't she? Why do you let her upset you so? You're a grown woman. Won't she be pleased to see me back! It's almost worth the boredom of Baltimore to be here so that I can annoy her with my presence."

Meg's soft voice in reply was barely audible and Emma could not hear what she said. Looking at Dorcas Emma saw a malicious grin on the black woman's face. Dorcas, catching her eye, said, "Don't nobody but Miss Cordelia talk to Miss Margaret that way."

"It's Mrs. Drummond?"

"Yes'm. She just got here. I think Miss Margaret would want you to go and meet her."

Emma, entering the room, saw a tall woman, as tall as herself, standing against the brightness of the windows. Meg, sitting in her usual chair, said at once, "Emma, I'm so glad you've come. Cordy, this is Dr. Wycliffe. Emma, Mrs. Drummond."

The tall woman, whose big hat lay with her gloves on the table, came towards her. They exchanged greetings. What a handsome woman, thought Emma, noting the large, dark eyes, the head with its mass of glossy dark-brown hair poised elegantly on the long neck, the deep bosom, the erect back, the restless white hands.

"Ah," said the seductive voice, "so this is Dr. Wycliffe. I am delighted to meet you at last. I have been so intrigued."

Emma, aware of something vital, unpredictable, unmanageable in the woman before her, answered briefly.

"You have made the most remarkable impression on my friends and relatives here in Baltimore, Dr. Wycliffe. Mrs. McHugh thinks you are a gift from heaven. My uncle John Lightfoot thinks you are a menace to the medical profession. The newspapers say you're an angel of mercy sent to succor the ill and needy, Mrs. Harms is certain that you're —"

"Cordy." Meg's voice was sharp and Cordelia stopped in midphrase but shot a knowing smile at Emma. She went on,

"Altogether a most remarkable woman. I see the reason for some of it." With a sort of bold deliberation her alert dark eyes traveled over Emma from head to foot. "Yes, it's readily apparent."

"Cordy, don't be outrageous!"

"Outrageous! Why, Maggie, I'm sure Dr. Wycliffe has been told many times that she is beautiful." Emma, uncomfortable, was aware of the look in Cordelia's eyes, a look that seemed to invite intimacy, that seemed to say that already there was an understanding between them, that naurally there was an alliance between them, as women more knowledgeable, more sophisticated than those amongst whom they found themselves.

Emma turned away from her challenging scrutiny and Meg interposed, so that the conversation flowed on to Paris, to the new gowns, to the Drummonds' trip home, to Cordelia's quick, caustic comments on the welcome they had received from their relatives and friends.

Cordelia ended by saying, "I've not seen Susanna yet."

"You will on Sunday," said Meg.

And shortly after Cordelia took her leave.

During the next few days Emma was often aware of Cordelia's presence, though she did not see her. She was in and out of Meg's house, as if it were her own. The Drummonds were staying at the Belvedere Hotel. Cordelia, said Meg, was disinclined to take up housekeeping in the large, gloomy old house in Monument Street which had been uninhabited for some years. Chiefly Cordelia's visits seemed concerned with the dresses she had brought from Paris, viewing them on Meg, demanding little alterations to make them come up to the standards of elegance she required for herself. Emma, coming into the main part of the house from her consulting room late in the day, was aware of Cordelia's perfume, Parisian and subtly pervasive, floating in the air, even clinging incongruously to Meg herself — the fastidious, austere Meg. She was aware also of the docility with which Meg seemed to accept Cordelia's sway. Cordelia's throaty voice seemed to echo, just below audibility, in the drawingroom, in Meg's upstairs sittingroom, in Meg's bedroom. Even Dorcas gave Cordelia's opinions, Cordelia's preferences the greatest importance.

The dinner for the Harms on Sunday was elaborate and sumptuous. Obviously Meg had planned carefully that it should be so. She had hired extra servants to help Dorcas. Flora was renowned in Baltimore as a cook. Meg had added to her natural gift a wide acquaintance with French cuisine. Miss Bell's dinners, Emma had learned, were an exotic, much-sought-after feature of the Baltimore social season.

Usually on such occasions Meg was calm, decisive, in command of all the preparations herself. Now, superficially, there was nothing to betray her state of mind. But Emma observed the extra sharpness with which she spoke to the servants, the side glances, half-anxious, half-knowing, that Dorcas cast at her. Dorcas took an immense pride in Meg's social preeminence. Oh, yes, Dorcas' manner seemed on such occasions to say, Miss Bell might be retiring, spinsterish, known chiefly for her competence in managing the financial affairs of charitable societies. But she was also one of the most skilful and sophisticated of hostesses, unruffled, indomitable in any emergency. It was plain to Emma that this time Dorcas was troubled.

There was nothing during the first part of the evening, while Meg's drawingroom filled with her guests, that indicated any of the tension that lay beneath the surface. Yet, thought Emma, I certainly feel thunder in the air.

Cordelia sought her out almost at once. She sat so close to Emma that Emma was enveloped in her perfume.

Cordelia's eyes took her in carefully. "Ah, one of the gowns Meg had made for you in Paris. How clever she is in choosing for you! If she could only do as well for herself."

Emma glanced across at Meg. "I think tonight she could not look better. You had something to say there, I'm sure."

Cordelia's eyes flashed. "I always seize an opportunity. Maggie was in Paris only long enough for a first fitting. I saw to it that the dresses she had ordered were properly finished — what I consider properly finished. Maggie simply refuses to spend sufficient time with the couturier."

"She is not really interested in clothes."

"She is merely stubborn. She wants to make herself into an old woman. It is ridiculous. However —" Cordelia paused to glance at Emma. "We had very little chance to talk the other day. Maggie shut me up. But I am most anxious to talk to you. Anyone who can make Maggie drop everything at a moment's notice and take ship across the Atlantic must have an extraordinary attraction."

"Did she?"

"One moment she was talking to me in our hotel and the next

she ran out of the room to pack her trunk. I was never more astonished in my life. Maggie does not act on impulse. Oh, she sometimes wants to! But she long ago was taught harshly to repress her impulses, poor darling.''

"Something must have come up to make her act so.''

"She saw the account in the Baltimore paper of Clara Minton's death and the inquest demanded by Frederick Minton.''

Emma answered stiffly, "I'm sorry to have interrupted Meg's trip. I would not for the world have interfered with her plans.''

"Well, it was taken out of your hands. I can see why Maggie was so alarmed. You are a stranger to Baltimore and our closed society. She was instantly aware of the danger you were in.''

"Of course I am very grateful to her.''

"Oh, Maggie is your champion. You needn't be uneasy. No one can gainsay Maggie — not even Susanna — or my uncle, Dr. Lightfoot, who, I'm sure you know, thinks of you as one of those dreadful women who are undermining the medical profession.''

"Dr. Lightfoot certainly has not welcomed me.''

"Nor will he ever. Dear me, what an example of the closed mind. As for Susanna —''

Emma was uneasy. "I really don't think you should be discussing all this with me.''

"Oh, you need not be shy. Maggie and I understand each other very well. Of course, Susanna will never approve of you. Well, cheer up. She has never approved of me and I've not died of it.''

Emma laughed in spite of herself.

Cordelia went on. "Susanna is used to having a great deal of authority over the lives of those closest to her. She does not like the fact that Maggie has been displaying a will of her own. I'm sure she thought she had disposed of that some time ago. I can tell you a good deal of what has happened to Maggie in the past.''

"Please don't!''

Cordelia laughed. "Well, certainly not here. But, perhaps, for Maggie's sake —''

She broke off to follow Emma's gaze across the room. James stood there, talking to his uncle. His eyes, Emma was aware, had been on them ever since Cordelia had sat down beside her.

Cordelia said, "Ah, yes. James. Susanna perhaps deceives herself that she can control James.''

Emma, in an agony of embarrassment, pleaded, "Mrs. Drummond, could we talk of something else?''

Cordelia looked at her speculatively. "Of course. But you are needlessly alarmed. I see we must find another opportunity to talk."

With practiced ease Cordelia broke up their tete-a-tete and presently Emma found herself listening first to Mrs. McHugh and then to several people who were strangers to her. Across the room she saw James hovering over Cordelia, apparently entirely engrossed with her, and heard Cordelia's laugh above the sound of other voices.

At the dinner table Preston Harms made a heavily jocular comment on the number of French dishes served. Quite a change, he said, from the terrapin soup, the crabs, the spoonbread, the wild duck they had been enjoying down on the Eastern Shore. There was a mild but unmistakable tone of criticism in his voice.

As an ordinary thing, Emma knew, Meg would have ignored his remarks. Now she replied, the sharpness in her voice causing her words to ring clearly down the table, "I don't deny, Preston, that Maryland has provided some remarkable dishes for the gastronome. But much of our native cookery I find barbaric."

There was a sudden silence. Emma, glancing at Susanna, saw her turn to look at Meg. Glancing away again quickly she met Cordelia's eyes, full of laughter.

*   *   *

The next afternoon, when Emma arrived at the house in the midst of another thunderstorm, she saw Susanna's carriage at the door and the coachman, sheathed in a glistening raincape, soothing the horses and fastening down the horse blankets he had spread over them. Mrs. Harms did not use the motorcar for social visits in town.

Emma turned up the walk to the door of her consulting room, anxious to avoid Meg's sister. When the rain cleared, several patients arrived and it was dinner time before she left her quarters to join Meg. Meg was taciturn and preoccupied and they sat chiefly in silence, sipping their wine.

Presently Meg said, "Susanna was here today. She is not very well pleased. She does not like the fact that Cordelia has come back to Baltimore. She thinks it extraordinary that Martha McHugh is still such a staunch friend of yours, after the scandal of Clara Minton's death. She does not like my new gowns. They are quite unbecoming, she says, and she supposes Cordelia had something to do with them. She thinks it highly objectionable that I brought some dresses back for you. I make too much of you. She finds Dorcas too uppity these days and that is my doing also. In fact, nothing about me pleases Susanna just now."

Emma, her first impulse being to laugh at this recital, checked herself at the despairing note in Meg's voice. "Are you still so much swayed by your sister's criticism?"

"I try not to be. But it is hard to go against lifetime habits."

Emma thought, You've fought her all your life, haven't you? She has made you an old woman before you could have any youth and carefreeness. Aloud Emma said, "Perhaps you've never really tried to get out from under her thumb."

Meg did not reply. Emma watched the brooding look on her face. So self-absorbed did she seem that, though they were physically separated from each other by only a few feet, they might as well have been miles apart. I suppose I could get up and go out of the room, thought Emma, and she would scarcely notice. The thought saddened her and she got up and went over to kneel by Meg's chair. She took Meg's fine-boned hands in her own.

"Meg, can't you shake off this mood? For days now you have been depressed and nervous. Is there any real reason for it?"

Meg let her hands lie in Emma's warm, loose grasp. "Yes, yes. I suppose I should shed these feelings. Oh, Emma, ever since I can remember I've had to struggle with these feelings of not being quite what I should be — of always being guilty of something I can't quite define — of never being completely in the right about anything —"

"In fact, being the cause of your mother's death and the disruption of your sister's life. Meg, I'm sure your sister never meant to burden you with a sense of guilt for something over which you had no control, but the result has been the same as if she had. If she cannot change her attitude, you can change yours. You know you cannot undo the past or the actions of others. Don't let her make you unhappy, Meg. If she feels she must punish you, you need not accept the punishment."

"Susanna has another weapon to use against me—something more damaging than my mother's death."

"And what is that?"

"I cannot tell you."

"But what if she does? Why should she want to?"

After a silence Meg said, "She thinks she must save me—no matter how drastic the means."

"Save you? From what?"

"Myself." Suddenly Meg burst out with involuntary energy. "Why won't she let go of me? She doesn't want me. But she won't let go!"

Emma tightened her hold on Meg's hands. "Then you must ignore her. She cannot hold you against your will." She studied Meg's face for a moment. "Meg, do you ever think of me?"

Meg stared at her. "I have every thought of you." She took her hands out of Emma's grasp. "I will not allow her to do it."

"To do what?"   ·

"To drive you away from Baltimore — from me."

"You have said before that that is what she wishes to do."

"She is more determined than ever."

Dorcas interrupted them, summoning them to dinner. Emma, eating with a good appetite, saw that Meg picked at her food in silent abstraction. Emma saw Dorcas watch her with worried eyes, once or twice trying to coax her to eat her dinner. But Meg put her aside with a gesture of her hand.

When they went upstairs together at the end of the evening, they both stood for a few moments in front of Meg's door. Emma, looking down at the silent Meg, felt her heart full of a longing to lift the cloud that had settled over her, to comfort her with the warmth of her own love. But Meg turned away and Emma, rebuffed, walked slowly to her own room. For another moment she lingered, half-hoping that Meg would relent. But presently she heard Meg's door close.

*   *   *

There followed a succession of days that for Emma had an unreal, spirit-deadening quality. Professionally she found herself very busy. The remnants of a typhoid epidemic lingered in the city's alleys and back streets and kept the beds in the free wards of the hospital filled. Her private patients, returning from their summer absence, filled her waiting room. Like Mrs. McHugh, most of the women who had consulted her before, continued to come to her, tacitly indicating that they took her part in the controversy over Clara Minton's death. Mrs. McHugh reported to her that Frederick Minton's disregard for his wife's reputation had acted in his own disfavor. Few people could sympathize with him in his brutal assault on his wife's memory. Only a few, like

Susanna, believed that Clara's own actions had put her beyond
pity and forgiveness.

Yet under the stress of these unavoidable demands Emma felt
the division between Meg and herself. She saw very little of Meg
in the days immediately following. Meg's afternoons and
evenings seemed filled with teas and dinner parties as her friends
and relatives returned to town. When they were together Meg
seemed too absorbed in her own thoughts to notice Emma's
silence. Once or twice Emma, vexed beyond control, made a
sharp remark. Meg glanced at her as if suddenly aware of her
presence and yet not fully aware of her feelings. This gave Emma
a momentary shock. Meg, who had always seemed to have some
special antenna to detect her moods, to guess at her state of mind,
was now remote and insensitive.

But chiefly anger burned in her like a slow fire out of sight. Her
break with Alison had provoked no such feelings as these. With
Alison she had felt ill-used, defrauded. Meg's rejection was far
more devastating. Her inmost self seemed diminished by Meg's
withdrawal. Meg not only rejected her. She seemed to forget her,
to have banished her from thought and feeling. Before this, even
in the moments of their most intense conflict, she had felt the
deeply buried longing in Meg's heart to give in to her, to leap
forward to meet her own ardor. Meg now seemed to have gone far
away, to have left her bereft altogether.

It must be, Emma thought miserably, that she regrets what she
has done for me in the past year, that her sister has convinced her
that she has been unwise, that she wants to undo the situation she
has created. Susanna has made her feel that she has stepped too
far outside her natural sphere. She cannot stand the strain of being
anyone other than the Miss Bell all Baltimore knows.

And Emma stood for a long moment with her nightgown in her
hand, mourning. She was twice as desolate now as she had been
on parting with Alison. For now she had no understanding,
sympathetic Miss Bell to bolster her sense of herself, of the value
of her life and work.

Slowly she put on the nightgown and got into bed. As she lay
down she realized that sleep would not come, in spite of her
fatigue, until she had reached some conclusion about what she
was going to do. It was impossible during the day to find the time
for serious thought. So it must be now. She knew she wanted to
evade the task. If sleep would come, she would postpone it. Yet I
cannot, she thought. If I am to preserve any sort of dignity, I must

decide and act before it gets any more apparent that Meg regrets
my presence here. I must leave Baltimore.

Of course she could stay in Baltimore but move out of Meg's
house. She could find another location for her consulting room.
Her hospital appointment had still several months to run. Perhaps
Meg would want her to continue at the Shelter. Presumably Mrs.
McHugh and the other women who had given her their moral
support would continue to do so — even Meg herself might do so,
on an impersonal footing.

But even as she argued this out with herself she knew she
would not be able to carry out any such plan. Unless she was to
Meg what she had seemed to have become she could not stay in
Baltimore. She could never steel herself to be within sight and
sound of Meg, to live within a few streets of her house, and treat
her and be treated by her as a casual acquaintance. The very idea
was monstrous.

She would have to go away and make another start somewhere
else. Somewhere else meant another city where she could be alone
and anonymous and where her professional life would
undoubtedly be lived in some large institution, with little prospect
for advancement and no real authority. She knew what the scope
in the medical world was for a woman physician. She had seen
women older than herself, dedicated, able women, spending their
lives as assistants to young men who used them as stepping stones
to greater success. Nevertheless, she had no choice. In her first
free moment she must write the necessary letters of inquiry.

Having settled the matter, she should now set it aside and go to
sleep. She needed sleep, to strengthen her for the demands of her
day and also to drown the sorrow, the despair that otherwise
would overwhelm her. Could it indeed be possible that Meg could
be so dominated by her sister that she could abandon the love she
had seemed to feel? Emma's heart cried out against the idea. Yet
the remembrance of Meg's coolness, Meg's remoteness, Meg's
preoccupation with undisclosed thoughts, came back to her. She
must not go on trying to deceive herself —

The ringing of the telephone beside her bed came as a relief, a
deliverance. Her inner debate had made her so restless that she
knew she would never find sleep. She answered the call briefly
and with a sigh of relief reached for her clothes.

*   *   *

The next afternoon, as she crossed the hall on her way from her consulting room, Emma met Cordelia coming out of the drawing room. The sound of voices told her that there were other guests still with Meg. Cordelia's rich contralto voice called out to her, "Ah, my dear doctor, you're certainly elusive! I've seen Maggie every day and not a sign of you. I was beginning to think that I would have to become a patient of yours in order to have another talk with you."

Emma stood still. "Is there something in particular you wanted to say to me?"

"Need there be?" Cordelia walked over to her and putting her hand through Emma's arm, gently urged her towards the window that overlooked the back garden. "You know, everyone tells me you are a very clever young woman. I can quite believe it. I like clever people. There are so few, I'm sorry to say, amongst my nearest and dearest."

Emma said nothing, breathing in the cloud of Cordelia's perfume and bodily presence.

Cordelia went on, speaking almost in her ear. "Is it true that you may desert us? I've heard speculation that you may soon be looking for greener pastures — that our narrow little world here won't be able to hold you much longer. Martha McHugh is in despair."

Emma looked into the dark, inquisitive eyes. "May I ask from whom you heard this?"

"Oh, you don't deny it? Why, I believe Susanna—Mrs. Harms—spoke of the possibility some days ago and since I've heard it mentioned by others. It seems all too reasonable, if lamentable, a possibility. What can possibly hold you here, except Maggie's wishes. Naturally you would not want to repay her kindness with ingratitude."

Emma said boldly, "Why are you saying all this?"

Cordelia was smiling. "Maggie and I are very old friends, you know. And it has occurred to me that perhaps you do not hear everything that is said about you." She stopped and glanced quickly over her shoulder towards the drawing room door. Her ear had caught the sound of movement. "Susanna is here this afternoon. She comes almost every day. Do you know that? And to tell you the truth, it is rather hard on poor old Maggie. She doesn't look very well. Surely you have noticed that."

But before Emma could speak Susanna came out of the drawing

room, followed by Meg and James West. Cordelia dropped her
hold on Emma's arm and they both walked back to the middle of
the hall. Emma stopped at the foot of the stairs and stood with her
hands clasped loosely around the newel post. A subtle change had
come over Cordelia. She spoke banteringly to Meg but her eyes
were on James's face, as if to judge the effect of what she said.
James greeted Emma without a smile. His eyes stayed fixed
somberly on her. Emma saw that Susanna noticed the fact.
Susanna herself gave Emma the barest of nods.

Cordelia said, drawing on the gloves she held in her hand,
"Well, I shall have to have a cab. James, do you suppose you
could find one for me?"

Susanna said in an abrupt voice, "I have my carriage here. I
can take you home, Cordelia. James, will you come with us?"

It was phrased as a question but there was a tone of command
in Susanna's voice. James, at last shifting his gaze from Emma to
Cordelia, said, "If you'd rather have a cab, I'll be happy to get
you one."

"Oh, no! If Susanna insists on being so kind, I shall be glad to
go with her." Cordelia stepped over to Meg and bent over to kiss
her. "Au 'voir, Maggie dear. I shall see you tomorrow, no
doubt."

She waited for Susanna to go first out of the door and then
followed her, talking to James as she went. Dorcas, before she
closed the door, peered after them, watching Cordelia tap James
lightly on the cheek as he handed her into the carriage.

Meg stood mute in the middle of the vestibule. Emma said,
"Mrs. Drummond and James seem on very good terms."

Meg, turning away impatiently, said in vexation, "Cordelia is
an idle, pampered woman. She has brains for more than trifling
with men, if she'd only use them."

Emma, watching her go up the stairs, stood for a moment
longer and then, making up her mind, followed her up to her
bedroom. Meg stopped inside the door, surprised to find Emma
behind her, but waited for her to come in. She gave Emma a look
of anxious inquiry.

Emma said, "I had meant to wait until I had made inquiries and
had my plans in order, but I think I should speak to you now."

The anxiety deepened in Meg's face. It is true, thought Emma.
She does not look well.

"In fact," Emma went on, "we've seen so little of each other lately that I have not had a chance to tell you what is in my mind."

"Yes, yes. I realize it. We have scarcely been alone together. But what is it, Emma? What is it?"

"I've come to the conclusion, Meg, that I must leave Baltimore."

She saw what little color there was in Meg's face drain away. Meg tried to speak but could voice no words.

Emma plunged on. "Apparently my presence here is becoming an embarrassment to you. I cannot allow that to continue."

Meg blurted out. "Cordelia has been talking to you."

"What she had to say only showed me that the time for me to act has already come."

"Emma, there is no reason for you to feel this way. No right-thinking person can hold you to blame over Clara Minton's death. Martha McHugh does not and Clara was her favorite niece. If she does not —"

"This has nothing to do with Clara Minton's death. I should not leave here for that reason."

"Then why, Emma, why?"

"Because my continuing to be here in your house seems to offend your sister. Her disapproval has made you so unhappy it is affecting your health. I have considered leaving your house and staying elsewhere in Baltimore. But that is impossible. I cannot be near you, Meg, and yet be a stranger to you. I must go away entirely and try to rebuild my life without you. I cannot stop halfway."

Meg suddenly sat down, as if she had lost the strength to stand. "Oh, no! Oh, no!" was all she could say.

"From what Cordelia has said, I gather that your sister wishes people to believe that I intend to leave Baltimore."

"Emma, you would not give up your practice?"

"It will be a great waste, won't it? The loss of more than a year of work, of all the money you have invested in me. But I have no choice. Meg, you've put me in limbo. That is not where I want to be."

Meg's hands were shaking and she turned away. After a moment, in better control of her voice, she pleaded, "Emma, don't leave me."

"How can I stay? Your sister has not succeeded in ruining my professional reputation. But she has already succeeded in destroying my happiness in being here with you. She has turned you away from me. With other people she has treated me as a mere hanger-on of yours—someone who has taken advantage of your generosity —''

Meg cried out, "Emma, no! Don't talk like that! I can't stand it. Susanna dislikes you. She dislikes women who take part in any public affairs. Her ideas will never change.''

"But I am right, aren't I? I cannot stay here and be the object of her enmity, the cause of her harassing you. Meg, if you accepted me as you once did, nothing could drive me away. But I cannot stay here as a — a pensioner of yours.''

"Emma, you must not go away! I cannot tell you why I must give in to Susanna. But don't leave me, Emma! I can't bear to lose you.''

"You can't bear to have me and you can't bear to do without me. There is no answer I can give you except to put the choice beyond you. You will learn to do without me. You can be again what you were when I first came here.'' Emma spoke as confidently as she could but the words rang hollow in her own ears.

Meg dropped her head into her hands. After a moment she looked up. Emma was alarmed by the white-lipped distress in her face. "I cannot stop you. But, Emma, you will kill me if you go away.''

She got up shakily from her chair and moved to where Emma stood. She caught hold of Emma's arm to steady herself and leaned her head against Emma's shoulder. "Oh, my darling, I cannot do without you!''

Emma, feeling the soft sobs that began to shake her, put her arms around her. She strove to hold back, calling on her own stifled rage to help her stand aside from Meg's misery. But Meg's body clinging to her own, Meg's shattering grief, reached to her heart and her arms tightened around Meg's shoulders.

She said into Meg's ear, "I've wanted to be everything to you but you will not have it.''

Meg's only answer was to cling to her more fiercely. She began to moan and tremble, and Emma, realizing that she was in the grip of a nervous spasm, said calmly, "Meg, you're overwrought. Come and let me put you to bed.''

Half-carrying her, Emma took her to the bed and placed her on it. She touched the button that would summon Dorcas and began

to unfasten Meg's dress. Meg lay shivering and speechless, her
teeth chattering. She must have a raging headache, thought
Emma, taking off her shoes and stockings.

The door opened and Dorcas looked in and exclaimed, "Oh,
Miss Margaret, honey, are you sick?" Seeing Emma's upraised
hand she stood silent, dismayed. "Bring her a cup of tea,
Dorcas."

By the time Dorcas returned Emma has undressed Meg and put
her between the sheets. Taking the hot tea from Dorcas' hand, she
held the cup for Meg to drink, steadying her head with her other
hand. Dorcas walked softly about the room, picking up Meg's
garments and putting them away. At a gesture from Emma she
closed the curtains to shut out the last of the daylight. Emma sat
down beside the bed. Drawing the covers over Meg she said,
"See if you can sleep. I have given you a sedative. I shall sit here
with you."

Sometime later, when Emma came out of the room, she found
Dorcas hovering about the landing.

"Miss Emma, is Miss Margaret real sick?"

"If you mean, is she ill with some disease, no. She is
nervously upset."

Dorcas said softly, "It's her feelings. Miss Margaret can get
real sick with her feelings."

"Has she had attacks like this before?"

"A long time ago she used to get like this, even when she
wasn't more than a girl."

They stood together silent for a while, each absorbed in her
own thoughts. Then Dorcas said, in an urgent voice, "Miss
Emma, don't you leave Miss Margaret. She needs you. Don't let
Miss Susanna drive you away."

Emma astonished, stared at the fierce black eyes. "Well, no,
Dorcas, I won't leave her—at least, not till she is well." As
Dorcas moved to go downstairs, she added, "She must not have
any visitors for a while—especially not Mrs. Harms."

"Yes, *ma'am*," said Dorcas, going down the stairs.

Emma stood for a while longer, irresolute, and then went back
into Meg's room. A nightlight glowed out of Meg's range of
vision. She sat down in Meg's armchair. She realized now that,
though she had tried to qualify it, she had told Dorcas the simple
truth: she could not leave Meg. In facing the fact she had a sudden
longing to be away, away from the constant rasping of this too-

intimate yet distant awareness of Meg. The strain was coloring her thoughts, distorting her judgment. In time it might affect her work. No financial loss, no professional setback, would weigh in the balance against freedom from this emotional harassment.

And at once her feeling changed. She recoiled suddenly from the thought of being away from Meg, of not being daily in her presence, of being out of earshot of Meg's voice, forever banished from Meg's friendship. This hanging in between was an exquisite sort of torture, but it was a torture she could not escape from by leaving Meg.

*   *   *

Meg did not get up the next morning nor for several mornings thereafter. Even when she did leave her bed she clung to the privacy of her room. She is afraid of Susanna, thought Emma. Dorcas, by one artifice or another, succeeded in keeping Susanna away. Meg, pale and miserable, kept to her room as to a refuge, the one spot where she could be safe.

But Dorcas' wiles were not sufficient to keep Cordelia out. One afternoon when Emma opened the door to Meg's room, she heard Cordelia's voice.

"Of course, Susanna despises Washington. But I think I should find it amusing for a while — Why, how nice to see you, Dr. Emma! Don't you think Maggie should get out for some fresh air?"

Meg had retreated to her bed and lay there under a coverlet. Emma walked over to her and touched her forehead lightly with her fingertips. "Is your headache worse, Meg?"

Meg's lips barely moved in reply. Emma said, "Try and sleep again." She took Cordelia's arm. "She must have absolute quiet for a while longer."

"Ah, you are showing me out! All right, Maggie, I'll come and see you tomorrow. There is nothing like having one's own physician-in-residence, is there?"

Her tone was goodnatured and she made no protest at leaving the room with Emma. Out in the hall she asked, "It is just a nervous headache, isn't it — a migraine?"

"Yes."

"She used to have them quite often years ago. I thought she had outgrown them."

"Then this is unusual now?"

"I think so. Unfortunately, it has been quite a number of years since I have seen anything of Maggie except for brief visits when she has come abroad. And there, of course, she was away from Susanna."

"You think Mrs. Harms is the cause of her distress? Why should that be?"

Cordelia looked at her from under the massed feathers on her hat. "It will take quite a while to explain." She put her hand on Emma's arm and looked towards the door of Meg's study. "Let's go in there." She walked quickly across the hall and opening the door went in. Emma, following her, sat down and waited for her to speak.

Cordelia put her purse and gloves down on Meg's desk and walked about the room, examining the books on the shelves. "Poor old Maggie. She at last has a place of her own for her toys." Cordelia turned around to face Emma. "She would never have brought herself to make this change if it had not been for you."

"I know that Mrs. Harms upbraided her for making over her father's office for my consulting room."

"I always thought it a mistake for her to continue to use that gloomy old room as her study. She must constantly have been reminded of her childhood and her grandfather and her father and Susanna—she could not get away from any of them there."

"Her grandfather — I've been told it was he who taught her Greek and Latin."

"Yes. He was a sweet old man and very fond of Maggie. But the only thing he knew anything about was Greek and Latin."

"Well, he seems to have given her a gift she has valued all her life."

Cordelia's hat feathers nodded as she agreed. "Oh, yes. But in some ways it was the wrong sort of gift for her. Too unsocial, you know. She really has always needed to be brought out of herself. However, the Greek and Latin have been a useful refuge from Susanna. I'm sure even now Susanna doesn't know what Maggie learned out of those books, from those old authors. I've often been astonished myself."

"Then she has always needed a refuge from Susanna."

Cordelia sat down in Meg's chair. "I remember when we were children together at school, whenever Maggie came back from spending a holiday with Susanna she was so nervous and miserable that she would stutter and burst into tears at the least thing. Fortunately, Susanna found it more convenient to let her come and spend most of her holidays with me. Susanna was newly married then and she was enjoying her release from being her father's housekeeper and Maggie's governess.''

"Was he hard to deal with?"

"Oh, no. It was simply that Susanna hated being left on the shelf. Mr. Bell did very little socially after his wife died. He preferred the company of his mistress.''

Emma answered Cordelia's inquiring look. "Yes, I've heard about that.''

"In fact, he had more than one — not at the same time, of course. Susanna knew nothing about them at the time.''

"But Mrs. Harms was devoted to her sister.''

Cordelia's dark eyes glanced quickly at Emma. "No one has ever doubted Susanna's devotion to duty. Oh, she loves Maggie and always has. But there is something about Susanna's interest in you that is very unnerving. She never doubts the rightness of her own view of anything. There is no softness in Susanna. She despises softness. And poor little Maggie was all softness sometimes. My dear doctor, I understand you have been in Vienna. You must be acquainted with the ideas of that very clever doctor — Freud, is it? — and his disciples. They accuse us all of having such wicked feelings underneath our best behavior.''

"I don't agree with all of Dr. Freud's opinions. But he is right in saying that we must look beneath the surface for our real motives, in many cases.''

"You think then that Susanna wasn't as self-sacrificing as she seemed. Or at least that her motives were not purely self-denying. But why would she want to make poor little Maggie unhappy?''

"I don't think she consciously wanted to do that. I would say that she did not. I suppose she did not — does not — realize how she affects Meg.''

"You mean you don't think she really wishes to punish Maggie for having been born!''

Emma smiled. "You can put it that way.''

"Dear me. What depths you suggest! Do we all act so?''

"I'm not a specialist in such things, but to some extent I suspect we do.''

Cordelia, enjoying herself, laughed. "Now I like to be candid. But candor is not often well received, at least in my world. Except with Maggie. But then Maggie and I have always been on a special footing. Susanna has never approved of that fact, either. When we were children she always believed that it was I who taught Maggie a lot of wicked things she would otherwise not have known."

"Really? You and Meg are the same age, aren't you?"

"You would hardly think it, would you? As a matter of fact, Maggie is six months younger than I and I'm not yet forty."

"Perhaps it is her temperament."

"What? To act like a grandmother?" Cordelia broke off and studied Emma's face. "I really do believe that I must tell you everything."

Emma waited.

"I remember, when she first came to the school where I was, she was like a little old owl—solemn and dignified and very bookish. At first she was formal and polite with me and everyone else. The other girls used to make fun of her. I am afraid I joined them in the beginning. But there was something about Maggie even then. I made her mad one day, teasing her beyond endurance, and we had an awful fight. I hadn't realized that Maggie had such a temper. But after that we were the best of friends. Nobody made fun of Maggie to me after that. She became, to me, somebody different, the first human being I had come across who was particularly mine and who saw me the same way. We seemed to grow together, in an astonishingly quick space of time. At least, it seems to me now, looking back, that it was astonishing and yet to children time has no real meaning. One day Maggie and I were new-met strangers and the next we had become so close as to be one. If I had stopped to think about it, I could not have imagined what it was like not to have had Maggie."

Cordelia stopped and gazed at Emma. "Surely, doctor, you know what little eleven-year-old girls do together when they are left to themselves and have no one else to satisfy their curiosity but each other?"

Emma smiled. "I have a fair idea."

Cordelia laughed out. "I find you most refreshing! Well, Maggie and I learned all about each other. We explored every inch of each other's body. We learned from each other the answers to a lot of things nobody else was willing to tell us. We understood instinctively what the other thought and felt. We could communicate with each other without words when we needed to disguise feelings and intentions. The amazing thing is that nobody suspected anything. I suppose our elders, the people in charge of us, were rather naive and after all we were almost related and it seemed natural that we should choose each other for bosóm companions. I was a tomboy and Maggie was the demurest little thing you could imagine. I was always accused of being the initiator of any mischief we were caught at. Maggie was supposed to be my enslaved disciple. It was nothing of the sort. Maggie was the one with the brilliant and bold ideas. I was the one who imagined the means to put them into effect. We used to laugh together in secret over what we could get grownup people to believe."

Cordelia became pensive. Emma had not seen her in such a mood and watched her with interest. When her silence lengthened Emma said encouragingly, "Young girls often have these attachments."

Roused, Cordelia said, "Oh yes, I know that. A common stage of female growing up, isn't it? But it was something more in our case. That was our undoing. We had an importance for each other — I wonder if I can convey to you what it was. As we grew older our feeling for each other seemed to grow too. It ceased to be just a childish alliance against the adults around us. We were a unit, body and soul. It made us women long before the other girls were beyond childishness. We lived together in the fullest sense of the word. I've known nothing so satisfying since. When I came to marry I wasn't an ignorant, immature maiden. I had had Maggie for years."

"Years?"

"Yes, years—until we were seventeen. Maggie nearly always came home with me in the holidays. Susanna did not want her underfoot and since I had a mother and Maggie had only a father who couldn't cope with young children, it was natural enough." Again Cordelia was thoughtful for a while. "Part of the explanation was, I think, Maggie herself. Maggie must have been born with the mind of a grown person. Who was it in ancient Greece who sprang full grown from her father's head?"

"Athena, the goddess of wisdom."

"Well, Maggie was always ahead of me in intellectual things. When she first came to school she was a phenomenon. It was her grandfather's fault. She was his only companion and I believe the old man forgot very often that she was only a little girl and not a scholarly contemporary of his own. So she had very sedate ways even then. I was the one who discovered what Maggie was underneath. Nobody knew the Maggie I did—that passionate little thing who could make me forget everything—time, place, people—when we were together."

"What happened to bring an end to this?"

"Susanna began to suspect us, when we were almost old enough to leave school. I don't know why. We were old hands by then at disguising ourselves. Perhaps we got careless and it showed more than we realized. It may simply have been that after the first few years of her marriage Susanna began to give more thought to Maggie, especially since she was getting to be of marriageable age. Susanna did not like me. I was Maggie's only real friend of her own age and Susanna thought I put ideas in Maggie's head. She thought Maggie was very inpressionable and easily led. Susanna has never understood Maggie. And then there was the row over her father's quadroon mistress."

"I have heard something of that."

"Not from Maggie, I'm sure."

"No, Dorcas."

"Ah, yes, Dorcas. Maggie had known about the woman for some time, ever since she was fourteen. But she said nothing about it until Mr. Bell died and there was the scandal about his leaving some property to the woman, which she claimed. Maggie should never have let on that she knew but she did, in a moment of weakness, no doubt, when Susanna had upset her. I have no idea why it came as such a surprise to Susanna that her father kept a mistress, a woman of color. Anyone might have guessed it. Susanna was enraged when she did learn about it and doubly enraged when she found out that Maggie knew about it all along — seventeen year old, innocent Maggie. She accused Maggie of being deceitful, underhanded, evil-minded. Then she accused me of having corrupted Maggie, of teaching Maggie vicious habits. It seemed to be the only explanation that occurred to her for Maggie's precocious knowledge of sex. I've no doubt Maggie babbled out a lot of things she should never have mentioned, about us — enough to confirm Susanna's wildest suspicions. That has always been the effect Susanna has had on Maggie."

Emma, watching the sober expression on Cordelia's handsome face, waited silently.

"It would have been bad enough if Susanna had simply said all she had to say to Maggie and me, but she went to my mother and there were all sorts of scenes. My poor mamma always thought I was perfection itself. She would never believe I would do anything bad. She rejected all of Susanna's accusations. It made me just defiant. I was sorry my mother was upset. I hated Susanna then with all my heart. It wrecked Maggie's life. She has never really got over it. We weren't allowed to see each other after that — that much Susanna got out of my mother. I was sent to a French boarding school and Maggie had to stay home with Susanna. After a year or so Susanna let her go to the Women's College here. I hooted when I saw the College's statement of purpose. Susanna might have written it. Going to the theater or the opera wasn't allowed and neither was dancing or playing cards or seeing young men. Poor Maggie.''

"Did you keep in touch?"

"Oh, yes. We weren't supposed to write to each other—we were supposed to be dead to each other—but we did. I sent my letters to Dorcas' sister and Dorcas gave them to Maggie and mailed her letters to me. We never felt a real estrangement. But when we finally met again, after Maggie was of age and she had more freedom, I had a real shock. My Maggie was gone. I was ready to take up where we left off—at least, until I got married, which everybody expected me to do. But one glance told me that Maggie had been shattered. I've very seldom seen Maggie cry but she burst into tears in my arms and told me we could never be to each other what we had been. I saw then that I would never have Maggie back. My mamma died soon after that and after a few years of amusing myself—the way one does at that age—I married John Drummond, not because I was in love with him—I've never been in love with anybody but Maggie—but because he was safe and reliable and doted on me. I knew he would take me abroad and that was what I wanted, ever since I came back from the French boarding school and found what had happened to Maggie. And Maggie became Miss Bell of Baltimore, whom everybody holds in some awe.''

"You are worried about Maggie now."

Cordelia thought for a moment. "I don't think I am worried about her. Maggie is very self-sufficient. Nobody can really rule her, you know. She must always do what she thinks fit. That is what Susanna has never learned. That is the source of the conflict between them. So Maggie gets migraine headaches.''

"Then if you are not worried about her —?"

"Why have I told you all this? Well, I thought Maggie had finally learned not to let Susanna upset her." Cordelia got up and picked up her purse and gloves. She cast another glance at Emma. There was the usual vivacity in her eyes. "In fact, I know she had. She has been very secure for the last few years. I wonder, doctor, whether it is you who have upset the apple cart."

"I?" Emma had also got up.

Cordelia suddenly touched her fingertips to Emma's cheek, a soft, lingering caress. "You're a great beauty, my dear. And charming and intelligent and Maggie can't bear to part with you. Do you suppose Susanna could approve that?"

Emma laughed uncertainly. "Really, Mrs. Drummond —"

"Cordelia, if you please. Let me tell you, Susanna cast a spell on Maggie. For years she has lived in a shell, asleep to her real feelings—until you came along and breathed on Sleeping Beauty and awakened her." Cordelia smiled at Emma's consternation. "Well, I shall be back to see Maggie tomorrow."

*   *   *

The shortening days brought early dark and the lamps were lit when Emma came into the main part of the house and climbed the stairs to Meg's room. When she opened the door she saw Meg in her dressing gown standing by the window.

"You are feeling better, Meg?"

Meg had turned at the sound of the door. As she walked into the glow of the lamp Emma saw that she was pale and her bright eyes were dark-shadowed. On impulse Emma started towards her and then checked herself. It was a new experience, this self-check. I've never felt like this before Meg, she thought. Not even when I first knew her and we were strangers to each other.

Meg had noticed it. She took another step towards Emma. Emma, somehow ashamed, went over to stand beside her. Meg reached up and took hold of her shoulder.

"Emma." Emma felt the nervous tension in her fingers. "Yes. My headache is much less and I am not nauseated."

"Good. I shall tell Dorcas to bring you some food."

She had made no move to go but Meg, as if alarmed, gripped her tighter. "I shall ring for her, Emma. Stay here with me."

"Yes, of course."

Meg let go of her and walked across the room to ring the bell.

Turning back she said anxiously, "Emma, what we were talking about before I — about your leaving Baltimore —"

Emma cut her short. "I don't think we should discuss that now. When you are more recovered —"

"No! I cannot go on worrying about it — living in fear of it. Emma, you must not go away. You cannot leave me. I should have nothing then."

She had come back to Emma and now put her arms around her neck. The warmth of her body in the loose robe, the slight tremble as she clung to Emma overcame Emma's reserve. She took Meg in her arms and held her close. "Hush, Meg. Don't distress yourself so. Yes, yes, I will stay."

Meg raised her head to look up at her. "You are not going away? You promise me that?"

"Yes. I will stay as long as you want me." She thrust her fingers into Meg's soft hair, pressing Meg's head against her. "Let us. forget what we have said before about my going away."

After that Meg seemed to pull herself together. The next day she dressed and left her room. When Cordelia came to visit she was in her sitting room. In the evening, when Emma came into the house from her consulting room, she found them there. Meg was still pale and taciturn but she smiled occasionally at Cordelia's flow of talk. Her eyes stayed on Emma.

They seemed then to return to their old companionship. The interweaving of their lives was complete. Everything of their everyday lives they spoke of, discussed, agreed upon. What lay beneath they did not touch upon. Whenever they were alone together they caressed each other lightly, a mere touch of Meg's narrow hand in Emma's shapely large one, of Emma's lips on Meg's soft mouth. But as if they were both frightened now of the consequences of a greater contact, they drew away at once after such an exchange, Emma with a sense of frustration, Meg as if under compulsion. The wall between them was at once like gossamer and like iron.

In the weeks that followed, Emma, most of her day absorbed in professional activities, came in and out of the house aware in only a general way of the fact that both Susanna and Cordelia were daily visitors. Meg never spoke of Susanna and Emma believed that Meg's sister chose moments for her calls when it was unlikely that Emma would be present. But she did not escape Cordelia. They were often there together with Meg, neither ready to abandon the intent to be dominant. It was Susanna who always left first. Cordelia always lingered. On these occasions, when Emma came in to the house to find Susanna newly gone, the atmosphere of the drawing room made her think of a battlefield strewn with invisible wreckage. Cordelia then was more than usually brilliant, talkative, vivacious. She would seize Emma in her arms and kiss her vigorously, uninhibitedly. Meg wore an air of weary determination, silent, watching Cordelia's ebullience with brooding eyes.

Once, when Emma came home unexpectedly, she found Meg's sister about to leave. She stood hatted and gloved in the vestibule, suppressed anger apparent in her gestures, her voice. She scarcely acknowledged Emma's greeting and continued what she was saying to Meg.

"It seems to me that Cordelia must surely have more to occupy her than coming to idle away her time in your house. It would be far more appropriate if she were to open her own and not force her poor husband to live in a hotel."

Meg said mildly, "I think John likes the Belvedere."

"For a temporary stay, no doubt. But for months —"

"You forget, they may be going to Washington. It would be foolish for them to open the house when they may be leaving Baltimore again so soon."

"You always have excuses for her." Susanna's anger rose to the surface.

A faint color showed in Meg's face and she answered sharply, "Cordelia is welcome in my house whenever she chooses to come."

When Susanna had left and Meg had gone back to the drawing room, where Cordelia could be heard humming a popular song, Emma became aware that Dorcas was still standing by the door she had just closed. A sly smile was on her face and amusement in her eyes.

Dorcas said, "Miss Susanna don't like being answered back."

"They disagree over Mrs. Drummond?"

Dorcas ignored the question. "But Miss Margaret ain't going to back down this time. It's all Miss Cordelia's doing. That's what makes Miss Susanna mad."

The tug-of-war — it must be a tug-of-war, thought Emma, — exhilerated Cordelia, though Meg merely grew even less talkative. Emma had no doubt that, alone together, they spoke without disguise, of Susanna, of themselves. With herself they were both uncommunicative. Cordelia had never spoken again to her of the past.

Then for a while Cordelia was away from Baltimore. Her husband, said Meg, although he was not a politician, was being considered for a post in the new Federal administration. He was a great friend of Mr. Taft's.

"He likes John. They are the same sort of men. I'm afraid Mr. Taft doesn't quite understand politics nor the resistance he will get from members of his own party, since John is a nominal Democrat. So I don't think matters will get very far and perhaps Cordelia does not want them to. But in the meantime she is in Washington and is being greatly amused by what she observes."

* * *

With Cordelia away, Susanna's visits obviously were longer, and when Emma joined Meg of an evening, she had an air of fatigue, of anxiety. One evening she said abruptly, almost before Emma had sat down, "Emma, have you ever discussed with James your views about family limitation or the need to change the laws on spreading such information?"

"Why, no. Why on earth should I?"

"Susanna tells me that you are rumored to have prescribed contraceptive devices for some of the women you treat at the Shelter. I thought perhaps it was from James that she would hear of such a thing."

A mixture of alarm and anger took possession of Emma. "That is a very serious accusation to make."

"She does not accuse you of doing so. She merely says someone has spoken of it."

"She does not say who?"

"Oh, no. She would not speak as frankly as that. I told her there is certainly no truth in the rumor, how foolish it would be of you to do such a thing. I believe there had been mention in the newspaper of another woman doctor who has got into trouble over something of the sort —"

"A doctor who prescribed a pessary for a poor woman who was tubercular and for whom another pregnancy might well be fatal. Yes, I know of that. But no matter how I long to take some action to prevent such things, I would never endanger the Shelter and your interests, Meg. I would risk myself but not you."

"It is a wretched business, Emma. But, Emma, the worry is, who is spreading such tales about you?"

"Obviously someone who dislikes me. Is that why you thought of James?"

"I thought perhaps in the past, when you felt more confidence in him than you do now, you might have expressed your views. I know it is something about which you feel very strongly and that might make you indiscreet with someone you like well."

Emma was forced to smile. "You mean, in a soft moment with James I might have talked too much. Oh, no. I never felt like that about James. And really I would not accuse him of such underhanded dealing. There is another possibility —"

When she failed to go on, Meg urged her. "What is it?"

Emma said carefully, "It is not a nice thing to say of your sister."

Meg looked at her silently for a long moment. "I see. You think it may be Susanna herself who is spreading these rumors —"

Emma interrupted, "Perhaps not spreading them. Perhaps only making you think that they are being spread, to frighten you, to make you less willing to back me."

Meg got up suddenly from her chair and walked away from her. Emma sat quietly, wondering what was taking place in her mind. After a while Meg returned and sat down again without speaking. Her face in the lamplight was splotched red and white. Why, I have never seen her in a rage before, thought Emma.

In the days that followed Emma noticed a decided change in Meg's manner. She was still preoccupied and thoughtful but she was more decided in her way of talking and acting. Dorcas watched her with obvious approval. It was only a week later that Dorcas told her that Susanna had not been to visit for several days.

*   *   *

Cordelia came energetically into the room with a loud rustle of skirts, talking as she came. "Well, certainly that was an experience." She gave her wrap to Dorcas and kissed Meg.

"Washington?"

"Yes. I know Susanna despises Washington and I must say you find some very funny people in Congress and their wives are even odder. And the civilized people all seem to be from the North.

But I found it highly amusing—for a short stay."

"At least a change."

"I don't know that I'd want to change for long, even Baltimore. But I mustn't complain of our old Baltimore. It is simply not Paris or London or even New York. Do pity me, Maggie. I do get tired of listening to our aunts and uncles and cousins who have thought of nothing new since the Civil War. You're the only one I can really talk to. In any case, we're here till the New Year. Gracious! Christmas is almost here."

"But if John doesn't go to Washington?"

"Oh, I shall escape somehow. Where is Emma? Is she ever visible? It seems to me that I hear of nothing but Dr. Wycliffe, the extraordinary Dr. Wycliffe. She cannot be the only medical woman in Baltimore."

"There are very few in private practice. It is a difficult thing for a woman. And besides Emma has accepted a good many public responsibilities. She has great tenacity where it comes to getting money out of politicians for things that must be done."

"Oh, yes, she is everywhere. And she succeeds chiefly because of you, Maggie."

"I did not give her her intelligence and her skill."

"But you give her your financial and moral support. The redoubtable Miss Bell, of whom practically everybody in Baltimore is a little afraid, who is a member of the boards of the Female House of Refuge, the Almshouse and the Visitors of the City Jail."

Meg laughed. "Cordy, where did you get all that?"

"Oh, anyone can tell you. I suppose, Maggie, if I had your passion for good works I should not be such a grasshopper. But I cannot find it in me."

"But why not, Cordy? It would be better than getting into mischief through idleness."

Cordelia's dark eyes sparkled. "You mean James. Somebody has been carrying tales to you about James. Well, he is paying me some attention."

Meg nodded.

"And you are wondering why I bother with James again. It's vanity, of course, Maggie. It intrigues me that now that I am five or six years older than when I had my first affair with him, I can still have him at my beck and call."

"Only as long as it amuses him, Cordy. You are still one of the handsomest women in Baltimore. That appeals to James. Only the best will do for his pleasure."

"Maggie, you can sometimes say some very wicked things."

"You know it is so, Cordy."

"And then there's Emma."

"Emma?"

"Don't be alarmed. She has no time for him. But he hasn't got over Emma."

"Does he complain to you about her?"

"Complain? Well, not exactly. I tease him about her. It puts him out so. As you say, he collects us, doesn't he, as if we were fine mares."

Meg spoke sharply, "Cordy, there are more worthy occupations than being a man's amusement."

Cordelia laughed. "Oh, there is no doubt of that! But you see, he is my amusement right now also. Of course, one must be careful that he does not leave one to pay the penalty — like Clara Minton."

"Was he responsible for that?"

"I really don't think so. It is a pity she did not consult Emma sooner. She could have learned to prevent herself from getting pregnant."

"Cordy!" This time there was real alarm in Meg's voice.

"Of course, it is easy enough in France to learn what is necessary, even in the boarding school I went to. Don't look so shocked, Maggie. Don't you remember how we used to wonder what Susanna did to avoid children?"

"I'm not shocked about that. It is your remark about Emma. Emma cannot give advice like that without risk. Please don't make remarks like that indiscreetly. Don't you know that there are several well-meaning, honorable doctors who have been sent to prison for doing such a thing?"

Cordelia said drily, "Of course I know that. But nevertheless doctors do tell their patients what can be done — the better class anyway. It is the poor devils with ten children and no food in the house who have to be kept in ignorance. I am sure Emma has told you that. And I am sure she does what she does discreetly. In fact, she has taught me a very much safer way than the one I was using. You know, I would be lost if I ever got pregnant. Everybody knows John is incapable. My, what hypocrites we all are!"

"You have consulted her?"

"Why, of course. Everyone else I know has, why shouldn't I? Oh, there, now, Maggie, don't look so worried. I'm sure Emma is very careful. She must be, mustn't she, because of you."

"Cordy, have you said anything about this to anyone else?"

"Anyone else? Who on earth should I say it to, except you? Why are you so anxious, Maggie?"

"Susanna has spoken of rumors about Emma."

"Susanna!" In spite of the frown on Meg's face, Cordelia burst out into a deep laugh. "Maggie, you can't possibly think I'd talk about anything like that to Susanna!"

"No, Cordy, no. But to someone who might have said something to her?"

Cordelia's laughter was gone. "Maggie, I've said that I would not speak of such a thing to anyone but you. I'm not really shameless. And I value Emma much too highly to think of saying anything about her. One of these days Emma's convictions may carry her beyond discretion but —"

"Emma has promised me that she will work quietly for the revision of the laws on contraception, that she will not try to overturn things by defiance."

"And if she has said so, so she will. But Susanna —"

Cordelia stopped and watched Meg's face. Meg sat silent, her lip caught in her teeth.

Cordelia said, "You've had a row with Susanna."

Meg did not answer.

"Well?" Cordelia demanded.

"Yes, but I've begged her pardon."

"But you haven't forgiven her. What did she say to you, Maggie?"

"Cordy, there are no rumors about Emma. Susanna tried to make me think so —"

"Because she wants you to take fright and send Emma away. Maggie, she'll not rest till she can get rid of Emma."

Meg said somberly, "I think she realizes now that she will never succeed."

They both looked up at the sound of the door. Emma stood on the threshold. Cordelia walked towards her with her hands outstretched.

"Emma, how delightful!" She caught Emma in her arms and kissed her.

Emma, trying gently to disengage herself, said, "You're back in Baltimore."

"We came back yesterday. It looks as if we shall spend Christmas in Baltimore. Dear me, these family feasts. I am rather out of practice with them. I suppose, Maggie, we shall be at Susanna's?"

"No. I am having my own Christmas dinner this year. You will come to me?"

Surprise echoed in Cordelia's laugh. "Yes, of course. But what will Susanna think of that?"

"I don't know."

"Forthright Maggie. Well, I can guess."

Cordelia's eyes, inquiring, met Emma's, amused. They talked on, Cordelia satirical, skillfully probing, Emma wary, Meg preoccupied, inattentive. When Cordelia got up to leave she bent down to kiss Meg. Then she caught Emma around the waist and kissed her on the mouth. Emma, too surprised to resist, saw the invitation sparkle in the dark eyes so close to her own.

"You're such a darling," said Cordelia, laughing at her surprise.

Emma saw her exchange a glance with Meg over her own shoulder but she could not tell what it held.

"Tomorrow, Maggie," said Cordelia, and sailed out of the room.

And tomorrow she was again at Meg's, and every day thereafter. Whenever Emma came home she found Cordelia. Cordelia's full-throated, unrestrained laugh reached her ears sometimes before her eyes found Cordelia's voluptuous, vigorous body clad in the most fashionable of Parisian dresses. Frequently she found her in Meg's sittingroom, when she came into the house after her last patient had left. This was cartainly a change, thought Emma, from the muted decorum of Meg's house when she had first come to live there. Meg's friends then had all been long-settled matrons, intent chiefly on the charitable and civic improvements of which Meg was the guiding light. They still came as always — Mrs. McHugh, Mrs. Vickers, and the other women she remembered from her first visit. In fact, Meg seemed to be even busier with such activities.

But besides these decorous teas, disguised committee meetings, there was Cordelia. Cordelia was rarely present then. But when they had left she was there with Meg, commenting, joking. Her good humor was infectious and hearty. Her range of anecdotes frankly scandalous, but at the same time invariably and irresistibly diverting. Emma found herself looking forward to these momentary breaks in her overburdened day. Cordelia made her laugh. Cordelia seemed always to guess her state of mind and to set herself to relieve the tension, the sense of overwhelming responsibility, the memory of the grim realities she faced all day, that Emma often brought with her into the quiet elegance of Meg's house. In Cordelia there was a suppleness, a quickness to understand, a wish to enliven, that drew Emma out of herself, grateful and relieved.

At first Emma did not realize that Cordelia had a way of finding her alone, of waylaying her when Meg was otherwise engaged. At times when Emma returned home and found Meg's drawing-room full of the sound of women's voices, it was Cordelia who appeared in the hall or in Meg's sittingroom, laughingly conspiratorial. Her strong, well-tended hands caressed Emma through the fine soft fabric of her shirtwaist. It was Cordelia who kissed and fondled her, holding her against he own robust body.

She knew she should not tolerate this petting and yet she could not resist it. Cordelia aroused her and Cordelia knew that she did. At first Emma had hesitated, anxious not to offend Meg's dearest friend. But she soon had to admit to herself that this was not the real reason she did not pull away, did not tell Cordelia to leave her alone. There was a wonderful feeling of comfort in being held against Cordelia's deep bosom. There was nothing small and grudging in Cordelia. Emma felt her feet to be on a very slippery path. Even her attempts to avoid meeting Cordelia were halfhearted and she knew herself glad when she failed. Cordelia felt her response no matter how she strove to hide it. She could not escape Cordelia's grasp without throwing her violently off. Cordelia's caresses, Cordelia's soft endearments said as plainly as possible, Come and let me have you.

Even when they were in the presence of Meg, Cordelia scarcely disguised her actions. Under Meg's brooding stare she was both bold and subtle, often smiling in amusement at Emma's embarrassment. Emma wondered miserably at such times why Meg said nothing. Only Meg could put an end to Cordelia's blandishments. But Meg seemed frozen in a mood of remote disdain. Her silence seemed to prompt Cordelia to even more open courtship. Emma, feeling at sea in the face of their so obvious,

wordless understanding, on such occasions sank into a state of
silent wretchedness.

It was Dorcas who brought it out into the open to her. One
morning as she served her breakfast, Dorcas said, "Miss
Margaret's right highhanded these days, Miss Emma."

Emma looked up to see the ironical gleam in the black eyes
looking down at her. "Highhanded?"

"She don't have much patience with anybody. She's real sharp
with Miss Susanna. And she's not much better with Miss
Cordelia."

"Why, Dorcas?"

"Why? Don't you know, Miss Emma? She's upset with both of
them—Miss Susanna because she don't like you and Miss
Cordelia because she likes you too much."

*   *   *

Dorcas had built a fire in Emma's bedroom grate. Outdoors the
day was cold and grey. From the window the long Baltimore
street looked cheerless. No one was tempted to be out strolling
about in the wintry chill. New Year's Day, thought Emma, and
cast back to the last, which she had spent nursing Meg. She was
glad that she had been able today to take a respite from all her
responsibilities. Meg, with her old thoughtfulness, had said, Why
didn't she stay home, comfortable and at ease. There was no need
for her to spend her precious few moments of leisure maintaining
conversation with Susanna's guests.

Gratefully, Emma stretched herself on the sofa in front of the
fire. She felt tired and dispirited and unequal to the daily drain on
her physical vitality. She longed for Meg, the same longing, she
recognized, that she had felt before she had come to know Meg in
the flesh, the Meg of the letters, the Meg who had seemed a
refuge to her in the days when she sought to forget Alison. Meg
had been gone most of the afternoon, busy on the round of family
visits demanded by Baltimore tradition. Emma dropped off her
slippers and the warmth of the fire felt good on the bare soles of
her feet.

She was roused from a half-doze by the sound of the door
opening softly. She looked up to see Cordelia come into the room.
Cordelia was dressed in a sleek dark gown of satin and lace. The
delicate scent of her perfume came with her. She closed the door

behind her and came at once to sit down on the edge of the sofa beside Emma.

"Oh, Emma! How charming! Dorcas says Maggie is still at Susanna's. How lucky you are not to have to engage in our tribal customs. Now, if I had a taste for rye whiskey, like my uncle John Lightfoot, I shouldn't mind it so much. I've just passed him, sailing down Mount Vernon Place, whistling and swinging his cane in greeting to everyone he meets. Ah, New Year's Day in Baltimore! He must have made a dozen calls already and had a glass of something at every one."

Emma laughed. "That is one way to pass a dreary day."

"It is dreary, isn't it? But Dorcas has made you a nice fire. And good company, they say, makes nothing of bad weather."

She leaned forward and, taking Emma's head in her hands, kissed her several times on the mouth, light, tantalizing kisses, with a flicker of her tongue between Emma's lips. Emma tried to draw away, but her effort was half-hearted.

Cordelia laughed gaily. "I'm so glad I am not a man! You would not tolerate me for one moment then, would you, Emma?"

"Of course not. I have a reputation to preserve."

Cordelia laughed again. "But that's not what I mean and you know it. You can't stand being touched by a man. How do I know? Because you like me. It's quite a joke on the men. You are a glorious woman, Emma. Your body provokes the greatest response. But you don't let a man come near you. James will never forgive you. Oh, don't be cross. You can't hide anything from me. You are a blessed angel—as pure as the sky. Kiss me, Emma. You want to, I know you do."

She caught Emma up in her arms, strong, unyielding arms. Emma lay still. Cordelia's fragrance enveloped her, the rise and fall of Cordelia's breasts against her own robbed her of the will to resist. Cordelia's voice said softly in her ear, "You're not a statue, Emma. You are not made of marble. You're a living woman and that beautiful body of yours craves caresses, loving tenderness. You stir when I touch you. It is a great lie that women don't want to be stirred, to feel the touch of a lover's hands. I've known that from a child."

"You discovered it with Meg." Emma heard her own voice as that of someone else.

She felt Cordelia's embrace loosen for a moment. But it grew at once more urgent. "Poor Meg. What she is sacrificing. But you must not let her sacrifice you to the ideal of self-denial.''

Emma, gently pushing her face away a bit, said, ''Self-denial is not something you have practiced, is it?''

''No. Why should I? I detest sanctimonious people. It seems to me that they are really evil—that they must harbor the most evil thoughts. Otherwise why should they enjoy thwarting their fellows?''

''Meg is not sanctimonious.''

Cordelia relaxed her embrace enough to hold Emma a little away from her. ''Of course not. Meg, of all people. But we are straying from the point, which is you.'' Cordelia's fingers delicately stroked the back of Emma's neck as she passed her hand around Emma's head. ''What glorious golden hair you have! It is finer than pure gold. It is unfair, really, Emma, that you should have such beauty as well as brains and character. It is too much of an endowment for a mortal woman.''

''It is an accident of nature, a question of genes.''

''And not a divine gift? You do disappoint me. I'm always seeking some evidence of divine action to fortify my belief in the faith of our fathers and here you shatter another earnest effort.'' All the while she was speaking Cordelia's luminous dark eyes were on Emma's face. Gently she fondled Emma's neck and shoulders. Emma, feeling her nerves respond to the inviting touch, tried hard to remain impassive. At last, unable to withstand the teasing, she reached up and caught Cordelia's hand in her own and held it. Cordelia, aware of the reason for her action, chuckled and said in her ear, ''You darling. Don't hold back so. You are as eager as I am.''

Emma, cradled on her bosom, sank in acquiescence further in her arms. Cordelia said, ''You want Maggie, don't you? Well, you'll never have her. Susanna has spoiled all that.''

Emma, still struggling for calm, said, ''Meg is much more to me than a bedmate.''

''Ah, but you still want her in bed, don't you? Of course you do. And she denies you, turns that stern side of her to you and lets you know you must be content with a platonic love. You're not made for that. Self-denial is nonsense. It is worse than nonsense. It engenders all sorts of madness.''

Cordelia suddenly stopped speaking and, relaxing her embrace, sat up straighter. Emma became aware that she was listening. The door opened and Meg came in. She had already removed her hat

and gloves. Surveying the two of them, she said, "Cordy, you did
not go to the Lightfoots."

Cordelia smiled at her. "I didn't?"

"You had no intention of doing so, when you told Susanna that
you were going to visit your aunt. You heard me say Emma was
home. You came straight here."

"You read me like a book, Maggie." But Cordelia's lightness
began to wilt under Meg's furious eyes. "I don't have to account
to Susanna for what I do. I'd rather talk to Emma than listen to
my aunt Kitty."

"You don't have to seek occasions to see her behind my
back."

Cordelia showed a spurt of anger. "You don't think you own
her, do you?"

Meg's anger blazed out. "That's a disgusting thing to say!"

"Then don't attack me as if you caught me poaching on your
property." She lifted her hand which had rested on the back of the
sofa, and gently caressed Emma's head. The several rings on her
fingers flashed in the firelight.

With an involuntary movement Emma sat upright. Cordelia,
with an amused glance at her, removed her hand.

Meg's voice shook with anger. "Cordy, I know perfectly well
what you are doing. And you think I'll go on standing by and
watching you without a protest."

"You haven't shown much sign of objecting."

"That's not so! You know that's not so! I don't have to speak
for you to know."

Emma saw that something in Meg's voice had touched an inner
chord in Cordelia. The big woman rose abruptly and stepped over
to stand close to Meg's slight, trembling figure. They stood facing
each other, Meg's white face and blazing eyes lifted up to
Cordelia bending over her. Emma, watching them, was aware of a
strong current of unspoken feeling passing between them, a
tension made of intimate conflict, attraction, remembered inter-
knowledge. They were old lovers, old antagonists, so closely
interwoven that no passage of time and separation could nullify
this instinctive response to one another.

Cordelia said, her voice laden with rebuke, "Rather, I
wondered how far you'd let me go, how dead you are to any real
feeling. Whether you'll ever escape from Susanna."

For a while the room was absolutely quiet. She cannot speak, thought Emma, anxiously watching Meg's struggle to breathe. Cordelia seemed likewise aware of the grip of emotion in which she was, because she took hold of Meg's arm. Finally Meg gasped, "Don't taunt me. I cannot stand it, Cordy."

Cordelia took her hand away and said in a more offhand way that showed her relief. "If you mean, I can't understand the wish to die of unfulfilled love, you're quite right. You can have your romantic friendships, ever on an ethereal plane. But I think you've chosen the wrong partner. You've got hold of a flesh and blood woman. Don't try to make her into what Susanna has made of you."

"I don't need to be told what to do."

"You might let me tell you, while it still can do some good. Maggie, I've tried to make you listen to me before, a long time ago, when it might have made all the difference between us. It's too late now. Don't go on repeating your mistake —"

Emma saw, as they stood eyeing each other angrily, that, though they spoke of her, they had forgotten her in the interplay of their own feelings. She was astonished to see that it was Meg who first gave in. Her anger seemed to desert her and she pleaded, "Cordy, don't! You must not!"

Cordelia's anger also seemed to evaporate. It was transformed into sudden awareness. "You don't mean to say, Maggie —!" She broke off and cast a brief glance at Emma. Her dark eyes were wide with surprise. "So that is what you're sickening over! You've already been to bed with her. You've done it, Maggie! And all you can think of now is what Susanna would say. Maggie, what has happened to your backbone? Do you have to grovel like this?"

Meg said crossly, defensively, "Cordy, you don't have to bring everything down to one thing."

"One thing? What are you talking about? Of course it's not one thing. But you can't ignore it—not you, of all people, Maggie! Don't talk nonsense — to me."

Again there was a moment of silent confrontation between them. Then Maggie said uncertainly, "Cordy, I've tried to think it wasn't important — that it was just something we had learned to do as children that we shouldn't have —"

"Rubbish. Don't talk to me like that, Maggie, or I shall really come to hate you!"

Emma could not see Cordelia's face, but she was aware, by the expression of Meg's, that there must have been real rage in Cordelia's eyes.

Meg cried, "No! No! Cordy, I cannot forget — I've never forgotten you — I've never forgotten what we were —"

"Then don't talk like that. Susanna tried to convince you that it was wicked and you tried to believe her. Wicked, Maggie? What we were, you and I? You were never a hypocrite. Don't talk like one now."

"Cordy, don't rake it all up!"

Cordelia softened and took a step closer to her. Putting her arm around Meg she said, "Come, give me a kiss, Maggie. You are not going to be angry at me?"

Meg returned her kiss. "No. But you'll have to give me a little time to get over this."

"Not I, but Emma." Again Cordelia glanced briefly at Emma. She turned back to Meg. "Maggie, don't ruin everything for yourself. And don't ruin Emma's life. You might find yourself with nothing where you could have everything."

She turned away and went across the room to pick up her hat, which she had laid aside when she first came in.

"I shall now," she said, carrying the hat to the looking glass, "go and visit Aunt Kitty."

There was silence while she pinned the hat carefully into place, turning her head about to see if it suited her. At last she finished and went over to kiss Meg.

"Don't be foolish, Maggie. And don't spurn your blessings." At the door she paused and blew a kiss to Emma. Her smile had returned, the same bantering, provocative smile Emma had always seen. "Such a pity, my dear, we were interrupted."

As the door closed Emma looked anxiously at Meg. Meg still stood where she had, her hand on the back of a chair, gazing at the fire, absorbed in her own thoughts.

*   *   *

They lay in the center of Meg's big bed. The world they lived in seemed as remote as the night darkness beyond the curtained windows. The room was very quiet, in the silent house in the silent winter street. Even the fire in the grate had sunk to a mass of red coals, with no more fragments of wood to fall and crackle and throw out showers of sparks.

Emma nestled her head between Meg's pink-nippled small

breasts and gathered her soft bottom into the palm of her hand. This is bliss, she thought, pressing Meg's body against her own, feeling the tickle of Meg's silky hair against the pit of her own stomach. How many nights she had spent alone, her arms aching for just this warm, yielding body to comfort her loneliness, her frequent discouragement. What a long drought it had been, before she reached at last this spring of life.

She felt Meg stir, felt her fingers clutching her head, felt her move against her in the last tremors of their lovemaking. "My love, my heart," said Meg's soft voice. With a final effort of wakefulness Emma drew her even more closely against her. Together they settled more deeply in the bed. In a half-dream Emma saw Meg's face, the unquenchably proud gaze of the brown-flecked green eyes, turned towards her in the soft indulgence of love. Dreamily, happily, she sank into sleep, conscious of Meg's voice murmuring into her ear.

*   *   *

Dorcas opened the door for her as she hurried up the steps. She was late for the meeting of the Ladies' Committee, as she seemed so often these days to be for everything. As Dorcas took her doctor's bag and wrap from her, a fleeting memory came to her of her first visit to Meg's house. It seemed very long ago.

Dorcas, grinning proudly up at her, said, "They're waiting for you, Miss Emma. It don't seem like they can do anything nowadays without you."

Emma smiled absently down at her. Still in the thrall of memory she thought, And when I got to London, I could not even remember what she looked like. She crossed the vestibule quickly and stopped for a moment in the doorway. The tumult of women's voices sank for a moment and welled up again. Emma's eyes searched the room. Then she saw the slight trim figure standing by the fireplace, a little apart from the women clustered about her. Meg. Her own Meg, never to be lost again. Meg turned to glance in her direction. Even across the room Emma saw the soft radiance of welcome come into her face.

Reassured, she turned courteously to reply to those who greeted her.

Publications of
THE NAIAD PRESS, INC.
P.O. Box 10543 • Tallahassee, Florida 32302
Mail orders welcome. Please include 15% postage.

Contract with the World by Jane Rule. A novel. 340 pp.
ISBN 0-930044-28-2 $7.95

Yantras of Womanlove by Tee A. Corinne. Photographs. 64 pp.
ISBN 0-930044-30-4 $6.95

Mrs. Porter's Letter by Vicki P. McConnell. A mystery novel.
224 pp. ISBN 0-930044-29-0 $6.95

To the Cleveland Station by Carol Anne Douglas. A novel.
192 pp. ISBN 0-930044-27-4 $6.95

The Nesting Place by Sarah Aldridge. A novel. 224 pp.
ISBN 0-930044-26-6 $6.95

This Is Not for You by Jane Rule. A novel. 284 pp.
ISBN 0-930044-25-8 $7.95

Faultline by Sheila Ortiz Taylor. A novel. 140 pp.
ISBN 0-930044-24-X $6.95

The Lesbian in Literature by Barbara Grier. 3rd ed.
Foreword by Maida Tilchen. A comprehensive bibliog.
240 pp. ISBN 0-930044-23-1   ind. $7.95
     inst. $10.00

Anna's Country by Elizabeth Lang. A novel. 208 pp.
ISBN 0-930044-19-3 $6.95

Lesbian Writer: Collected Work of Claudia Scott
edited by Frances Hanckel and Susan Windle. Poetry. 128 pp.
ISBN 0-930044-22-3 $4.50

Prism by Valerie Taylor. A novel. 158 pp.
ISBN 0-930044-18-5 $6.95

Black Lesbians: An Annotated Bibliography compiled by
JR Roberts. Foreword by Barbara Smith. 112 pp.
ISBN 0-930044-21-5   ind. $5.95
     inst. $8.00

The Marquise and the Novice by Victoria Ramstetter.
A novel. 108 pp. ISBN 0-930044-16-9 $4.95

Labiaflowers by Tee A. Corinne. 40 pp. $3.95

Outlander by Jane Rule. Short stories, essays.
207 pp. ISBN 0-930044-17-7 $6.95

(continued on next page)

Sapphistry: The Book of Lesbian Sexuality by
Pat Califia. 195 pp. ISBN 0-930044-14-2 $6.95

Lesbian-Feminism in Turn-of-the-Century Germany.
An anthology. Translated and edited by Lillian Faderman
and Brigitte Eriksson. 120 pp. ISBN 0-930044-13-4 $5.95

The Black and White of It by Ann Allen Shockley.
Short stories. 112 pp. ISBN 0-930044-15-0 $5.95

At the Sweet Hour of Hand-in-Hand by Renée Vivien.
Translated by Sandia Belgrade. Poetry. xix, 81 pp.
ISBN 0-930044-11-8 $5.50

All True Lovers by Sarah Aldridge. A novel. 292 pp.
ISBN 0-930044-10-X $6.95

The Muse of the Violets by Renée Vivien. Poetry. 84 pp.
ISBN 0-930044-07-X $4.00

A Woman Appeared to Me by Renée Vivien. Translated
by Jeannette H. Foster. A novel. xxxi, 65 pp.
ISBN 0-930044-06-1 $5.00

Lesbiana by Barbara Grier. Book reviews from
The Ladder. iv, 309 pp. ISBN 0-930044-05-3 $5.00

Cytherea's Breath by Sarah Aldridge. A novel. 240 pp.
ISBN 0-930044-02-9 $6.95

Tottie by Sarah Aldridge. A novel. 181 pp.
ISBN 0-930044-01-0 $5.95

The Latecomer by Sarah Aldridge. A novel. 107 pp.
ISBN 0-930044-00-2 $5.00